The Sexual Division of Work

The Sexual Division of Work

Conceptual Revolutions in the Social Sciences

Shirley Dex

Lecturer in Economics
University of Keele

ST. MARTIN'S PRESS   New York

All rights reserved. For information, write:
St. Martin's Press, Inc., 175 Fifth Avenue, New York, NY 10010
Printed in Great Britain
First published in the United States of America in 1985

ISBN 0–312–71349–5

Library of Congress Cataloging in Publication Data
Dex, Shirley.
   The sexual division of work.
   Bibliography: p.
   Includes index.
   1. Women——Employment——United States.
2. Women——Employment——Great Britain.
3. Sexual division of labor——United States.
4. Sexual division of labor——Great Britain.
I. Title.
HD6095.D47   1985   305.4'3'0941   85–8301
ISBN 0–312–71349–5

Contents

Acknowledgements

I particularly want to thank Colin Bell, Pauline Hunt and Chris Phillipson for their helpful comments and encouragements at an earlier stage. Many thanks are also due to Chris Booth and Kim Pickerill for their patient word processing on temperamental machines.

1 Introduction

Prior to the 1960s much research was premised on the unwritten assumption that women's economic role was unimportant, that gendered divisions in the working population were not particularly interesting and that everything that needed to be known about women workers could be captured in a few stereotypes. Things have changed. The new developments have not merely added the study of women to a list of research topics, they have raised questions about the earlier conceptualisation of problems which has provoked new ideas and new approaches to the study of the economic relationships of women and men. By taking women seriously, rethinking and restructuring has been taking place in social science which is proving to be very fruitful, as this book intends to illustrate.

A large part of the impetus for promoting the study of women has come from feminists, and this varied group—largely composed of women—are producing empirical research in a variety of fields. Undoubtedly another major factor which has served to promote research into women's economic activity is the fact of their new and increasing participation in the labour force since the Second World War. It is no longer possible to ignore women's employment. Women are now an important and visible workforce; in this respect they are a mirror of contemporary socio-economic change, since the changes taking place in women's employment are linked to simultaneous changes in fertility rates, birth patterns, family size and family or household relationships. Women's increasing economic activity is also related to structural economic changes in Western economies in ways which so far have been inadequately explored.

The subject matter reviewed in this book comes largely

1

from industrial sociology, labour economics and, of course, women's studies. Whilst the main aim has been to produce a textbook which is accessible to undergraduates, it is hoped that other academic readers will be able to find some stimulation from the organisation of the material and the perspective adopted. Whilst the subject matters of industrial sociology and labour economics have been treated separately, on the whole, as they usually are in practice, the organisation around certain substantive research questions is intended to promote a more interdisciplinary perspective. By drawing this material together one cannot but hope that readers, and critics especially, will be impressed by the frequency and scale of conceptual changes which are in progress and which emanate from the same source.

The scope and objectives of this book make it a very ambitious project: it attempts to be both relevant and accessible to students of sociology and economics on both sides of the Atlantic. Combining the research efforts of British and US economists is not too difficult, but the same is not true of sociological studies, which tend to be very different. US sociology is more quantitative and less conceptual than the British tradition. It is beyond the scope of this book to tackle two of the questions raised by these differences; namely, why are there differences between women in British and US societies and sociologies? There are important differences in the legal-political position of women in the USA and Britain, in addition to differences in their level of opportunities, tax concessions for child care and the frequencies of part-time work. These differences are reviewed more extensively in Dex and Shaw (1984), and they go some way towards answering the 'why' about society. It is perhaps not surprising that sociologies of different societies vary to some extent, but this is far from being a thorough explanation. There is obviously considerable scope for research which tackles these differences in societies and sociologies head-on, and the explanations would be likely to go beyond the bounds of sociology and economics—at least entering history, politics and demography.

Producing a textbook which is both stimulating but not

superficial and which has the right balance between describing substantive issues and results whilst giving an overview, presented a serious challenge. The reader is left to judge whether this aim has been achieved. There has been far too much material to include it all. The scope was not intended to be comprehensive and has been restricted to the author's own areas of interest and to the areas where the most far-reaching changes have occurred. Important aspects of the sub-disciplines have been omitted nonetheless, the most obvious example being the focus in industrial sociology and labour economics on industrial relations. Also, there is no discussion of migrant women's work included. It would have been appropriate to include more about part-time women's work in Britain, but despite its scale, the phenomenon is relatively under-researched to date. The many policy implications of both the old and new conceptualisations of women's work are too extensive to be included.

CHANGES IN WOMEN'S EMPLOYMENT

The actual changes which have been occurring in women's employment are at least partly responsible for some of the conceptual changes which will be described in this book. Whilst women's growing visibility in the workforce has occurred gradually, the recognition of women as employees or workers has been more sudden, dating from the late 1960s onwards. A more detailed description of some of these changes is provided in the appropriate place in the chapters which follow, but a broad outline of the women's employment changes is provided here as a context for what follows.[1]

The number of women employees in Great Britain has grown from 6.7 millions in 1948 to 9.2 millions in 1980. At the same time the number of male employees has fallen from 13.3 to 12.8 millions, although the fall has been steepest for men between 1966 and 1980. Women constituted 33.6 per cent of the total number of employees in 1948 and 41.7 per cent of the total in 1980; the equivalent proportion of women in 1881 was 27 per cent, so it is clear that the biggest changes have occurred since 1940.[2] In 1980 a survey of women found that 65 per cent of women were economically active, 60 per cent being employed and 5 per cent unemployed at the interview.[3] A breakdown by age of women's labour-force participation rates show that young women's participation rates have not changed very significantly over time, except insofar as the school-leaving age has risen and the population as a whole now receives more education on average. The participation rates have increased most markedly for women between the ages of thirty-five and fifty-four. Most commentators on these changes describe them as an increase in married women's employment and, indeed, in 1951, 38 per cent of the women's workforce were married women, whereas in 1971 the percentage was 63 per cent. However, it is important not to attach explanatory significance to these figures. It is not changes in women's marital status behaviour that have caused these aggregate-level changes, however, but changes in women's child-rearing practices.

Women's participation rates by age in the aggregate figures display an M-shaped profile, which has sometimes been called a bimodal pattern. The first peak occurs between the ages of twenty and twenty-four and the second peak between the ages of forty-five and fifty; the height of the second peak has been rising over time, and the trough has also been rising and moving towards earlier ages. The general M shape remains, but it is experiencing a shift which corresponds to demographic and behavioural changes.[4] Women now marry earlier but continue working until they are pregnant instead of stopping work at marriage; they have fewer children per family and return to work after childbirth sooner. In addition, the sequence patterns of not working and working over childbirth have been changing from being bimodal, or sandwich-like, to being predominantly tiered, with returns to work occurring between childbirths.[5] Birth-spacing is also changing.[6] The net effect in aggregate of these changes is that the women's labour force has, on average, been growing older.

One of the crucially important things to note about British women's employment rates is that a large proportion of employed women are in part-time work, and this percentage has been growing over time. Figures giving the proportion of part-time workers have only been available in Britain since 1961, and they have only been systematically and reliably collected since the Census of Employment started in 1971. Over the period 1961 to 1980 the number of part-time jobs has increased by approximately 2.3 millions. Over the same period the number of full-time jobs fell by approximately the same amount. Part-time jobs as a percentage of all jobs grew from approximately 2.2 per cent in 1961 to 4.5 per cent in 1980, but the proportion of part-time jobs of all women's jobs if far higher.[7] In 1971, for example, 33 per cent of women employees were in part-time jobs, whereas in 1981 the percentage had risen to 42 per cent.[8] The growth in part-time work has been a growth of women's jobs and in Britain these have been predominantly in the service industries and the public sector.

A comparison of British and US women's participation rates reveals that important differences exist between the two countries.[9] By examining women's employment rates— that is, both full- and part-time work—older British women in their forties and fifties are somewhat more likely to be employed than their US counterparts. However, British women are far more likely to be in part-time jobs at this age than US women, and the US women are far more likely to be in full-time jobs than British women. Among younger women in their late twenties and early thirties, American women are much more likely to be employed than British women, by a difference of between 10 and 20 percentage points. American women work far more than British women—and in full-time jobs—over their family-formation period. US women return to work sooner after childbirth and are more likely to work between childbirths than British women. The same trends in women's employment rates and patterns are visible both in Britain and the USA, but US women are ahead of British women in their level of attachment to the labour force. Childcare constraints in the two countries explain the difference as Dex and Shaw (1984) illustrate. US women work full time, pay for childcare and get tax deductions against childcare expenses. British women have to work part time and get husbands or relatives to care for young children.

Women's unemployment rates have been difficult to assess—especially in Britain, for reasons which are discussed more fully in Chapter 3. In Britain, until recently, women's unemployment rates were always below those of men, whereas in the USA women's unemployment rates have traditionally been higher than those of men. In Britain studies of published statistics have also suggested that the average duration on the unemployment register was greater for men than for women. US figures are a more accurate reflection of unemployment than the British published unemployment-count statistics since the US figures are obtained from a regular survey of households. When British survey data of a kind which is equivalent to US data is examined, the conclusions about the relative experiences of unemployment in Britain can sometimes change.[10] Unemployment figures are based on whether the individual is seeking work or not, and insofar as women say that they seek employment to a lesser extent than men, their unemployment will be lower. The estimates of women's registered and unregistered unemployment in Britain in 1971 were 318,000 and in 1979 the figure was 654,000.[11]

Women's unemployment, however it is measured, appears to have been increasing during the 1970s relative to men in both Britain and the USA. The reasons for this shift are not clear. In Britain, at least part of the increase is a growing propensity to register as unemployed, when women previously did not bother; since 1977 women have been unable to opt out of paying national insurance, and they are therefore now entitled to unemployment benefit. Some commentators have suggested that women have suffered disproportionately more than men in the recessions of the late 1970s, but other analyses in Britain and the USA contest this conclusion.[12]

Women have tended to be located in a narrow range of occupations, notably clerical work, semi-skilled factory work and semi-skilled domestic work; semi-skilled domestic work is likely to be part-time work. In Britain the Women and Employment Survey of 1980 revealed that 30 per cent of all working women were in clerical jobs, 10 per cent were in semi-skilled factory work and 11 per cent were in semi-skilled domestic work. Of the working women in part-time jobs, however, 20 per cent were in semi-skilled domestic work and only 20 per cent were in clerical jobs.[13] A comparison of British and US women of the same age found that although women in both countries were heavily concentrated in such stereotypically female occupations as clerical work, differences in the occupational distributions could be observed. American women were somewhat more likely to be employed as professionals or teachers and about twice as likely to be employed in the intermediate non-manual category. This latter difference was thought to be a result of the fact that American women have found increasing employment in management positions in recent years, sometimes as a result of sex discrimination suits brought against large employers. Although clerical work was the largest occupational category for women in both countries, American women were more likely to be clerical workers than their British counterparts. British women were somewhat less likely to be employed as skilled manual workers and somewhat more likely to be employed in semi-skilled factory work, as well as in sales, semi-skilled domestic and unskilled work. In summary, American women are somewhat more likely to work in the better-paying occupations and British women in the lower-paying occupations.

Women are disproportionately employed in service industries in both Britain and the USA. In Britain in 1980, 77 per cent of working women were employed in services, and 82 per cent of part-time working women were employed in services.[14] This is the result of a steady growth in the employment of services over the post-war era and a decline in manufacturing employment. American women are more likely to be employed in services and consequently less likely to be employed in manufacturing than British women, but American women's services jobs are not part-time to the same extent as British women's jobs. Within the service industries, British women are more concentrated in miscellaneous services and American women are more often in insurance and public sector jobs. The distribution industry provides similar percentages of employment for women in both Britain and the USA—around 18 per cent.

A brief review of women's employment in Britain and the USA has been provided here. The changes which have occurred are common to both countries, but the structure of women's employment, and consequently women's economic role, is slightly different; notably, British women play a part-time worker's role to a far greater extent than American women. This difference is clearly linked to the child-care provisions available, since in Britain women rely heavily on husbands and relatives for child care whilst they are working part-time, whereas in the USA where child care is tax-deductable, women can better afford to work full-time. The switch from full-time to part-time work in Britain takes place largely over the first break from work for childbirth, and studies have shown that this transition is often associated with downward occupational mobility, particularly in Britain.

However, the above discussion has been concerned with only a part of women's work: their waged work. This book wishes to take women's unwaged work equally seriously, although since researchers and large-scale surveys have not given unwaged work equal attention in the past, there is less information to document about women's unwaged work. One of the themes of this book concerns the way this situation is beginning to change.

RECONCEPTUALISATIONS

In going back through the traditions of analyses in sociology and economics, the revolutionary nature of the current changes in the disciplines become more apparent. The traditions can be criticised for their reliance upon common stereotypes about women, treating women as a problem, for their reliance upon false assumptions and for just plain ignorance. These things pervade not only abstract theoretical discussions, where their presence might be at least understandable, but also the assumptions are evident in empirical work directing the focuses of studies, the research questions asked, influencing the selection of samples and the writing up of the results and conclusions. As Feldberg and Glenn (1979) have pointed out, where women have been included, they have been examined from the perspective of 'a gender model' in contrast to the 'job model' discussions about men's work. Brown (1976) and Beechey (1984) have both documented some of these characteristics in certain fields. A reworking of the tradition's foundations reveals that studies of women were initiated, but somehow they have been lost from subsequent reviews—'hidden from history'. Empirical samples of workers have sometimes contained women, but their only mention has been in the first description of the personal characteristics of the workforce. Much of the tradition has thus built upon the notion of a unisex worker.

What has changed? The reconceptualisation now taking place is at different stages in the various research areas and disciplines. The first step in taking women's work seriously has sometimes been to ask similar questions of women as have been asked of men or, in quantitative work, to consider sex as one of the explanatory variables. Studies of this sort, (e.g. studies of occupational attainment) have helped to fill in some of the gaps in our knowledge about women. Other developments have gone beyond this to suggest changes in the fundamental concepts of analysis; for example, seeing the home as a sphere of production and an origin of orientations to work rather than solely focusing on the workplace, and seeing the notions of skill and productivity as essentially socially constructed. However, it would be erroneous to suggest that all of the changes have been accepted and adopted by the mainstream. In some cases a thorough-going critique of the tradition has been followed by empirical studies of women and a new direction established as a result. The consideration of housework and motherhood as occupations is one such development. In other areas, resistance to change is being expressed partly because the exact nature of the desired reconceptualisation is unclear; class analysis is a good example. Women's studies has a lot of catching up to do, so it is not surprising that the reworking is still in its infancy in some fields and non-existent in others; for example, we know relatively little about older women, ethnic minority women and women's participation in part-time work.

On the whole, sociologists have been more receptive to the changes advocated than economists. Consequently, the nature of the reconceptualisations occurring have been more fundamental in sociology than in economics. But this is not to deny the magnitude of conceptual changes in economics. We are only at the beginning of what is likely to prove a far-reaching reorientation of these disciplines, and women are at the vanguard of both societal and conceptual changes. The process by which these changes have come about is complex and we should beware oversimplification. It would be a gross misrepresentation to suggest that only feminists have contributed to conceptual change, or that women's studies can only produce good work. The women's critique has sometimes been one of a number of advocates for change. The reintroduction of the notion of 'segmented labour markets' owes its origin equally as much to American blacks as it does to women. There are a series of healthy debates within the women's movement over what objectives are desirable and which changes promote the objectives. Concepts like 'deskilling' have risen to fame as they were thought initially to offer a more serious treatment of women, only to fall later after a more thorough critique.

Although the book spans two disciplines and many research fields, recurring themes and debates emerge throughout. In all we see that empirical research has been given a new boost by the desire to find out about women's work, and this development has spread even into areas described previously as arid abstract theory. A similar thrust has been given to interdisciplinary study. One very encouraging outcome from these developments is that seemingly alternative and opposed perspectives have reached similar conclusions. Both Marxist-feminists and neoclassical economic analysis are now treating the household as a unit of production and reproduction. Similarly, neoclassical analyses of pay differentials reveals the importance of the sexual division of occupations and trade union organisation, as does the segmented labour-market perspective.

Women's studies has been contributing to critiques of structural-functionalist and Marxist-functionalist analyses, and is part of a more widespread conceptual change which seeks to take the actor's perspective seriously. A challenge has come to the view of women as passive, and the image of active, creative, resisting women is being substituted. The issue of whether capitalism or patriarchy is responsible for women's subordination is also a recurring debate which is part of a more general question which we shall now examine.

WHAT IS FEMINIST METHODOLOGY?

The question of whether feminists have or should have a unique and specific approach to social science is receiving considerable attention.[15] The question is sometimes discussed in general terms with respect to all social science. In other cases the merits or disadvantages of particular approaches like that of Marxist-feminism are discussed. The general issues will be considered first in this discussion. There is a set of questions which are discussed under the more general question about a feminist methodology, and one can usually find opposite viewpoints being expressed on each of the separate questions. Most feminists agree that part of their task is to uncover and criticise sexism in social science. If sexism is in our society, it is expected that it will influence our thought forms and enter into social science analyses, but its existence in society is not a reason for accepting it in social science.[16]

One question which can be asked is, should a feminist methodology focus solely on women? What in fact has happened since feminists began to criticise the sexism within the traditions of social science is that many empirical studies of women have taken place. These studies form a major part of this volume. Given that women were not the subject of earlier studies as content analyses have shown,[17] the women's studies approach has been to fill in the gaps and help our understanding of women. Most feminists accept that this has been a necessary and valuable contribution, but they see dangers in such an approach. It is easy for women's studies to become ghettoised, cut-off from research and ideas and then ignored by the mainstream. A feminist approach is thus argued to be one which differs from women's studies, since it aims at researching men as much as women. It is not content to simply add on an extra dimension to social science; it seeks to transform it. Bell and Roberts (1984, pp. 6–7) have suggested that this is part of a 'strong' programme of feminist research which claims to produce 'better' social science. The subsequent chapters of this volume will demonstrate that transformations have occurred, although feminists have not been solely responsible for all the changes.

Whilst there is a measure of agreement on distinguishing feminist social science from women's studies, there is less agreement on the implications which emerge. Disagreement exists over the question of whether men can be feminists. The Roberts (1981) volume appears to argue that men can be feminists, and Stanley and Wise (1983, p. 18) categorically deny the possibility. Stanley and Wise argue that it is impossible for men to be feminists because 'what is essential to "being feminist" is the possession of "feminist consciousness". And we see feminist consciousness as rooted in the concrete, practical and everyday experiences of being, and being treated as, a woman.'

The alternative position, which I find more persuasive, is that men can appreciate and agree with the aims and objectives of feminism, as Morgan's (1981, p. 84) account of his experiences at a BSA Summer School confirms; he suggests that men can experience the essential qualities of being treated as a woman. Moreover, if one does not allow that men can be feminists, and yet one wants to include the study of men within the feminist ambit, a dialogue is being closed-off which could relegate feminism to the ghetto—just what the same writers are anxious to avoid. There are, therefore, unanswered questions and potential contradictions implied by the view that men cannot be feminists.

Another question which is raised about a feminist

methodology is, should it be for women? Should it be specifically aimed at improving women's position and contributing to their liberation? A weaker affirmative answer to this question can be found in Kuhn and Wolpe (1978) and a much stronger version in Ehrlich (1976). Insofar as feminism is a political philosophy it is likely to want to change the world, but the extent to which that desire should enter any analysis is, as Kuhn and Wolpe recognise, a problem.[18] Stanley and Wise (1983) also express the same desire to change the world but do not appear to like any of the well articulated attempts to do that, from feminists or anyone else. Ehrlich wants to expose the new research on women which can be seen to be merely exploiting this new interest with a view to satisfying personal ambitions. Ehrlich advocates that the condition for feminist research must be that it is conducted from within the women's liberation movement or not at all. Research which goes on outside, so-to-speak, has been called 'rip-off' research.[19] The discussions of this issue have tended to conflate two things: knowledge and the uses to which knowledge is put. If one holds this to be a valid distinction, then the answer to this question about the nature of feminist methodology is that, as far possible, a correct understanding of women's position should be sought. This will be 'feminist' only insofar as the topic selected for study may be specifically of interest to feminists. On the basis of the knowledge obtained, feminists may seek to argue for changes, using some of the knowledge, or the subjects themselves might want to use the knowledge obtained. I am advocating here a realist, objectivist position along with Kelly (1978), recognising, of course, that many would not agree.

In fact, some feminists have made quite fundamental criticisms of the objectivist position, claiming that it is a sexist view of knowledge. Spender (1982, p. 2) in particular takes this view:

Gone are the days when we could believe that all knowledge existed 'out there' in the wilderness, merely waiting for brilliant men to discover it and to make impartial records uncoloured by their own opinions and beliefs. Like it or not, we have come to terms with more recent discoveries (to which feminism has made an enormous contribution) that human beings invent or construct knowledge in accordance with the values and belief with which they begin.

Some of the dangers of this position are noted by Kelly (1978). What is somewhat ironic about the attack on objectivity noted above is that it has come at a time when few (male) sociologists would support the notion, although Berger and Kellner (1981) have argued for its retention. My main objection to the anti-objectivist position is that it is inconsistent and ends up cutting off a branch upon which one also wants to sit. The quotation from Spender aptly demonstrates the inconsistency by first denying that there is any such thing as objective knowledge. At the same time she clearly does want us to take notice and believe that she (unlike others) is telling us a truth which is of the hard 'like it or not' objective variety. She ends up by affirming what she set out to deny.[20] The dangers of feminists insisting that there are no objective facts arise because, unlike many sociologists, the rest of the world still operates with the notion of objectivity. Why should the feminist's position be taken seriously if it is claimed to be subjective?[21] It is understandable that women should want to leave behind the arrogance of men's claims to knowledge as so aptly charactured by Stanley and Wise (1983, p. 5): 'I can see and conceptualize the truth about things but those poor falsely conscious morons can't'. You'd think all these years of men saying that women can't understand what's going on in the world would have had some kind of impact on . . . how feminists do theory and research'. But criteria of truth and falsehood do not necessarily imply arrogance, since they are open, unlike subjective opinions, to rational dispute. If feminists want to change the world, they are going to have to be able to say to the false claims; 'You are wrong for this, that and the other reasons'. It may or may not be liked.

Another question has been raised about the methods used in sociological or anthropological research. Should they seek to obtain 'hard' or 'soft', quantitative or qualitative data?[22] The argument is that the sort of data which are suitable for quantitative analyses do not tell us much about women's experiences. Oakley (1981, p. 40) has made a similar point about the interview, calling it 'a masculine paradigm':

'interviewers define the role of interviewees as subordinates; extracting information is more to be valued than yielding it; the convention of interviewer–interviewee hierarchy is a rationalisation of inequality; what is good for interviewers is not necessarily good for interviewees'.

Oakley thinks that the interview neglects the sociology of feelings and emotion and is therefore particularly damaging and unsuitable for women. Finch (1984) has reiterated some of the same points and suggested that they raise an ethical dilemma for feminists. It may well be the case that researching women's experiences stretches the interview method of data collection beyond its limits. The point which is being made is a general one, however, and it is not specific to feminist analyses. Data collection will be more difficult in some research fields than in others, and susceptibility to reflexivity will vary depending upon the subjects. If one is seeking the actor's view of the situation, or the actor's feelings, whether women's or men's, the difficulties increase. Providing any sort of social science account involves a sense of detachment which is more difficult the more one identifies with the subjects, but the difficulty is a matter of degree rather than being different in kind. It may well be the case, however, that women are the only interviewers who are likely to be able to interview other women about certain topics. But the same general point will be true about men, ethnic minorities, etc. There may be other topics when women (men) have a better response when interviewing men (women). A method has to be chosen which is appropriate to the nature of the data being sought. Morgan (1981) makes a useful point that there is nothing inherently sexist in any of the methods of data collection and analysis available for use to social scientists, with the exception of personal experience. He suggests that the use of terms like 'hard' or 'soft' data may well have sexist overtones, however. Spender (1978) rightly considers these terms an unproductive and false dichotomy.

A feminist methodology has been proposed as one which considers gender divisions as important to any analysis. Bell and Roberts (1984) describe this as the 'weak' programme of feminist research (p. 6)' and whilst they think it is likely to be more acceptable to the sociology profession, they recognise that in practice it is not (yet) a condition of research applications. Dissention from this position has been expressed by Matthews (1982). Matthews suggests that sociology and feminist sociology will be making a mistake if it adopts gender divisions as a matter of course, because gender is socially constructed and the women's movement hopes ultimately to transcend gender classifications, which are oppressive to women. The value of feminism, as seen by Matthews (1982, p. 29), is in 'accumulating evidence that gender is not a good index to understanding the social world'. She is critical of feminist work which has served to accentuate a gender dichotomy by highlighting the differences in empirical results rather than the similarities, even when the similarities are greater. The discussion of orientations to work in Chapter 2 clearly illustrates this point. It is an important point that research should not start out with too many *a priori* assumptions, but if the mistakes of the past are to be rectified, then it would seem to be crucial that gender be considered as a potentially important division, whilst allowing the empirical work to demonstrate that it is not.

This discussion about the nature of a feminist methodology has sometimes taken place in the context of the Marxist-feminist desire to inject a feminist perspective into classical Marxism. There appears to be general agreement that classical Marxism has neglected women, but Marxist-feminists think that the essential components of Marx's analysis are worth retaining.[23] Marxist-feminism is not seen as an attempt to add on a discussion of women to Marxism, however, but as an attempt to transform it by a consideration of the sexual division of labour in all its aspects. Some of the efforts at transformation are reviewed in this volume.

Some commentators have implied, if not openly suggested, that Marxist-feminists are not genuine feminists, because of their adherence to Marxism and because they fail to stress the existence of sexual inequality and subordination prior to the era of capitalism. The concept of 'patriarchy', which describes the subordination of women by men, has been shown to be age-long, going back as far as historical records are available.[24] Hartmann (1976, 1979) and Delphy (1981) have criticised Marxist-feminists using this concept, and a complex debate has been taking place.[25] There has been a convergence between these groups insofar as all agree that the forms of sexual oppression under capitalism changed from earlier forms, but they clearly differ in what they regard as the aims of feminism and feminist research.

In conclusion, an acceptable feminist methodology has been argued here to involve a critique of sexism where it is found in social science, raising the potential importance of gender divisions for analyses and promoting studies of women when they have been neglected. Fulfilling this mandate will mean that feminist methodology operates in the selection of subject matter and the uses made of research, that it adds to our knowledge about women, that it encourages all research in the disciplines to take women seriously and that it also has a transforming effect on the discipline as a whole which is beneficial to all. The latter point is not merely wishful thinking, since the rest of this book documents some of these reconceptualisations. There are the pitfalls of a ghetto mentality and arrogance to be avoided. All social science research has a duty to choose the methods of data collection sensitively and appropriately to the subject matter, recognising that the built-in sense of detachment which data collection involves may possibly pose more problems for studies of women by either women or men than when other subjects are the focus.

PLAN OF THE BOOK

The material has been organised around a series of questions. A focus on substantive research questions has helped to draw together the analyses of the two disciplines of sociology and economics and to allow a discussion of both theoretical and empirical answers to these questions. The questions are also intended to help us focus on social phenomena instead of focusing on the tradition itself.[26] Part of the aim of this book is to illustrate the tradition of neglecting women in sociology and economics, but we do not want to get locked into traditional modes of thinking. A review can easily cement a tradition of analysis rather than help to liberate it. It is hoped that the organisation of the material will both accurately reflect the various traditions but at the same time illustrate the expanse of the liberation, much of which cuts across traditional boundaries.

The nature of the subject matter has meant that somewhat arbitrary boundaries have sometimes been drawn in chapters. The questions of why work or why not work in Chapters 2 and 3, for example, are clearly different sides of the same question, and answers to one will equally be answers to the other. In other cases the nature of certain theories means that they have implications for a wide range of research interests, so that they could conveniently be described under more than one heading; segmented labour-market theories are at one and the same time partial explanations of pay differentials, occupational segregation, career profiles of individuals and class analysis; labour supply is part of an explanation of pay differentials and an indication of why and how much individuals want to work; orientations to work are part of a class analysis which treats the actor's perspective seriously—and so on. Needless to say, there is usually only one extended discussion of each topic, although cross-referencing is often given to some of the other implications. Authors whose work has been more wide-ranging tend to appear repeatedly.

The opening quotations have been chosen because they reflect the traditional analysis and to help to side-step the potential criticism of firing at straw men. Obviously there are limits to the extent to which arguments can be documented, but it is hoped that the necessary minimum of support is provided for the claims made.

Chapters 2 and 3 mostly consider the subjective experiences of working or not working. Chapters 4 and 5 consider the occupational division of labour and its associated pay differentials. Chapters 6 and 7 consider the various theories of social change, class analysis being treated in a separate chapter because it has been so central to the tradition of sociological theory.

NOTES

1. For a more detailed discussion *see* Joseph (1983, Ch. 3).
2. *See* Clark (1982, p. 3).
3. These figures are from the Women and Employment Survey; *see* Martin and Roberts (1984).
4. *See* Elias and Main (1982) for a display of these changes.
5. *See* Dex (1984).
6. *See* Bhrolchain (1983).
7. The figures are quoted from Clark (1982).
8. The figures are quoted from Dex and Perry (1984).
9. The figures are quoted from Dex and Shaw (1984).
10. *See* Dex (1978).
11. *See* Roberts (1981), Annex I.
12. *See* Dex and Perry (1984) and Rosenfeld (1980).
13. The figures are quoted from Martin and Roberts (1984, p. 23).
14. The figures are quoted from Martin and Roberts (1984, p. 24).
15. *See* Roberts (1981), Stanley and Wise (1983), Matthews (1982), Bell and Roberts (1984) and many other articles.
16. Allen (1982) suggests that sexism is morally repugnant and so should be resisted in society and in social science.
17. *See* Stanley (1974).
18. Kuhn and Wolpe (1978, pp 5–6) say: 'The problematic relationship between theory and "practice" always poses itself quite acutely for the women's movement, precisely because it has been one of the projects of the movement to construct knowledge of the nature and causes of our oppression, with a view to changing that situation'.
19. See Stanley and Wise (1983, p. 25).
20. I have argued this position more fully in a paper 'Objective Facts in Social Science', 1983, Mimeo—unpublished, presented at a workshop on Philosophy and Objectivity. The paper argues that even more sophisticated statements of relativism involve the same contradiction.
21. For a description of 'subjective viewpoint', *see* Stanley and Wise (1983, p. 10).
22. *See* Roberts (1978) quoting Bart on the terminology of 'soft' or 'hard'.
23. *See* Kuhn and Wolpe (1978) and Beechey (1977).
24. *See* Middleton (1979) for a useful discussion of relationships between the sexes in the Middle Ages.
25. For a discussion of patriarchy and for details of the debate, *see* Beechey (1979) and Hartmann (1979). Beechey (1984) suggests that the concept of 'patriarchy' has been more popular in the USA than in Britain.
26. For an alternative approach to some of this material, via a discussion of paradigms, *see* Beechey (1984).

2 Why Work?

The orientations and aspirations which the individual finds prevalent in family, school, relatives, friends and other groups to which he looks for clues on how to live are themselves strongly shaped by work experience of the past as well as present generations, and this experience will have been derived from the same class stratified division of labour as he is himself entering or about to enter.

(Fox, 1980, p. 156)

This might seem to be an inappropriate quotation if we are concerned with the question of why people work. But in fact it accurately represents a tradition of research in industrial sociology which has focused on men's employment and men's orientation to work. If one starts off by assuming that men are always employed, then the question of 'Why work?' seems less interesting. The tradition focused, therefore, on examining the meanings men attach to their work and where these meanings originate.

The question of 'Why work?' can be meaningfully asked of women, especially if they are assumed not to work. The question has therefore been included in large-scale surveys of women's employment but not in men's surveys.[1] If women are not necessarily employed, it becomes less relevant to investigate their orientations and attitudes to work. The quotation from Fox illustrates that women can have an implicit, although undiscussed, role in the family socialisation process. The failure to discuss the family in industrial sociology suggests that it was regarded as unimportant—or certainly less important than the work-place—in forming men's orientations to work.

These assumptions about men and women dominated at least half a century of research in the subjective aspects of industrial sociology; so we have had few, if any, answers to

20

why men work. We have more knowledge about men's experiences of not working since this is a deviation from the norm which thus attracted interest from sociologists. For women, until recently, there has been little sociological investigation of women's working experiences and certainly no consideration of why women might not be working at any particular time. There have been a set of parallel consequences in discussions of policies with respect to, for example, retirement or child care. The literature reviewed in this chapter and the next examines these two related areas of sociological concern, charting their liberation from these restricting assumptions. However, the picture is slightly more complicated than painted so far.

A perspective on the breadth of interest in the subjective aspects of working can be gained from the list of headings under which such things are discussed: attitudes to work, orientations to work, motivations to work, alienation from work or the ideology of work. These cross the boundaries of sociology into psychology, but we shall not.[2] These subject matters have drawn interest from various groups. For instance, management has been interested in people's motivation to work, with the aim of removing all restrictions on output; for example, by decreasing absenteeism and decreasing industrial relations strife. Sociologists and psychologists have been employed to help in these tasks. Sociological theorists have been interested in workers' attitudes towards their work as evidence of their class consciousness and class awareness, for the political implications such attitudes might have (e.g. in voting behaviour) or for the identification of segments within labour markets. These are just some of the areas with an interest in workers' orientations to work.

The managerial interest has remained constant throughout this century and it is bound up with the process of industrialisation, the introduction of new technology and the changes in skills which have resulted. The early Scientific Management school, the Human Relations school and the Technological Determinism school are all part of this tradition of interest. More recently, sociologists from an action-theory perspective have wanted to give more priority to the meaning individuals attach to their actions, and there has been a more radical questioning of why people tolerate monotony, boredom and the lack of control in their working experiences. In reaction against so-called crude Marxist determinism, radical sociologists have also become interested in worker's active resistence to management.

These developments have gone to and fro across the Atlantic, sometimes cross-fertilising each other, in other cases developing simultaneously on both sides. One recent line of development, workers' orientations to work, has been more predominantly on the UK side, partly through the linkage which British industrial sociologists have been making between workers' attitudes and class analysis (as part of the European tradition of class analysis). The topics which are currently of interest include the issue of how to interpret earlier results which found that large proportions of workers said they were satisfied with their jobs. Sociologists are also considering the origins of orientations to work and how far these orientations are influenced or formed by technological change, work design, prior socialisation, expectations of work, workplace experiences, the worker's capacity for independent action and resistance, and the worker's willingness to accommodate himself to changes. There is also an interest in discussing whether orientations to work exist at all in any meaningful sense and, if so, whether they are static or flexible, weak or strong. Men are the focus of all these discussions in the main, although things are starting to change.

Brown's review (1976) of the treatment of women as employees suggests that where they have not been neglected altogether, women are treated as unisex and indistinguishable from men; alternatively Brown suggests that married women have been treated as a special or social problem. Feldberg and Glenn (1979) describe this treatment of women as part of a 'gender model'—in contrast to the 'job model', which is used to study male workers. Women workers are now starting to get mentioned in the textbook reviews of industrial sociology. Hill (1981, p. 120) summarises what he sees as the present state of affairs by saying; 'not a lot is known about the orientations of women workers as distinct from men'. The Brown *et al* review (1983) repeats Hill's point about women's relative neglect, adding that part of the reason for this disregard is the focus on manufacturing by industrial sociologists. However, these reviewers have missed an important point.

As well as being neglected (relative to men) as a subject for study within the workplace, the research on women workers has gone relatively unnoticed and unrecognised by industrial sociologists. There are many more studies of women workers than those listed by Hill (1981). The Brown *et al*. review also tends to underplay the number of studies which contained women, partly because their review starts in 1968 but also because their main conclusions are drawn from a smaller sample of studies than the total ones reviewed in the annotated selected list in their Appendix B. This longer list of studies contains more women than one is led to expect in the main-text review. Why then, one wonders, have women been lost from the record.

Brown's claim (1976) that many researchers have treated workers as unisex and male is part of the reason, no doubt, although this phenonemon itself needs to be explained. Presumably at some stage these studies have been thought uninteresting and insignificant. It is not clear, however, which criteria were used to exclude them, or why the studies of women are given less prominence in reviews than those of men. One might be tempted to think that neglected studies of women workers have been less scholarly, except that some infamously unscholarly work has become a household name and gets pride of place in reviews of industrial sociological literature. Anthony's point (1977) about the influence of prescriptive views of what work ought to be may also be part of an explanation. Anthony shows that, broadly speaking, work has been seen either as a necessity and something which has to be done or as a moral duty and valuable in and for itself. As such, employment has tended to receive pride of place, not only in our society but also in sociological analyses. Women are seen as marginal to these two traditions of work and so are given marginal attention by sociologists of work.

Whatever the explanation, however, it is clear that some

blatant sexism runs through the discipline in this respect (which is also evident in society). It is worth noting that some of the more recent findings that large proportions of men do not give work a pre-eminent place in their lives has not served to narrow the gap between the sexes, presumably because the tradition of ignoring women is deeply embedded.

. The rest of this chapter will now review chronologically some of the work in industrial sociology concerned with workers' orientations to work in order to illustrate that this tradition has either neglected to study women, or treated workers as unisex but male, or treated women as a social problem or failed to recognise studies of women workers. The consequences of these approaches to women workers are wide-ranging, and their effects have served to restrict both the scope of the discipline and discussion of policies about workers. Industrial sociology has been infused with erroneous and confused deductions and assumptions about women as a result of this tradition; as Brown (1976) pointed out, in effect we know little about the division of labour, which is primarily a sexual division, as a result. A new wave of empirical studies of women employees is beginning to challenge the errors of the past, part of which involves a new recognition of earlier studies which were previously ignored.

SCIENTIFIC MANAGEMENT

Scientific management is often the starting point for reviews of the stages of development in industrial sociology. This development in management strategy and work design owes much to F.W. Taylor, sometimes called 'speedy Taylor'.[3] Braverman (1974) argued that scientific management was not the science of work but the science of management. On this ground one could argue about whether this approach to work should be included in a review of the study of sociology rather than the historical practice of management, but it is important to include it here as the background against which later developments took place. Also, Taylor did base his ideas on observations of the work process, and on this basis scientific management is rightly included.[4] (Taylor's study was the beginning of a long tradition of focusing on male manual workers in industrial sociology, although the workers have often been described in unisex terms.)

In his observations first of the armed forces and then at Midvale Steel Company in the 1880s, Taylor decided that industry was inefficient and wasteful. He began to theorise about the nature of this inefficiency, which he called 'soldiering' in an *ad hoc* manner, and he suggested that it arose either because of men's natural laziness or because a group of men encouraged each other to control and reduce their joint output. They could get away with this strategy, which Taylor thought was rational in the circumstances, because managers were on the whole incompetent and had to use guesswork or rules of thumb to set tasks and target times.

Taylor suggested a package of changes intended to promote efficiency; they concerned the organisational structure, the design and measurement of work tasks and the motivation of workers. Thus, Taylor suggested two measures: first, a type of supervision and foremanship which was to complement, second, a work-study method of work tasks. In the whole study he set out to observe men skilled in certain tasks in order to define the elements of their work task and to time each component with a stop-watch. In some cases the task might be split into components and the sequence of completing components altered. At the end of the study, the best and quickest method for completing this task would be known, and when combined with the 'best' pauses for rest the manager could calculate the maximum amount of work possible in a day. The fulfilment of these targets depended upon having the third element: recruiting a 'first-class man' for the work and paying him 'a fair day's pay for a fair day's work'. Taylor only gave scanty guidelines on how to recognise first-class men for any particular job, although he recognised that elements of training would contribute to his make-up, as well as inherent or natural characteristics. Rose (1975, p. 36) quotes Taylor's prescription for a first-class pig-iron handler: 'Now one of the first requirements of a man who is fit to handle pig-iron as a regular occupation is that he shall be so stupid and phlegmatic that he more nearly resembles in his mental make-up the ox than any other type.' The reward for a fair day's work should be above the going rate for similar work in the locality and be on a sliding scale according to the proximity to the target, with bonuses being awarded for reaching the target. Taylor got a chance to put these ideas into practice when he was appointed as a management consultant to the Bethlehem Steel Company in 1898, although he did not implement the ideas without some struggles. His influence on management strategy and work design, however, goes well into the twentieth century.

There are some obvious flaws in Taylor's reasoning which are more visible in hindsight, and Rose (1975) amongst others has listed criticisms of his schemes. What is important to note for our purposes is that Taylor's observations and his theorising was based on a model or image of a typical worker. Some of the components of this model worker have been noted already; the worker ideally was rational and essentially economistic in his motivation; he should also think individualistically about his work and his contract of employment. In addition, workers could be hedonistic in their use of leisure and they would need intricate bonuses to keep them at work. In Taylor's view, therefore, men were seen essentially as machines, and they were supposed to function in a clockwork fashion, if given adequate servicing. Taylor also recognised that workers might have different priorities, and this implied that there might be segments within the labour forces of the kind noted by early classical economists.[5] It almost goes without saying now, however, that Taylor's typical worker is a male manual worker; not surprisingly, perhaps, in view of his work experiences in steel and metal manufacturing processes. The applications of these principles, as well as their theory, was initially on *male* manual work processes. The industrial sociology reviews have not thought it worthwhile to mention this male-centred focus of Taylor's work, and this is a clear example of treating workers as unisex, even though it is men who are being described.

HUMAN RELATIONS

Taylorism is the background against which the Human Relations school of thought emerged, and it is interesting that similar developments emerged simultaneously on both sides of the Atlantic. The British work had more of a psychological flavour, the US work was more sociological; but the lessons learnt were similar, and in both cases the basis of the changes lies in a series of empirical studies of work in industry. The British school became known as 'human factor industrial psychology', but the American term 'human relations' gradually became the predominant label of both developments. The contribution of the British human factor industrial psychology, according to Rose (1975), was that it substituted a different image for Taylor's picture of a worker. Taylor's image of a greedy robot was substituted by the image of a worker as a complex organism; a human factor was thus injected back into the picture. How did this development occur?

The British development had its origins in the Health of Munitions Workers Committee, which was set up in 1915 after the start of First World War to study the decline in output, absenteeism and increasing reports of sickness in the industry. They published a report about the conditions of work, making various suggestions for changes and further investigation. At the end of the war two institutions were set up to pursue some of the committee's suggestions; they were the Industrial Fatigue (later Health) Research Board of 1919 and the National Institute of Industrial Psychology of 1921. Charles S. Myers was an important influence in both of these institutions, in initiating a large number of studies and as a publicist and fund-raiser for the work. The studies undertaken by these institutions were on topics like fatigue, monotony and boredom at work, the effects of the menstrual cycle, the effects of lifting heavy loads on women's capacity to work and sickness in different working conditions.

One theme which began to emerge in the results of these studies, and which explains the label attached to this development, is that subjective psychological perceptions of workers and their environment are crucially important in the work process and need to be injected into purely physiological descriptions of phenomena, like fatigue. Physiological accounts were the most common theories explaining human behaviour and experiences at the time. This was an important step in the development of industrial psychology, therefore, and it revealed that grossly oversimplified work processes were embedded in Taylor's theories. These studies introduced a social/psychological aspect, or a 'human factor', into what was previously either a wholly physiological or a crude machine-like image of a worker.

This development and the large number of studies subsequently produced have been neglected on the whole. Current textbooks on industrial sociology fail to mention this work, and even industrial psychology texts give Myers only a brief mention. Rose (1975, p. 65) draws attention to this neglect and suggests that it is understandable because the studies produced were 'heavy reading', having the air of a 'museum piece', despite their being, as Rose sees it, an important historical innovation based on painstaking work.

Rose fails to mention that a large proportion of these studies were of women. The initial Munitions Committee report emphasised its interest in the far-reaching issue of the social and economic conditions of women's labour, and subsequent work specifically took up the recommendations to investigate the conditions of women's work. I would suggest that these studies have not been lost, relatively speaking, from the tradition, because they make heavy reading. By that criterion much of what is revered should also have disappeared into oblivion. More likely, they were lost because they largely contain information about women workers, who after all were only marginal to the workforce.

The study of this marginal or hidden workforce, however, made a valuable contribution to the discipline. Studies which took women's work seriously in the early part of this century served to overturn crude robot-like images of workers. The 'human factor' which was injected into the image of industrial workers was one which came largely from women; the credit has gone unacknowledged.

It is fascinating to discover a similar development in the

USA occurring at the same time, which, whilst being well known and regularly included in review material, owes its origin to the study of women; a fact which is less often noted. This development is the Human Relations tradition, often associated with the name of Elton Mayo, although the link is somewhat tenuous.[6] A series of experiments were enacted at the Western Electric Company in 1924–25, commonly known as the Hawthorne workers' experiments. These experiments were primarily concerned with the effects on output of certain environmental changes and with testing the effect of work incentives. Thus, the artificial lighting was changed in one case, and in two other experiments in the Relay Assembly Test Room and one in the Mica-Splitting Test Room, investigations were carried out to examine the bio-psychological influences on output. These experiments were the first phase of a much larger development. In the mid-1920s, and overlapping with these earlier studies, a series of fairly detailed interviews began which, as they developed, had more in common with psychotherapy counselling. Another phase of experiments and observations began in 1932 using anthropologists' observation techniques. This later set of observations became known as the Bank Wiring Room experiment.

Most commentators describe the content of this set of experiments in terms of unisex worker's responses, and the 'Hawthorne effects' which were thought to be discovered are similarly described. The first Hawthorne effect suggests that a person's knowledge of being an experimental subject modifies the subject's behaviour. The second Hawthorne effect suggests that production output rose because the experiment transformed the subject's total industrial situation, especially in the lighting experiments, by having the observer become a friendly supervisor. Broadly speaking, the results suggested that a complexity of factors influences the attitudes and behaviour of workers at work. In this sense the results are identical to the British 'human factor' results described above.

Most of the subjects of these experiments were women. In particular, the early lighting experiments on the basis of which the two Hawthorne effects were formulated were all women, and the researcher observing them who was thought to initiate these effects on their output, was a man. The research reports of these experiments did not see fit to attach any importance to this gender division. Nor did they suspect a gender explanation for some of their other findings; for example, the results from the observation of male workers in the Bank Wiring Room differed from those of the women workers in the Relay Assembly Test Room. In the same report, however, Roethlisberger and Dickson do recognise that men's and women's attitudes to work differ.

The methods of conducting this set of experiments were very sloppy, and the results are a case study in the problems of allowing lapses in experimental control rather than being a substantive contribution to our knowledge of worker's behaviour. This did not prevent Elton Mayo and many managers from pursuing these ideas, thinking that gener-alisations about supervisory style, productivity and worker morale had been found through these experiments. They did not stop to consider, even though they were aware of gender differences between workers, the extent to which their conclusions applied to both sexes. Later studies which followed in this tradition were of a better quality generally, but in this aspect of gender-blindness they remain the same. For example, Coch and French (1948) and British studies influenced by these developments such as Lupton (1963) and Cunnison (1966)[7] all have women factory workers in their samples as well as men. Often, the findings were still presented as having general applicability to the unisex worker when this may not necessarily have been the case. The opportunities for drawing out gender distinctions were often ignored, as were the opportunities to make a contribu-tion to our understanding of men's and women's positions in industry or society, and the sexual division of labour.

We have in the Human Relations school, therefore, a further example of the treatment of workers as unisex, which had the consequence that our understanding of social relations in the workplace was restricted, confused and even incorrect in some cases. The failure to recognise and examine gender differences meant that the potential of these often detailed studies was never realised. What is worth noting, however, is that the model of the worker changed from one which was individualistic to one which recognised the importance of social groups and the complexity of a worker's motivation and behaviour. This change of image has been used to characterise the Human Relations school's contribution to the discipline, and the changes again owe their origins to the study of women workers. As we have said, the study of women workers injected a 'human' element into the model of a worker. The long-term practical effects of the Human Relations conclusions were that managements tried to enrich the working environment of workers. Whilst some of these enriching measures are of dubious value, there undoubtedly have been some benefits to workers, men and women alike, from such changes. Perhaps it is ironic that management had very little grounds for expecting that such changes would influence working men's behaviour.

ORIENTATIONS TO WORK

The studies of workers' attitudes to work took a great leap forward in Britain in the 1960s, one which promoted the term 'orientation' into sociologist's vocabulary and dictionaries. The development came with the work of Goldthorpe *et al.* (1968) and the foundation work of one of the authors, Lockwood (1966)—the Affluent Worker study, as it has become known. It is worth describing some of the results of this study, partly because it is attributed such prominence and for its undoubted influence on the succeeding studies of orientations to work. Also, it is worth highlighting some neglected asides in this study which in retrospect turn out to be important for our understanding of women's work and for the reconceptualisation of orientations to work which has been taking place. These notes were neglected at the time probably because the limelight focused on the vociferous debate between Goldthorpe, Daniel and others on men's orientations. These insights had to be rediscovered by subsequent studies in order for a reconceptualisation to take place.

Textbook reviews of the Affluent Worker study describe its contribution under the heading 'action approach' or 'actionalism'. By this they mean that the earlier Human Relations and Technological Determinism schools were to be superceded by the view that workers played an active role in determining their workplace experiences.[8] In an action framework the role of technology is de-emphasised. As such, the Affluent Worker study had antecedents in Etzioni (1960) and some French research, although these studies had not attracted the same publicity. The renown of the Affluent Worker study went beyond its action approach, however. The study demonstrated that an understanding of workers' attitudes to their work cannot stop with a description of the attitudes themselves but must look outside the workplace as well as inside it for explanations of attitude formation. The study took a step away from another area of social psychological literature which focused solely on such attitudes and their correlations with other largely personal characteristics.[9] Ironically, these conclusions about worker's orientations were incidental to the main purpose of the study, which had been to examine the embourgeoisment thesis about the new affluent working-class, and to study workers' class consciousness.[10] The conclusions about orientations to work drew most of the fire from other researchers, and not surprisingly, minor conclusions then went unnoticed.

The Affluent Worker Study

There are any number of summaries of this famous study because it 'went directly into the required reading lists for British sociologists' (Rose, 1975, p. 164).[11] A group of male manual workers were interviewed in Luton, from three types of production processes: mass-production, batch-production and process production.[12] They also included workers with varying degrees of skill. The investigators focused on the workers' patterns of attitudes and behaviour and found that there were hardly any significant differences between workers in different types of production. Even differences between workers of different levels of skill were relatively minor. There was a prevailing or dominant pattern of an 'instrumental worker'. The primary meaning of work to an instrumental worker is that work is a means to an end, the end being external to the work situation. The worker therefore gains mainly extrinsic rewards from his work.

What makes this description more unusual and innovative is the link which Goldthorpe *et al.* (1968, p. 175) made between this instrumentalism and a privatised approach to life for these workers: 'a privatised social life and an instrumental orientation to work may in this way be seen as mutually supportive aspects of a particular life-style'. The notion of 'orientation to work' which Goldthorpe is using here is defined as 'the meaning which men give to their work and . . . the place and function they accord to work within their lives as a whole' (Goldthorpe *et al.* 1968, p. 9). Other types of orientation were contrasted, but these came from other studies rather than being the empirical results of this study. Subsequent work has debated almost all of the elements of Goldthorpe *et al*'s research on the orientation to work, but before we move on, it is important to note some of the Affluent Worker study's conclusions which have since been neglected.

A highly instrumental orientation to work was linked to a number of social correlates. One of these was the life-cycle stage of these male workers, who were largely of a similar age, being married and having one or more dependent children. The authors cautiously drew the conclusion, because they had no source of comparison, that the life-cycle position of men influences their orientation to work. Some of the men were found to have left a previous job to take up their current job on having a family, and the previous job was preferred. Reviewers of this study in industrial sociology took up what they saw as the implication of this point at a general and abstract level; that is, that orientations to work are determined outside the workplace and not through the experience of work itself. Daniel (1969) in particular contested this conclusion. The ensuing discussions debated what they thought were the determinants of male workers' orientations to work. The results of Goldthorpe *et al.* were pointing to an influence of women in male worker's orientations, but this point was almost entirely lost. Platt's

(1984) discussion of how the Affluent Worker study became a classic is instructive about why certain aspects of the work were unrecognised as both the left and industrial sociologists disputed many of the findings of the study; also many erroneous summaries and characatures were published.

There was a further hint of the importance of women in an early summary of the sample by the authors. In comparing the economic position of the 229 male manual workers with the 54 white-collar workers, white-collar workers were found to have an advantage in family income but not in husband's income. This discrepancy resulted from the fact that more wives of the white-collar men worked and this group had fewer dependent children. The authors suggest that 'the advantage appear to result from some more or less deliberate family policy' (Goldthorpe *et al.*, 1968, p. 6). The implicit importance of women and the family was not taken up by the authors; nor, indeed, by subsequent researchers. However, these findings are in full accord with the more recent reconceptualisations of worker's orientations; that is, that men's orientations to work cannot be understood without reference to women and that the same is true of women's orientations.

Later Studies

It is important to pursue the tradition of studying orientations to work beyond the Affluent Worker study because it is in the context of those later studies that the study of women's orientations to work began. Subsequent researchers have sought to elaborate upon the Goldthorpe *et al.*'s list of three orientations by adding occupational orientations,[13] or by drawing finer distinctions between instrumental and economistic orientations.[14] Much of this work was done by research students supervised at least in part by authors of the original study. Others have suggested that workers have complex, multi-stranded orientations. Brown (1973) and Daniel (1969, 1973) have suggested that workers have a variety of expectations and that these lead to a complex set of orientations which are unlikely to be captured under a single label. Linked to this is a problem of whether an orientation has a stable and independent existence. The alternative view to seeing orientations as stable is to see them as fluid and brought about by certain circumstances which can be thought to contribute to their construction. As such, orientations are said to be unstable and more or less dependent on these circumstances. Debates have occurred, in addition, over the origin of worker's orientations,[15] as mentioned already, and over how to interpret the empirical findings about workers' attitudes.[16]

It is possible to criticise most of the Goldthorpe *et al.* critics on a number of grounds, but this is not our primary concern.[17] Insofar as these critics questioned whether orientations exist at all, the debate became largely semantic, and fortunately subsequent researchers have been prepared to strengthen the definition of an orientation if only in order to test for its existence. Platt (1984) noted that there is still no attempt to resolve the debate about the origins of workers' orientations using longitudinal data. The continuing arguments are therefore all hypothetical. There is a conceptual vagueness about the study of men's orientations to work over the decade following the Affluent Worker study.

Some clarity has been injected, more recently, from a study by Blackburn and Mann (1979) of a group of male manual workers in Peterborough. They considered as an empirical question the issue of whether men have orientations to work. They recognised that if an orientation to work is to be a meaningful concept, it must be regarded as a relatively stable property of people which underlies their choices rather than merely arising in the act of choosing. Orientations might, however, be strong or weak. Blackburn and Mann's study of Peterborough workers found that orientations to work did exist in their men's sample. They concluded about job choice, with some qualifications, 'not only that orientations exist but also that they have greater influence' (1979, p. 217). The orientations they discovered did not always coincide with earlier types, either those of Goldthorpe *et al.* or others.

Blackburn and Mann did produce empirical evidence that orientations to work exist in men. It makes sense, therefore, to discuss the origins and implications of such orientations.

The general view about orientations which has now emerged is that orientations should be examined within the context of social structures. Also, the idea of a dominant orientation should not be taken to mean that a person has no other thoughts on the subject. It is also generally agreed that if we are going to understand men's orientations correctly, we will need to distinguish between prior expectations and accommodated responses.[18] Very little, if any, consideration had been given since Goldthorpe *et al.* to the potential or actual role that women might play in men's orientation formation.

Women's Orientations

As we have noted already, discussions of orientations to work in industrial sociology texts have taken place, for the most part, in unisex terms. Reference is made to 'the worker' or 'workers' orientations', but most of the research has been carried out on samples of men. When women have been included, very little analysis was made of any differences between men and women.

Feldberg and Glenn (1979) provided two case studies which incorporated women, but they both approached the analysis of the women in a different way from that of men. As we have seen, Feldberg and Glenn (1979) called the two approaches the 'gender model' for women versus the 'job model' for men. The essence of the distinction which they chart from the studies of Blauner's (1964) *Alienation and Freedom* and Beynon and Blackburn's (1972) *Perceptions of Work* is that the job model treats the work people do as the primary explanatory variable of their attitudes and behaviour both on and off the job, whereas the gender model ignores the types of jobs and working conditions and explains workers' behaviour in terms of their personal characteristics or their family situation. Men are the workers who are analysed through the job model and women are examined using the gender model, and this use of sex-segregated models coincides with the view of men as primarily breadwinners and workers and women primarily as wives.

Other studies have suffered from making assumptions

about women's orientations to work which have had no empirical grounding. Such assumptions tend to suggest that women are less committed or less attached to work than men. The stereotypes about womens' attitudes towards work abound, and it is not difficult to find examples, either expressed or reported, from British and American sources. Sometimes the stereotypes even conflict. For example:

—Women 'find it hard to reject the notion that their prime role is in the home "servicing" male breadwinners'.[19]

—Women work only for pin money.[20]

—Women do not mind and even prefer boring work.[21]

—Women have an instrumental orientation to work: young women are only interested in work as a means to find a husband; older women work to finance home improvements.[22]

—Women only work for money and are not involved in work personally.[23]

—Women do not like to show initiative in their work and they are less interested in challenging jobs or promotion than men.[24]

Such stereotypes have effectively restricted the study of women's orientations to work and have had certain consequences in policy discussions of issues like retirement and child care. After all, if one knows everything about women to start with, or if they are only marginal workers anyway, why bother examining or worrying about whether they will have problems retiring. Not only are these stereotypes a false view of women, they imply an account of men's orientations, opposite to women's characteristics, which also turn out to be false according to the empirical studies available. Studies since Dubin (1956, 1976) and Goldthorpe *et al.* (1968) have drawn attention to the fact that many men do not see work as a 'central life interest', and men have instrumental orientations to work. If women are marginal workers on these criteria, then so are men.

The use of stereotypes about women's orientations to work, resting as they do on ignorance and false assumptions, have been criticised by feminist writers. Feminists have pointed out that these false assumptions about the differences between men and women workers have acted like myths and have perpetuated misunderstandings about the actual nature of women's and men's attitudes. This is not to say that there are no differences between women and men but that the actual differences are not necessarily the ones commonly assumed. The criticisms have been followed up by empirical work in Britain and the USA which has begun the task of destroying the myths and filling in the gaps in our knowledge. Studies have also begun to examine the issue of whether women have orientations to work whose origins and relationships with other experiences can be examined. The evidence has been accumulating on both sides of the Atlantic that the stereotypical views about women are at best half-truths and in some cases clearly wrong, and that women are not homogenous.[25] Some of the findings about women's attitudes have been summarised below.

The idea that women work for pin money fails to consider the sizeable and increasing proportion of women who are not maintained by an employed man. Recent estimates suggest that this is around 10 per cent of women with children in Britain in 1980. The Women and Employment Survey showed that the majority of women reject this view of their work and also that a large proportion of women work in order to earn money to buy basic necessities. In the USA there was little difference between men and women who were asked whether they would give up their job if they no longer needed to work. Martin and Fryer's (1972) study of redundant men found that the majority disagreed with the view that there is no reason for having a job if you have enough money without working. Studies show that more women than men declared that friendly and helpful relations with their fellow workers was important, and women's priorities about work differ from those of men. When the intellectual elements were controlled for, the dissatisfaction of women and men with undemanding jobs were equal. It is also worth noting that extensive studies of boredom and monotony by the Industrial Fatigue Research Board described earlier found no significant differences between the sexes as early as the 1920s.

There are a number of small-scale studies of workers'

attitudes in Britain which have contained comparisons between men and women. Brown *et al.* (1983) contains a review of the findings. Whilst there are some differences between the sexes, what stands out in the results are the similarities between men and women. One study found that pay was the most important feature of a job for 59 per cent of male manual workers, 40 per cent of women manual workers, 34 per cent of male non-manual workers and 44 per cent of women non-manual workers.[26] A study by Brown *et al.* of workers in Newcastle-upon-Tyne summarised in the same review reached the same conclusions. The studies Brown *et al.* review also found that 'the same kinds of reasons dominated men's and women's responses' on the question of reasons for dissatisfaction with a job (p. 29).

Where men and women differed, men attached more importance to working conditions or security whereas women attached more importance to convenience of hours and travel. One study found that men and women in Manchester had similar satisfaction scores for all features of work except promotion, women being less satisfied with their promotion prospects than men.[27] Brown *et al.*'s own study found that when second and third (and so on) choices were considered in an aggregate form along with the first choice, men and women's attitudes and priorities appeared to be more similar than dissimilar.

Further details about women's attitudes have become available from large-scale surveys, although there is no male sample for comparison.[28] Martin and Roberts's (1984) analysis of the Women and Employment Survey found that the majority of working women had a high financial dependence upon working and enjoyed working. High proportions of working women said that they were satisfied with their jobs, but whilst they were satisfied with the extrinsic features like hours and work-mates, they were not so satisfied with rates of pay or their prospects. On the question of why women work, which has always been thought to be an appropriate question for women, the Women and Employment Survey, like its predecessor by Hunt (1968), found that women say that they work for economic reasons. The Women and Employment Survey found that 67 per cent of working married mothers worked to earn money for basic essentials or to buy extras (Martin and Roberts, 1984, p. 110).

On the issue of whether women have orientations to work, a study by Beynon and Blackburn (1972) suggested that they do. Beynon and Blackburn also suggested that women who work part-time have different orientations to those who work full-time, largely because of a life-cycle effect. Goldthorpe *et al.* had suggested that men also have variations in their orientations to work over their life-cycles. McNally's (1979) analysis of temporary clerical workers drew the same conclusion as Beynon and Blackburn that women do have orientations to work. However, her results dismissed the idea that there is a single feminine orientation to work. From Brown *et al.*'s (1983) review of the studies on orientations to work we could conclude that there are a sizeable group of women who have orientations to work which are economistic, in the terms described for men. A study by Dex (1983) of the Women and Employment Survey also found that it made sense to call certain combinations of attitudes, orientations to work.

A study by Agassi (1979) made international comparisons between women in the workplace in the USA, West Germany and Israel in different occupations, examining in particular the incidence of instrumental attitudes to work in women. She found that less than a quarter of a population of women employed in jobs at lower than semi-professional level held a clear-cut instrumental attitude toward their work, and instrumental attitudes, where found, were suggested to be the outcome of resignation, higher in older workers and in jobs with the lowest content. The level of task characteristics of a job was found to be the most important factor explaining differences between women workers in the importance they attached to aspects of their job, and in their attachment to work and in their self-confidence. She suggests that these findings are in contrast to theories based on male (unisex) workers which suggest that the level of intrinsic work characterisation in a job is devoid of significance for unskilled and semi-skilled or industrial workers.

The increased availability of work-history data in the USA and more recently in Britain is facilitating more sophisticated analyses of women's attitude formation. Such analyses for men might have resolved some of the controversies over the Affluent Worker study a long time ago. Using the work-history data in the British Women and Employment Survey data, Dex (1983) found that women's orientations to work were correlated with their working status at the time, their life-cycle stage and their past working experiences. The US National Longitudinal Survey data are allowing researchers to test out whether orientations precede working experiences or are a product of working experiences. A study by Statham and Rhoton (1983) has found that women's past working experiences do affect their subsequent attitudes towards work. They found that the effect of work on attitudes was substantial and possibly increasing in 1972, but that the effect of attitudes on women's working activity was becoming a smaller influence. Women's attitudes were also influenced by their husband's attitudes.

Even taken at face value, studies have shown that many stereotypes are erroneous, or an incomplete account of a more complex set of results. There are probably far more similarities between men and women than was previously thought to be the case. Women have been found to be more economistic or instrumental than was thought to be the case, and men less so, and both experience life-cycle variations in orientations to work. The result is a convergence. When one considers that women's attitudes may also be partly a product of their different and often less demanding jobs, a difference which studies find difficult to control for since women and men are in different jobs, then the assumed differences between the sexes may be even smaller. We might add also that sociologists have been quick to point out the flaws of taking results about men's work at face value; in particular, they have questioned whether the high proportion of men who appear satisfied with the work means that they are actually satisfied.[29] Similar doubts about women's attitudes have not been expressed to the same extent and there has been a far greater tendency to accept a face-value interpretation for women. Studies like Beynon and Blackburn (1972) should also warn us away from drawing erroneous conclusions from the fact that women express job satisfaction; they found that satisfaction and the willingness to complain and industrial action did not correlate very well. The full-time women were the most likely to complain. Their study can be criticised, however, for the way it slips back into a gender-model interpretation of some of the results, as Feldberg and Glenn (1979) have noted.

Studies of women's orientations have been taking place within a local labour-market context (Cousins, Curran and Brown, 1982), within factories (Beynon and Blackburn, 1972; Coyle, 1984; Cavendish, 1982), within occupations (e.g. McNally, 1979; West, 1982) and, more innovatively, within the family (Hunt, 1980). As well as finding that there are many similarities between women's and men's orientations to work, these studies have found that women's orientations, like men's, were found to be influenced by non-work factors, work-related factors, work-history experiences and the character of the local labour market—its level of demand and recruitment patterns in particular. What is more, there are considerable overlaps in the conclusions of the different studies. These studies have also boosted the study of non-manual workers, which means that there is a move away from the tradition of focusing largely on manual workers. Many women have an extraordinary attachment to paid employment. Though women's work has been marginalised, even to themselves, the loss of work, as Coyle (1984) demonstrates, has often highlighted women's genuine attachment to work.

Hunt's (1980) study is worth highlighting since it is a good example of pathbreaking results in this field. This small-scale community study of women's class consciousness in a mining community has demonstrated the importance of the home in the formation of both men's and women's orientations to work and home. This comment by one of the men illustrates part of this point: 'I suppose my main function in life is to provide food and shelter for the people who are dependent on me. So obviously I've got to go and earn in order to do that' (Hunt, 1980, p. 123). What is more, Hunt's study made an important and unique contribution by treating the home as a production unit instead of a consumption unit, and thereby integrating industrial and domestic production. When attitude formation is examined through the socialisation process, the importance of the home and of women's central role stands out even further. MacKenzie (1974) also made this point, although it has remained undiscussed in more recent industrial sociology textbooks. These developments are moving industrial sociological research away from solely focusing on the workplace.

Conclusions

There is now a substantial body of research on women's orientations to paid work which has been filling in gaps in our knowledge about women's attitudes to work. Some of these studies have used similar strategies and approaches to those recommended by reviewers of the men's literature, and they have illustrated that men and women are more similar than was previously supposed. These studies have also demonstrated that common stereotypes about women's orientations involved erroneous views of both women and men. Whilst these studies were not particularly innovatory, changes have resulted in the wake of their findings. Questions previously reserved for women workers are now being extended to men; for example, studies are investigating men's attachment to work and their reasons for working; it is no longer being assumed that a stable commitment to work or an occupation will characterise men's working lives, possibly because of growing unemployment.[30]

Where women have been found to differ from men, feminists want to argue for a more positive view of the differences than has previously been the case; and, indeed, it now looks as if more men are demoting work in their priorities, agreeing with more women that paid work should only be one aspect of one's life rather than the 'central life interest'.[31] Some of the empirical work which supports these conclusions has been available for some time, but the male sociologists, committed to their notions of the overwhelming importance of work in men's lives and that men and women have grossly different attitudes to work, failed to recognise the significance of conflicting evidence.

The studies of women's orientations to work have gone beyond studies of men's orientations through being part of a new development in data collection and handling. There are still gaps, however, as we might expect; part-time women's work is as yet under-researched. It is not only in this respect that women are at the forefront of conceptual developments in industrial sociology, however. We can now see that the home and family are valid and important contexts in which to carry out industrial sociological research, alongside workplace studies, and that men's work cannot be understood without reference to women, just as women's work cannot be understood without reference to men. These are major conceptual changes in the discipline which owe their recognition to women's studies, although hints of some of these conclusions went unrecognised in earlier studies of men. A study of orientations to work is only a part of answers to the question of 'Why work?'. A more complete answer to this question requires an examination of fundamental societal relations, structures, socialisation and values. The discussion of unemployment in the next chapter returns to this theme.

NOTES

1. *See*, for example, Hunt (1968).
2. Hirszowicz's (1981) chapter on 'Motivations to Work' reviews some of the psychological interests in workers' attitudes which are ignored in this volume. He also considers the changing perspectives on workers' needs, the contractual obligations and inducements to work (Contribution Theory), outcome-orientated behaviour (Expectancy Theory) and the study of payment systems, all of which are similarly ignored.
3. This description appears in John Dos Passos USA, Penguin, 1966.
4. For a useful review of scientific management and Taylor, *see* Rose (1975).
5. Rose (1975) noted that Taylor's relation to the classical economists has not been fully explored or documented.
6. Rose (1975) gives a full account of Mayo's contribution, which was mostly as a publicist, sometimes in a vulgarised fashion, and of the empirical results and conclusions emerging from this work. Rose also discusses the overlap and interaction between the British and US

studies. He concludes that the US developments, whilst being aware of the British work, failed to benefit from their experience. It is not clear why this happened. Braverman (1974) makes the common mistake of attributing the Human Relations school to Elton Mayo.

7. Homans, one of Mayo's contemporaries, came to spend a year at Manchester University and stimulated a series of studies which took the Bank Wiring Room results as background—disputing their findings but using in many cases women workers as their samples.

8. The Technological Determinism school has not been reviewed here. It is largely associated with the name of Professor Joan Woodward (1958, 1965), who suggested that technology almost dictates management organisation and industrial relations within firms.

9. *See* Herzberg *et al.* (1957) for a review of the social psychological interests in workers' attitudes.

10. The embourgeoisment thesis current in the late 1950s suggested that the increased prosperity of manual workers in Western industrialised countries was changing the working-class into a middle-class.

11. *See* Hill (1981, Ch. 6), Rose (1975, Ch. 26) or Platt (1984).

12. This description is part of a longer list of the different varieties of production process which derives from Woodward's (1958, 1965) work.

13. For example, Cotgrove and Box (1966) for scientists and Sheldrake (1971) for computer personnel.

14. An instrumental orientation to work is one where the worker sees work as a means to an end, whereas an economistic orientation is one which gives priority to material rewards (e.g. Ingham, 1967, 1970). Fox (1971) drew a distinction between procedural and substantive orientations.

15. For example, Daniel (1969).

16. For example, Fox (1980) and Salman (1980) both suggest that orientations are an accommodation to what is realistically possible. Others debate the consequences of the various men's orientations for their trades union participation, for industrial relations and for political behaviour (e.g. Westergaard, 1970; MacKenzie, 1974).

17. Critics of Goldthorpe *et al.* took their conclusions and findings out of context, enumerated possible and alternative orientations without any empirical support and assumed falsely that Goldthorpe *et al.* were committed to the notion of a stable orientation.

18. Bennett (1974) has suggested a way of making this distinction in empirical work.

19. *See*, Salaman (1980, p. 107).

20. *See* Agassi (1979, p. 7).

21. *See* Beynon and Blackburn (1972, p. 159).

22. *See* McNally (1979, p. 6).

23. *See* Agassi (1979, p. 7).

24. *See* Agassi (1979, pp. 7–8).

25. *See* Crewley, Levitin and Quinn (1973), a US study which set out to test commonly held views on samples of men and women. In Britain,

Hunt (1968), a government social survey, and Martin and Roberts (1984) have provided detailed information from large-scale surveys of women.

26. *See* Brown *et al.* (1983, p. 25).

27. *See* Brown *et al.* (1983, p. 29).

28. Some sociologists have been critical of attitude surveys because they take individuals out of context, but if they are placed alongside case study material, there is no reason why they should not provide valuable large-scale information.

29. One sizeable area of literature which runs alongside the discussion of orientations to work, flitting in and out of its mainstream concerns, has been that of worker-satisfaction studies. These studies and their critiques have been neglected in this review for a number of reasons; their status within industrial sociology is somewhat ambiguous. Many researchers refer to the findings of such studies in order to criticise them. In the early days, satisfaction studies often found that the vast majority of workers said that they were satisfied with their work. Blauner (1960, 1964) engaged in a thorough-going critique and others (e.g. Fox, 1980) are still questioning the meaning of these results. On the other hand, some commentators have made more positive use of these results in that they have combined this declaration of verbal satisfaction with other instances of behavioural dissatisfaction and argued that together these results support a Marxian theory of alienation (e.g. Salaman, 1980). This work and discussion has tended to focus on male manual workers, often working on assembly lines. Occasionally, more psychologically focused studies have compared men and women and have often found that women appear to be more satisfied with work than men. This area of literature has treated women in a similar way to the other studies reviewed here. The focus has been largely on men, and the conclusions drawn claim to be unisex on the whole. The attempts to integrate these results into a more radical critique have also only been applied to men.

30. For example, Dubin *et al.* (1976); Cousins, Curran and Brown (1982).

31. *See* Dubin (1956); Dubin *et al.* (1976).

3 Why Not Work?

With a job, there is a future; without a job, there is a slow death of all that
makes a man ambitious, industrious, and glad to be alive.
> (E. Wight Bakke, 1933, quoted in Kumar, 1984, p. 185)

The converse of asking why people work is obviously to ask
why they do *not* work, so the theme of Chapter 2 is
continued here. A somewhat abitrary division between the
material is therefore being drawn. The tradition of studying
individuals' labour-market decisions has tended to assume
that women will not work. The last chapter reviewed some
of the effects of this assumption on sociological studies;
namely, that asking women why they work was a relevant
question because it was a deviation from what was expected.
Men were not initially asked a similar question because it
was assumed that men 'naturally' always worked. This
chapter will review the further implications and counterpart
to these gendered questions. If men are always assumed to
work, then it becomes relevant to ask questions about their
experience of and reasons for not working. It was thought to
make little sense to ask women about their not-working
experiences. Men's not-working activity has been extensively considered under the heading of 'unemployment'. The
definition of unemployment has been unequivocal for men
in this literature, with no thought being given to exploring
the possible definitions. The idea of investigating women's
unemployment is relatively new and it has raised conceptual
issues about the sociological definition and meaning of
unemployment. The conceptual discussions taking place on
this issue not only have wide-ranging relevance to policy-
making and forecasting of the macroeconomy but also to the
study of men's unemployment.

Economists have considered the question of why an individual will work or not as a quantitative issue of how many individual's will offer their labour supply, or are willing participate in the labour force. Labour-supply decisions are only part of an analysis of labour markets in economics, more of which is considered in Chapter 5. Individuals can choose to offer labour power in theory anywhere in the range from zero to sixteen hours, (eight hours for sleep). A standard neoclassical treatment of this choice allows individuals to divide their time between income earning or leisure, and the optimum hours of work for any individual with given preferences could be calculated algebraically. Criticisms have been made of this foundation, which uses an individual decision-maker. Labour-supply decisions were initially considered through examinations of the hours worked by individuals and estimates were calculated on men's data. Anyone who did not work was given zero hours of work, and since most men are assumed to work some hours, no significant biassing effect on the results was thought to emerge from this practice. The consideration of women brought to the forefront the potential biasses in this procedure (although much of the empirical work on women's labour supply has tried to explain only the dichotomous employed or not employed labour-supply decision of women). If one considers the hours of work only of those who are working, however, this gives biassed sizes of the effects of explanatory variables.

The consideration of women's labour-supply decisions has grown considerably in importance in labour economics, partly because the consideration of women has raised new technical and statistical issues which have demanded that new techniques be developed. Researchers who made the conceptual and technical breakthroughs in the analysis of women's labour supply now lead the profession, especially where new techniques are involved. It has also become obvious that the original variables used to explain men's labour supply were insufficient for women's labour supply. The collection and use of women's work-history data have aided supply analysis and have promoted additional conceptual and technique developments for the handling of longitudinal data and the description and modelling of supply decisions of both women and men.

UNEMPLOYMENT

prolonged unemployment is likely to pose less of a problem for the young woman. In the first place . . . work is not usually as important to them as it is for the young men.

(Ashton and Field, 1976, pp. 102–4)

Studies of unemployment exhibit a cyclical trend. They tend to be frequent during recessions and dwindle to nothing at the top of the cycle. The two main peaks of studies of unemployment are undoubtedly the 1930s depression and the recession of the 1970s and 1980s (given the normal lag between the initiation of a study and its publication). Between these major depressions women have become a visible labour force, so it is perhaps not surprising to see them largely absent from studies of unemployment in the 1930s but present in studies in the 1980s. There are, however, other factors which have contributed to both the neglect of women's unemployment prior to the 1970s and their consideration thereafter. These additional explanatory variables are identical to those described in Chapter 2 with reference to women's attitudes towards work. Women have been either neglected because they have not been thought to be serious workers; or they have been incorporated into analyses but not discussed; or on occasions they have been analysed but thereafter ignored by the tradition of research; or they have been considered briefly, if at all, as the wives of unemployed men; or, more recently, they have been assumed to have few problems with unemployment because they can become houseworkers. The early neglect of women can be partly explained by the fact that the traditional focus in industrial sociology has been on manual work in the manufacturing industry, and women have been a small minority of that workforce. The more recent neglect of women owes its origin more to the assumption that men and women workers are different and, in particular, that, despite the lack of evidence, they are assumed to react differently to unemployment, as the opening quotation to this section illustrates. Unemployment is assumed to be a problem for men but not for women. Marshall (1984) accuses feminists of being at least partly responsible for continuing the tradition of neglecting women's unemployment because they have argued against the division between paid and unpaid work. Marshall (1984) makes some very useful points about the tradition of women's neglect,[1] but unfortunately his parting swipe at women's studies is misplaced in the light of the five studies specifically on women's unemployment appearing in the same year as his article.[2]

Unemployment studies have been of different kinds. Economists have examined the amount of unemployment and what causes the difference in the stocks and flows. There is a long history of debate over the explanations for the size of the unemployed workforce which continues today in much the same way as it has since the 1920s—some would say earlier.[3] Certainly when one examines the history of economic thought there are familiar and recurring themes. The main debate in the 1980s is about whether unemployment arises largely because we have interfered with the 'natural' equilibrating mechanisms of the labour market, either by allowing trade unions to bid-up wage rates to levels at which employers are no longer willing to employ people or by offering excessive welfare benefits to the unemployed, which gives them a disincentive to work. Alternatively, it is argued tht unemployment can be partly and largely involuntary because there just are not sufficient jobs for all those who want to work and no built-in mechanisms to move the economy away from this demand-deficiency and towards full employment. The arguments are complex and will not be discussed any further in this volume, although this is not to say they are unimportant; they are merely beyond our scope. It is important to see that economists' interests in unemployment are part of this fundamental concern with the workings of the economy as a whole. Whether we recognise it or not, it is also the case that sociological studies of unemployment have the same context, as more recent sociological analyses are at pains to point out.[4]

Sociologists have asked a series of questions about the

phenomenon of unemployment. The earlier studies from the 1930s tended to ask questions about the experiences of unemployment. What is unemployment like? How does unemployment affect a man's morale and his family life?[5] Marshall (1984) suggests that some of the 1930s accounts were done by journalists rather than sociologists. Orwell's *The Road to Wigan Pier* is a typical example, written after a journey to see how the unemployed (men) lived. There are some modern-day examples of this tradition which serve to remind us of the serious consequences of men being unemployed.[6] Campbell (1984) has even repeated Orwell's journey in the 1980s, and she provides a woman's perspective on the effects of unemployment of both men and women.

Alongside this interest in the experience of being unemployed there have been regular analyses and surveys of unemployment statistics. The unemployment statistics have been manipulated to see what they tell us about the people who are unemployed. This tradition is also alive and well and sometimes performed by civil servants or market researchers as well as academics.[7] There have also been case studies of the organisational and institutional relationships during redundancies, which are not discussed to any great extent here, although some of these studies contain material on the topics under discussion.[8]

Whilst contemporary representatives of these older traditions can be found, some important changes have taken place which have moved away from this earlier focus on the personal and individual characteristics of the unemployed. Sociologists are now examining unemployment and its distribution for what it can tell us about the structure of inequality in society. Writers like Adrian Sinfield, especially, and Peter Townsend through his concern with poverty, have been pointing out that the definition and meaning of unemployment are socially determined and fluctuate accordingly over time. In effect their work has asked a more basic question. What is unemployment? The answer turns out to be complex, and unemployment is seen as clearly related to the value and nature of employment. In addition, a pressure group of policy-minded academics have been tackling particular issues thrown up in the politico-economic debates about unemployment; issues concerning whether there is widespread abuse and scrounging of the welfare benefits for the unemployed; how much unemployment costs and who pays; whether high unemployment is inevitable; and whether the unemployed are to blame for their own situation.[9] The answers to these questions build upon the broader framework for the analysis of unemployment which Sinfield has provided.

The recognition of women's unemployment as a research area has been linked to the conceptual changes in the study of unemployment. Women have been part of a stimulus to ask the more fundamental question about the meaning of unemployment. As Sinfield (1981a, pp. 141–2) points out:

Historical and comparative perspectives help to make us more aware of the ways in which changes in the demand for and supply of labour influence the social construction of definitions of the labour force in general and the unemployed in particular . . . The speed at which women return to the labour force after childbirth is influenced by job opportunities and the readiness of employers to permit flexibility in working hours and to provide creches and other facilities; or, in traditional working-class areas outside the textile towns, by the fact that their husbands are securely in work, and so there is less opposition to married women working.

Studies specifically of women's unemployment and of women who are made redundant have begun to emerge. The picture which they paint is complex. These studies reveal that unemployment as previously defined may not be a wholly appropriate concept for describing all women's experiences, that some women clearly have similar experiences of unemployment to men, and that some women have different experiences of unemployment from men but that the reasons for the differences are not the ones previously assumed.

More of the details of these changes in the traditions and of women's role in them will be described below. A summary of some of the findings of the recent studies of women's unemployment is also provided.

The Experience of Unemployment

The experience of being unemployed has been documented

vividly for men. It is not a pretty picture, and many of the same descriptions are found in the studies of the 1930s and in the more recent literature, as quotations from those interviewed illustrate.[10] Commonly recurring themes are that the men felt a sense of shame, stigma and injured pride about being unemployed and having to accept 'dole'. There could even be a sense of despair of ever working again, especially if the man's skills were obsolete. Sinfield (1981) points out that unemployed men have wanted to stress that they were redundant rather than unemployed. On the basis of these experiences, some researchers suggested that the experience of unemployment progressed through a number of phases. First there was shock and surprise. This was followed by optimism, but pessimism, anxiety and acute distress followed as no jobs were found. Fatalism and brokenness resulted in the end. This description of the psychology of unemployment in Eisenberg and Lazersfeld (1938) still has echoes in the more recent review of Jahoda (1982). Whilst one could undoubtedly find examples of men whose experiences followed this progression, commentators have pointed out that the evidence was largely snapshot data, at a moment in time, and it is strictly incorrect to assume that all men have the same series of experiences, in the same order, in a deterministic fashion.[11] The more recent studies stress that men's experiences of unemployment are quite varied and relate to their age at the time, their health, the duration of their unemployment, their resources, the level of settlement if they are made redundant, the labour-market conditions and their previous working experiences.[12] Longitudinal studies have provided better evidence of the developmental aspects of men's unemployment experiences.[13] A review of the literature by Brown *et al.* (1983) found no evidence of a decrease in the men's motivation to work.

The same studies have examined the job search of the unemployed men, their family relationships and the financial circumstances of the unemployed. On the whole, prolonged unemployment can be seen to place most families in poverty.[14] Wives of unemployed men often find their husband's unemployment particularly burdensome.[15] Recent policy-orientated studies have been anxious to point out that the link between unemployment and poverty which was evident in the 1930s is still apparent in the 1970s and 1980s.[16] The level of social benefits received have not been sufficient to keep families out of poverty. Again, recent studies have been concerned to correlate more details about the unemployed with their experiences of poverty and with the subsequent experiences in the labour market.[17] In particular, Townsend and Norris have examined the work histories of unemployed men to see whether they are recurrently unemployed, and how their previous occupations are related to their experiences of poverty and unemployment.

The general view in the 1970s was that women had been neglected in this tradition of study. Looking back, however, there are a few studies which did incorporate women. The famous Pilgrim Trust report, *Men Without Work* (1938) contained a sample of unemployed women, and forty pages were devoted to discussing them. One of the Industrial Health Research Board studies was of unemployed girls (Smith and Leiper, 1940).[18] The Jahoda *et al.* (1933) study of Marienthal also interviewed unemployed women. Until recently these studies had been lost from the record. More recent studies by Sheppard and Belitsky (1966), Daniel (1974), and Daniel and Stilgoe (1977), which contained samples of women, have received a similar fate; they failed to explore or publish the gender differences in their data to any great extent.

Some of the neglected studies of women's unemployment show that the idea that women experience unemployment differently from men is an oversimplification; a more complex set of relationships can be found in these studies.[19] The Pilgrim Trust study found that women's responses varied according to the local labour-market conditions, although the evidence was somewhat impressionistic. Jahoda *et al.* (1933) found that many unemployed women wanted to return to work for the money and for other social reasons. A more detailed study by Sheppard and Belitsky (1966) of US blue-collar workers who were laid off found that men and women differed in the proportions who said they were not intending to seek alternative employment. Many of the women who were not employed said that they preferred to stay at home, whereas few men gave this response. Daniel (1974, p. 156) concluded from his analysis of the unemployed:

The overall differences in the composition and situation of the sexes and different occupational groups made apparent differences in their experiences while out of work and in seeking new jobs somewhat misleading. Where it was possible to identify groups that were strictly comparable it appeared tht neither sex nor occupational level had very much effect on the unemployed workers' experiences.

Daniel and Stilgoe (1977) found that a higher proportion of women than men were still unemployed at their follow-up interview, often because they wanted to protect the dependent relatives' allowances of their unemployed husband; 38 per cent of the unemployed women said that they would have preferred to be working.

The conclusions from the case studies by Wood (1982) of two firms making women and men redundant were complex. He suggested that the women saw work as vitally important, although they did view work in terms of their family commitments. The women were thought to have a flexible orientation to work and did not think that their right to work was any less than that of men, although they saw men as having a 'breadwinning' role. The women did not have a uniformily passive response to their redundancy. Marshall (1984, p. 244) summarises Wood's conclusions as follows:

The women's reactions, like those of comparable men, were linked to the prevailing managerial profiles and structures of authority within the plants, the managerial strategies adopted for handling the redundancies, and to the available job opportunities that were perceived as being offered by local labour markets. They were unique in at least one respect, however, in that some women responded to redundancy by bringing forward their plans to have a baby.

This limited catalogue of comparisons between women's and men's unemployment do not add up to overwhelming differences between them. Also, when one considers the variables which were not controlled for in some of the studies, it is not clear that the differences are even as great as stated.

A further set of studies of unemployment and redundancy experiences of women have further elaborated some of the complexities of their responses. They contain far too much detail to adequately describe here. The assumption or the myth about women being cushioned by their housework from the effect of unemployment can be seen in those studies to be clearly false. Coyle's (1982) case study of redundancies from two Yorkshire clothing firms during the 1980s recession found that women were very attached to their paid employment. Women worked for financial need but they were found to derive satisfaction and status from their work. Women's unemployment could not be explained solely in terms of their family role, Coyle argued, just as men's unemployment cannot be understood solely in terms of their economic role, although unemployment may not cause a crisis of gender identity for women as it may do for men. It was exceptional for women to use the experiences of unemployment as the occasion to have more or a first baby. Unemployment was often experienced as 'a crisis of autonomy, as a loss of independence, and here women's domestic role is no compensation' (p. 121). Coyle concludes that there are many similarities in women's and men's experiences of unemployment.

Many of the themes found in studies of men are evident in the experiences of unemployed women in Cragg and Dawson's (1984) follow-up study of unemployed women from the 1980 Women and Employment Survey. The experiences quoted below from their study of unemployed women about poverty, hardship, pride in one's work, the degradation of welfare and the satisfaction of independence are all reminiscent of men's experiences:[20]

I go to the social security and they include the family allowance in your income, it's not an extra payment. Their figures are ridiculous anyway . . . They don't realise how much a pair of children's shoes cost. It's more like keeping another adult. (p. 50)

It's all right for Mrs Thatcher to say, do this and do that, but she doesn't have to do it, does she? She isn't living off scraps of food and what have you. I mean, we're triers, we're not scroungers. (p. 50)

When I went to work I made sure that whoever was going to eat what I was making was going to get the best of what I could do . . . You get involved in it. (pp. 30–1)

We just survive on social benefits. That's degrading, like charity. That's why I like working. (p. 22)

It was nice to know I'd got my own money and I could do what I wanted to do. It was because it was my money. (pp. 21–2)

Similar examples of poverty and hardship for unemployed women are vividly portrayed in Dennehy and Sullivan's (1977) study of two Liverpool streets and in Campbell's (1984) imitation of Orwell's journey.

A study of women's redundancies in five firms by Martin and Wallace (n.d.) confirmed that it is stressful, a finding also contained in the Women and Employment Survey (Martin and Roberts, 1984). The unemployed women in the Women and Employment Survey expressed negative attitudes to not working; they were dissatisfied with being at home, eager to start work again, and they had the highest financial stress score in comparison with other non-working and working women. Wood (1982) found that the women in his sample were optimistic about their future, and he expected that this would be the case even if the economic climate was worse and jobs were not so easily available for women. Martin and Wallace (n.d.), by comparing the experiences of women in different regions, with different job opportunities, found that women's optimism was clearly related to the local labour-market conditions. In Martin and Wallace's study, women in the south-east, where one of Wood's case studies was also located, were more optimistic than women in the high-unemployment area of the north-west, and non-manual workers were more optimistic than manual women workers. Martin and Wallace note that these findings are also evident in studies of men.

Many of the women from the redundancy studies of Coyle and Martin and Wallace took a period of rest after they stopped work, although most intended to look for work eventually. Sinfield (1981) describes the same phenomenon in redundant men.

These are just a few of the findings of recent studies which illustrate the similarities between men's and women's experiences as a result of redundancy. It may well be the case that the frequency of these various experiences differs between men and women. We are unable to tell from the studies which have been done. These studies begin to show, however, that a similar set of variables influence both women's and men's unemployment experiences; these include their age, their position in the life-cycle, the local labour-market conditions, their level of resources, their health and their attitudes towards work. It is important to note that women, like men, have a variety of experiences of unemployment.

There are other results from these studies of women's unemployment which go beyond the findings about men's unemployment experiences. The tradition of study of men's unemployment has tended to stress the negative effects of unemployment. Martin and Wallace (n.d.) and Cragg and Dawson (1984) show in their studies of women that there can be positive benefits from being unemployed in certain circumstances. Without wanting to minimise the problems of men's unemployment, this focus could be a helpful one to keep in perspective—for some men. The recent studies of women's unemployment, have also shown that women are not passive or merely acquiescent to redundancy. In the case of Wacjman's (1983) firm, the women took active steps to retain their jobs by setting up a cooperative. In Coyle's (1984) clothing firms the women said they would have been prepared to strike, but the union didn't ask them to. The conservative force of male trade unions is a theme which recurs when explanations of women's lack of militancy are being sought.

The studies of women's experiences of unemployment are far from being comprehensive. They are in their infancy. There are many unasked and unanswered questions for researchers to pursue, not least the question of what difference it makes to the experience of unemployment to have had a part-time job. The recent studies of women's unemployment are partly in the women's studies tradition and have filled in many gaps, destroyed several myths but also added new perspectives on the potential experiences of unemployment for men and women.

Who Are the Unemployed?

Academics, social scientists, politicians, civil servants and others have had a shared interest in asking this question, and it has become closely associated with the definition and measurement of unemployment. This is one area where there has been a long tradition of recognising the gender of workers, although the definition chosen to register and count the unemployed has been more suited to men's experiences. Garside (1980) has made a thorough catalogue of the sources of measures of British unemployment this century.

Garside points out that prior to 1914 no comprehensive accounts were available, and the extent of unemployment data were limited to enquiries about particular groups, for example, trade union members. Against this background, a survey was carried out by Rowntree and Lasker (1911) which attempted to quantify for the first time all those in the entire city of York who were unemployed on a particular day (7 June 1910), whether male or female. From 1923 onwards the range of official statistics was extended and regular supplementary surveys about unemployment took place which incorporated men and women more often than not. One document from the 1930 royal commission on unemployment insurance specifically examined a 1 per cent sample of married women claimants. Miscellaneous collections of statistics also took place and often recognised the different sexes. For example, after the 1902 Labour Bureau (London) Act, men's unemployment figures started to be collected in London, and in July 1915 a number of Women's Employment Bureaus were established. In 1910, employment exchanges were set up on a national basis and a gazette was published starting in April in which figures of unemployment and vacancies by sex and occupation became available following the 1911 National Insurance Act. The tradition of reporting unemployment figures by sex has continued until the present. Vacancies by sex were abolished after 1975 as part of the equal opportunities legislation in Britain. It is the case, however, that whereas extensive breakdowns and cross-tabulations of unemployed men are provided in the Department of Employment's publication, the same is not true for the women's statistics.

Who is counted as unemployed rests fairly clearly on the definition of what counts as unemployment. From the earliest days of unemployment records in Britain the measure and definition of unemployment have been linked, as we have seen, to the eligibility for national insurance benefits though the names of the benefits have obviously changed over time. There have been conditions of eligibility for benefits since their introduction. Again, these criteria have also changed, but what seems common to most of them is that they have discriminated, albeit indirectly, against women and have thus acted as a disincentive for women to be registered, to register themselves or to think of themselves as 'unemployed'.

Garside (1980, p. 120) describes how the 1923 disqualification from eligibility for benefit, after exhausting one's entitlement, varied in incidence by age and personal circumstances. Since women in industry were generally younger than men, this disqualification affected them more. After the Second World War and until 1977 married women were given the option of withdrawing from the insurance scheme, and this meant that they would not be eligible for unemployment benefit. They would therefore have no incentive to register as unemployed. The unemployment figures in this period in Britain are a record of the numbers registering as unemployed, so they are known to seriously underestimate the numbers of unemployed women and some other groups. US employment figures are not subject to the same limitation because they are collected from a survey of households every month. The British data source which is most nearly equivalent to the US source and which is a more accurate assessment of unemployment is the General Household Survey (GHS), but this is published only on a yearly basis. Estimates of women's underrepresentation in the monthly count in Britain are very large and can be as much as 60 per cent.[21] Women's unemployment registration has increased since 1977, which reviewers take to be an indication of the effect of removing the married women's ability to opt-out of the insurance scheme. Opting-out made a woman ineligible for unemployment benefits and thus less likely to register as unemployed.

The problem of women's under-representation on the unemployment register in Britain is well known. It undoubtedly has been responsible for the lack of attention by economists to women's unemployment. Economists are heavily reliant on published data sets, so a major fault in such a series would easily dissuade researchers from spending time and energy building a model on the basis of such an obviously erroneous data set. Some attempts to circumvent the problems have been made, however, but they are limited in scope.[22]

Another criteria commonly applied, certainly in Britain and the USA, in defining unemployment is that the ·individual must be seeking work or be prepared to accept a job if one is offered (within certain limits). This condition was not thought to be particularly problematic for women until recently. An analysis of the Women and Employment Survey has shown otherwise, however, and in the process, more of the value-laden, socially defined nature of unemployment is uncovered.

Roberts (1981) outlined the nature of the problems in a separate paper, and a special study of this problem was undertaken by Cragg and Dawson (1984). Women who were not working when interviewed in 1980 could be registered as unemployed and available for work, unregistered and available for work, or not available for work for domestic or other reasons. We would normally consider that the first two groups were unemployed. These women were asked whether they considered themselves as unemployed, and the women's self-assessment did not correlate very well with the conventional definitions: 21 per cent of non-working women thought of themselves as unemployed, but only 55 per cent of women who would normally be defined as unemployed thought of themselves in this way. Similarly there were those who would not be unemployed on the usual definitions but who saw themselves as 'unemployed'. The picture was more complicated by a consideration of the time period over which a woman might be expected to be looking for work. The GHS definition certainly excluded some who might otherwise be thought to be unemployed. On the whole, women failed to perceive themselves as unemployed because they were often actively doing housework and often not receiving any payment for their unemployment. As women pointed out: 'I don't think of myself as unemployed. I'm not, strictly speaking. I run the home. I think women are silly to think of themselves as unemployed because running a home is a job. In fact, it's a full-time job. It's a job that's unpaid' (Roberts, 1981, p. 10) and 'I think you class yourself as unemployed when you're being paid for being unemployed' (Cragg and Dawson, 1984, p. 17).

These findings highlight the way in which the conventional definitions build upon commonly held societal views that men ought to work and that the state of unemployment applies to those who fill a 'breadwinner's' role. There are serious political issues at stake here too. The total number of unemployed in the economy is one criterion of the success of a government's economic policies, so the definition of what counts as unemployed becomes crucial. There have been some controversial suggestions that certain groups, married women amongst them, should be removed from the figure since they are not really unemployed, even though they might meet the criteria in the current definition.[23] Elderly people are often subjected to this sort of debate.[24] In effect, these suggestions are advocating changes in the definition which are somewhat arbitrary, although they point up, at the same time, the fact that every criterion in the definition could be altered if society or governments so decided. Boulet and Bell (1973) made the most bizarre suggestion, that those on the register for between eight and twenty-six weeks should be excluded because they are voluntary unemployed. Those unemployed for up to eight weeks had already been argued to be excluded because they were considered to be only frictionally unemployed. Hughes (1975, p. 325) points to the arbitrary but political nature of these suggestions by saying of Boulet and Bell: 'Had they extended it (the cut-off point) to 104 weeks they could have reduced "real unemployment" to almost zero.' When the discussions have been about married women, they are effectively questioning women's right to take up paid employment. The definition of unemployment therefore has very fundamental implications.

Sinfield (1981, 1981a) and others have been noting some of these issues, pointing out that they are instructive to sociologists who are interested in the structures of industrial societies and in social inequalities. Analyses of the unemployment figures, either of the published register count or of special surveys, have been used to answer the question 'Who are the unemployed?'. Such analyses have usually been the first step in identifying inequalities and groups who have a risk of poverty. Researchers also need to consider how the definition of unemployment might be hiding other inequalities, and women who are unemployed are a good example of such oversights.

When Marshall (1984) suggests that the women's movement has contributed to the neglect of women's unemployment by questioning the division between paid and unpaid work, he is seriously underestimating the complexity of a problem which has deep roots in society. No one would deny that there is a great deal of difference between receiving pay for one's work and not receiving pay; nor that the absence of a paid job, having had one, is a major change for a woman. That this change should be researched for women as well as men seems only reasonable. At the same time the results of Cragg and Dawson's (1984) study of unemployed women show that the traditional concept of unemployment both in its everyday sense and in industrial sociology is not one which is wholly appropriate to many women's experiences. They suggest that the concept of unemployment has developed as a male, 'breadwinner' concept, often of a male manual worker in manufacturing. As such, it serves to reinforce the sexual division of labour and gender roles and to exclude certain areas of research. A large proportion of women are employed in jobs in the service industries, where redundancy is uncommon and part-time work is predominant. These women gain and lose jobs and have spells of not working but may not be unemployed according to the most common definitions. There are clearly a variety of women's experiences of not working and a variety of ways in which they arrive in such situations. A focus on 'unemployed' women which Marshall seems to desire would eliminate the recognition of the heterogeneities in women's experiences. The focus on unemployed men may have been having a similar effect on the study of men. The study of women has been helping to widen our horizons.

LABOUR SUPPLY

The traditional analysis of the supply of hours used the standard neoclassical instrument of indifference curve analysis to examine an individual's hypothetical allocation of time between work and leisure. Leisure in this sense is used as a label to represent all uses of time other than in the market of paid employment. It is, however, a peculiarly male choice of label.[25] The individual, as always, is assumed to wish to maximise his utility, whilst facing the constraint that there are a maximum of twenty-four hours in a day to allocate. Workers' preferences can be incorporated to the extent that an individual can weight his valuations of work relative to leisure time, and this determines the shape and position of the indifference curve or utility function. The optimum allocation is obtained by bringing together worker's preferences with the constraints which the individual faces because the wage rate is fixed exogenously. The fixed wage rate permits a budget constraint to be drawn which indicates the limits as well as the intermediate positions which are possible to the individual by spending all of the available time working and earning, at the given rate, or all of the time in leisure, earning and therefore consuming nothing. The optimum for an individual is where the budget line is tangential to the highest indifference curve, which is the highest level of utility. At this point the condition for optimality and equilibrium holds; that is the ratio of the marginal utility of an extra hour's income given up for an extra hour of leisure is in the same proportion as the ratio of the wage rate of working to the price of leisure. An individual in this position cannot increase his utility by either working an extra hour or taking an extra hour's leisure, unless of course conditions begin to change or preferences change.

This basic framework can then be used to introduce variations and complications which allow one to predict the effect on individuals of changes in wage rates, changes in taxation levels or structures, increases in the standard of living or unearned income, and so on. On the basis of this model we would expect that the effect of an increase in wage rates (or a decrease in taxes) might have one of two effects. The substitution effect, as it is called, results from the fact that the relative prices of leisure and consumption have now changed, and we would normally expect a shift to occur towards the activity that has become either cheaper or more remunerative—in this case, working. One could think of this wage increase as an increase in the opportunity cost of leisure or not working, which means individuals will choose to consume less leisure and more work. The income effect can have an opposite effect. The increase in the wage rate has effectively given an individual a higher income even for the same hours worked, and we might expect that a higher income would induce individuals to increase their leisure and reduce their working hours.

On the basis of this reasoning, economists tend to expect individuals to have a backward-bending supply curve; that is, the relationship between the wage rate (price of labour) and the quantity of hours supplied is such that at low levels of wages they will be positively related and increase together. At higher wage rates individuals will start to reduce their working hours and have more leisure, so the relationship will be negative. At these higher wage rates the income effect swamps the substitution effect to give a net decrease in hours worked or a net increase in hours of leisure. Any additional unearned income which an individual is given would be expected to have a similar effect to the income effect described above, so reducing the amount of working hours. Economists expect, therefore, that individual's working and not-working decisions are based on two main variables: the level of wage rates and the level of unearned income—but in combination with their preferences.

Generally speaking, however, apart from the existence of institutional disincentives to work like tax thresholds and high marginal tax rates, it is assumed that a rational individual—that is, a rational man—will prefer to work rather than not work so long as by doing so he can increase his income. Individuals would be expected not to work if institutional factors make it difficult to get an income increase by doing so. In an economy with social security provisions, if the level of social security for which an individual is eligible whilst not working is greater than the wage offered in a job, a rational individual man would be expected not to work. Alternatively, if by working at all, or by increasing the hours worked, an individual enters a higher tax bracket and so for the additional hour worked gains no extra income, again it is regarded as irrational to work or do the extra hour.[26]

Men's labour-supply functions were the first to be estimated empirically using data on hours of work and in simple models known as reduced-form equations, estimated by ordinary least squares (OLS) regression techniques. Most of the work was undertaken by US economists and it is reviewed in Cain and Watts (1973). Some of these studies had the motive of attempting to assess the effects of taxes on the incentive to work, and this interest has gone hand in hand with the development of labour-supply functions for men. These early studies have been labelled 'first generation studies' by Heckman *et al.* (1981) or 'Type 1' studies by Brown (1982). They found, as the theory suggests, that men's hours of supply depended upon the individual's wage rate, unearned income and his preference between income and leisure, as proxied by personal characteristics like marital status. The range of personal characteristics variables included was initially quite narrow. The estimates of the men's elasticities of (own-wage) labour supply were found to vary depending upon the data used, and they ranged between -0.45 and $+0.55$. The unearned income elasticities lay between zero and -0.16 for men.

When women were considered it was within the same framework, but since the participation rates of women were seen to be a lot lower than those of men, the labour supply function for women was estimated in two stages: first, on the basis of whether they participated in employment or not, and second, if they were working, their hours were regressed against similar variables to those included in men's regressions. Most studies of women's labour supply in Britain were within this tradition, although often the data restrictions have meant that studies have been limited to examining only participation as a dependent variable and not hours. A similar wide range of results were obtained. Women's own-wage supply elasticity was estimated to lie between -0.1 and $+1.6$, and the unearned income elasticity had a range of -0.1 to -0.75. On the whole, the range and values of women's labour-supply elasticities were greater than those of men.

Some significant changes have occurred to labour supply estimation since the late 1960s, and these are well documented in Heckman *et al.* (1981), Greenhalgh and Mayhew (1981) and Brown (1982). The changes have come from a number of sources and have only begun to be integrated together relatively recently, although overlaps of a sort have been occurring throughout the decade. There was a general desire to improve the data and reconcile differences between cross-section and time-series data-set results. Also, more realism was incorporated through the consideration of non-linear budget constraints. On the whole, these benefits were aimed at improving men's labour-supply estimation, especially with a view to examining the tax effects on men's work. Another structural development has been the consideration of marginal wage rates as endogenous, which they are in a system where taxation is related to the hours worked.[27]

What goes unnoted in the reviews is the way that several of the most important changes have resulted from a consideration of women's labour-supply functions. For example, the review by Heckman *et al.* lists three major changes, one of which is entitled 'Functional Form and Econometric Technique' (p. 81). The problem of first generation studies is described without any mention of the population to whom it was a significant problem (pp. 81–82):

it is necessary to consider a number of important questions about specification and estimation. In turn these questions raise further questions about the treatment of unobservables and the problem of self-selection bias or, more generally, sample selection bias . . . First generation empirical studies almost entirely ignored this basic consideration. In some studies, researchers instead proceeded to fit equations such as (1) to a random sample taken from the entire population, with the labour supply of non-working individuals set at zero . . . Hence this procedure mis-specifies the model and so will produce inconsistent estimates of its parameters.

The other major development in the analysis of labour supply came from the discussion of household decision-making and budget constraints building upon the work of Gary Becker's (1965) theory of the allocation of time. These discussions began to see men's and women's labour-supply decisions as interrelated and also recognised that the choice for women was between childcare or domestic work and employment. This area of discussion, as well as providing an alternative foundation for labour-supply analysis, had an input into the other individual utility-maximising tradition. A wider range of variables were injected into models; that is, personal preference variables. These new variables have been accepted to the extent that some reviews now list, as standard, variables which came in with the study of women's work and household-decision models: 'These preferences are proxied by means of personal characteristics and family circumstances, such as numbers and ages of children, education, health and race' (Greenhalgh and Mayhew, 1981, p. 46). Variables like the ages of children etc. are only found on the whole in models of women's labour supply. The rethinking of the whole foundations of neoclassical models which is implied by considering the households as a decision-making unit should not be underestimated, however, even if the full extent of these developments are not yet complete. We can explore these two developments and the relationship between them in more detail below.

Utility-Maximising Models
First generation models which considered the relationship between the hours of labour supplied and the wage rate, non-employment income and a vector of characteristics only explained a small proportion of the variation in hours

worked. A substantial part of the variation was assumed, therefore, to depend upon the error term in the regression. If the error was randomly distributed, then there was no problem, but if it was not, the estimates would be biassed. It became clear through a more serious examination of women's work that the error term was unlikely to be randomly distributed because the sample only included working women. There were systematic reasons why women do not work, it was thought, and a sizeable proportion of women are not working at any point in time.

Heckman (1974) analysed this problem and provided statistical techniques for correcting the bias which would be involved, but the developments did not stop there. A whole wave of what have become known as structural models was initiated and labour-supply decisions began to be regarded as a combination of discrete quantitative choices concerned with whether to work or not and how many hours to work. New models were devised to incorporate both the observed and unobserved aspects of these decisions, index-function models, and new statistical techniques for handling discrete choices were introduced; for example logit, probit and tobit. The concept and calculation of shadow wage rates became important as part of these developments. A shadow or inputed wage is one which is not observable, although it is thought to be influencing an individual's decisions. For example, if individuals are not working, they will have a wage rate which they could obtain if they worked, but it obviously cannot be directly observed. It could be the case, however, that an individual's potential earnings are too low to induce them to look for a job, in which case the shadow wage is in large part determining their behaviour. The question was raised that if women do not work, how much of their behaviour can be explained by this unobserved shadow or imputed wage? If this shadow wage for non-working women is calculated on the basis of what is known about working women's wages, biassing errors may be introduced. Heckman's work also corrected for this element of bias.

Other studies of women's status were also initiated which attempted to examine their durations of not working, and another new concept was introduced by Heckman's (1978) work on this topic; the concept of state dependence. The concept of state dependence derives from a mathematical model called a Markov process and it describes the extent to which individuals' behaviour over a period of time can be explained in terms of the state or status which they were in at the beginning of the period. For example, if a woman is not working in one year, what is the probability that she will not be working next year, just because she was not working this year? The concept tries to exclude the systematic reasons which explain women's working and not working and then distill out the cumulative effects of being in any particular state. The states can vary of course, between employment, unemployment or not working etc. A further set of sophisticated statistical techniques have developed hand in hand with these models. All of these developments have been fed into the mainstream of microeconomic analysis. They are having wide-ranging repercussions, therefore, on the study of employment, after largely originating in a study of women's employment. As a result of these developments, plus the wider range of variables and household interrelations from other areas of interest, we now know much more about women's and men's labour supply and their reasons for working or not working, as well as how much work they do. However, there are still differences in the results and gaps in the analysis, as Heckman *et al.* (1981, pp. 106–12) illustrate.

Studies have used a variety of types of model and different variables to capture and test the expected effects. The various models are linked on the whole to the type of data used to estimate them. Aggregate data on groups of women and men have been used, and more recently, household and individual data have become available. Both cross-sectional and time-series data have been used, as well as cohort data, in two recent British studies.[28] Since longitudinal data has become available, especially in the USA, a new type of investigation of labour supply has been taking place using longitudinal concepts like the duration of time spent working or not working and the attachment to work over the life cycle. Many of these studies have concentrated on the family-formation phase of women's activities. Of the major variables, income effects have the widest selection of proxy measures, ranging from housing tenure to husband's social class. Work experience, education and occupational status of women are all thought to be part of their potential earnings. In some studies occupation and education are included as separate variables, and in others they are used to calculate imputed or potential earnings. In view of the variations in the empirical work, it is perhaps surprising that there is so much agreement in the results, although the size of these effects is subject to more variation.[29] The issue of why women's participation has changed so dramatically over time is considered in Chapter 7.

Some of our knowledge about women's and men's labour supply can be summarised here.[30] The dependence of women's and men's participation and hours on their potential earnings has already been mentioned. A husband's increase in wage rates seems to depress the wife's participation; a wife's increase in earnings has a smaller but still negative effect on her husband's earnings. The main effect of the husband's earnings on the wife's labour supply is an income effect rather than a relative price effect. Studies have found that women's labour supply is more sensitive to changes in their own-wage rate than is the case for men, and second generation studies have demonstrated that the gap was larger than initially thought. Heckman found an own-wage elasticity for married women of 4.3, which is three times as large as the first generation OLS value. The own-wage elasticity has been found to be larger than the income elasticity of participation for married women. Greenhalgh and Mayhew (1981) suggest that this result may not be reliable. If it is trustworthy, it suggests that a potential wage increase of the same amount as an unearned income decrease (maybe through the husband's earnings falling) would have a net effect of increasing women's participation, other things remaining constant. The pull of higher wages is greater to women, therefore, than the desire for 'leisure'.

Children undoubtedly have a depressing effect on women's labour-force participation. One estimate calculated the loss of participation at 30 per cent for married women between sixteen and thirty-four years of age; the estimate of the total lifetime effect of a decrease in family size of one child suggested that participation would be raised by 4 per cent and lifetime hours by 12.5 per cent. The effect of children varies according to their age, however. The depressing effect of children on women's participation is greatest for children aged zero to five, smaller for children aged six to ten and not significant and even positive for children aged eleven to sixteen. However, there may be variations within these categories.[31] Joshi (1984) demonstrated that it is not the number of children in each age band that is important but simply their existence, so in some ways there are economies of scale in childrearing. Having more than one child in a particular age band does not decrease women's participation by a higher multiple. The effects of young children can be tempered by financial considerations, however; women in financial hardship will go back to work even with very young children. Another important result from the analysis of childbirth on women's participation is that when childbirth is taken into consideration, a women's age or her marital status have no further explanatory power on her participation. This result has yet to be recognised by the textbook discussions and reviews, which all consider 'married women' as a sub-group, as if their marital status is the most important aspect of their status. In fact, it is the existence of children which is the explanatory variable.[32] Whilst the presence of children decreases the utility of money income compared with leisure for women, the reverse is the case for men whose participation increases when they have children. This has led Greenhalgh and Mayhew to suggest that the main effect of children on a family is to encourage specialisation between the parents rather than inducing more or less participation per family.

Other effects on women's participation have also been noted. The ill-health of wives reduced their participation by 15 per cent and the poor health of a dependant was found to reduce a wife's hours of work by 11 per cent, as well as increasing the probability of retirement by 0.76 for women and 0.56 for men in Britain. Work experience, education and occupation, when they are included as separate variables, have effects consistent with human capital predictions, for example, longer work experience increases women's participation. Most studies incorporate a measure of labour-market demand, although the measures are thought to be inadequate for capturing the demand for women's labour. On the whole, the results suggest that demand increases raise women's participation, although few models have considered the simultaneous system problems of incorporating demand and supply in a one-equation model. Some of the longitudinal or life-cycle examinations find more varied results for the demand effects.[33]

Household Decisions

The whole basis of neoclassical labour supply has come under review since women have been seriously considered as decision-makers. As we have seen, much of the analysis uses as its basis the individual decision-maker. There are a number of reasons why this is unsatisfactory for both married women and married men, who constitute the vast majority of the working population, and attempts to improve models by considering household decision-making have started to emerge alongside the consideration of women's work.

The textbook on labour economics by Hunter and Robertson (1978) noted the unsatisfactory nature of focusing on the individual (pp. 16–17):

Most decisions about labour are based on the individual worker as the relevant unit of reckoning . . . For most of us, the income we earn becomes household income, and both the manner in which we want to receive it and the way it is spent are household rather than individual issues. Though it is conventional to discuss living standards and wages in relation to individual incomes, the effective unit ought to be the household rather than the individual.

Nevertheless, the individual decision-maker has provided, and still does provide, much of the backbone to neoclassical analysis, possibly because the focus on individuals' decisions means that complicated interaction effects between individuals' decisions can be ignored. If interactions were thought to occur, deterministic outcomes to models could not be assumed or assured.

A study of the history of economic thought on the fundamental decision-making unit in economics reveals that there has been much confusion over this issue. We can find many instances of the term 'household' dating back as far as Walras and Marshall, but this does not mean that the true nature of decisions was being recognised and incorporated into economic theory. Roston (1983) has documented some of the confusion, showing that terms like 'individual decision-making' and 'household decisions' have been used interchangeably. The analysis, whichever term was used, has always clearly been of an individual, however. The use of the term 'household' has been something of a smokescreen, and its use has helped to hide the neglect of genuine households for generations of economic analysis. In no sense have economists of the past tackled the issue of interactive or joint decisions within households. Addison and Siebert (1979) describe Gary Becker's 'new home economics' as having a household as its central concept, and since this is one of the new developments in labour economics, it will be worth assessing how far Becker has gone towards recognising the interactive effects of men's and women's labour supply or consumption decisions. The Leuthold model may have been an earlier attempt to capture household decisions.[34]

A series of applications of the 'new home economics' can be found in Levy-Garboua (1979) and Gronau (1973), and a review is contained in Joseph (1983). The analysis of household decisions which these models contain has been seen as a contribution to the analysis of labour supply, and it rests on Becker's (1965) theory of the economic allocation of time between alternative uses. The theory regards the household as a unit of production, and it suggests that we think of consumption decisions as being made in order to give people satisfaction. A variety of activities can contribute to utility, and these activities require the inputs of time or other goods. In this sense, the theory sees the activities as the output of a production process or production function, the inputs of which are time or goods, although the ultimate product is the satisfaction derived. To take a particular example; a family might be considering producing children, either a certain quantity of children or children of a certain quality. Children are the output from this production process, and they give their parents satisfaction. The inputs will be a series of consumption goods—for example, nappies, food, toys, shelter etc.—and a time input of child-care from at least one parent, or maybe a shared time input. The time spent in child-care will limit the time available for work by the parent concerned.

From this framework it is possible to use economists' techniques to calculate the optimum allocation of time and of consumption goods for any particular level of production for the various household members, and other predictions follow. If we are thinking of the costs of the inputs, then an increase in the wage rates raises the relative price (or opportunity cost) of time-intensive activities, and this would be expected to cause a substitution away from time-based activities in the household, making people work longer in the market. We see the link, therefore, between labour-supply decisions and consumption decisions. The difference in wage rates between the sexes would lead the theory to predict that necessary time inputs into the household are likely to be done by the partner whose foregone earnings are the lowest. Not surprisingly, this is usually the women. A more extensive summary of the predictions and results for women from this perspective can be found in Kahne and Kohen (1975), but we can see that the predictions on labour supply largely overlap with those of the individual models, as do the results.

This fairly novel approach has the benefit that it treats households as a unit of decision-making, but it does so by side-stepping the earlier problems. The household is now seen as a firm producing various items, and all household members participate in the production process. Women are just as essential as men in this model, which is an advance on earlier conceptualisations, but the way decisions are arrived at and the potential interactions between husbands' and wives' decisions has been either ignored or trivialised. There is a recognition that the necessary time spent on housework done by one partner involves an equivalent reduction in time available for work, or vice versa, but the causal mechanism is assumed and one could argue another case. It is not necessarily and only the case that women's lower pay in the market will cause them to be the ones to provide the input of domestic work at home; it could equally well be the case that women prefer to do homework and so have to accept a lower market wage because they allow their skills to depreciate by not working; it could alternatively be the case as Humphries (1977) argued, that keeping women at home is a strategy for increasing men's labour-market wages, and so on.

Becker's new home economics has the virtue of corresponding with the facts of labour-market participation, but it is far from offering us a clear explanatory theory with a causal mechanism which explains women's and men's relative wages or joint household behaviour. At best the theory illustrates the consistency of the patterns of wages and specialisations which occur. The theory is a standard economists' black box theory—but interesting nevertheless, especially since it recognises women's necessary role in the set of household decisions. Household decision-making has also been considered more recently by Blundell and Walker (1982) and Blundell (1983), and as such it constitutes a major conceptual development in the discipline.

There have been a wide range of conceptual and technical advances in economists' analyses of the labour supply resulting from incorporating working women, which help our understanding of the determinants of women's and men's working and not-working behaviour. The developments in the study of women's labour supply have been at the forefront of new directions and developments in labour economics.

NOTES

1. The main line of argument in this book were formulated before Marshall's (1984) article appeared. The points made here overlap with those of Marshall but contain important differences.
2. The recent studies of women's unemployment are Coyle (1984), Martin and Roberts (1984), Cragg and Dawson (1984), Wacjman (1983) and Martin and Wallace (n.d.).

3. For a review of economists debates *see* Trevithick (1980).
4. *See* Sinfield (1981, 1981a) and Marsden (1982).
5. For example, Beales and Lambert (1934), Hannington (1977), Wight Bakke (1933).
6. For example, Marsden (1982), Dennehy and Sullivan (1977), Hill *et al* (1973).
7. For example, Daniel (1974).
8. For example, Wedderburn (1964).
9. For example, Field (1977), Sinfield and Showler (1981).
10. For example, Hill *et al*. (1973), Sinfield (1970).
11. *See* Sinfield (1981).
12. For example, Wood, D. (1982), Martin and Fryer (1972).
13. For example, Daniel (1974), Daniel and Stilgoe (1977) and Wood, D. (1982).
14. Sinfield (1981) reviews these studies; *see also* Davies *et al*. (1982).
15. For example, McKee and Bell (1983), Marsden (1982).
16. Walker (1981), Hill *et al*. (1973).
17. For example, Townsend (1979), Norris (1979a, 1979b).
18. The history of the Industrial Health Research Board is described in Chapter 2 under the 'Human Relations' section (p. 27). The institution was linked to the development of human factor industrial psychology in Britain in the 1920s and 1930s.
19. Marshall's (1984) review of these studies concludes that women's response to unemployment was different from that of men. Some confusion is injected into Marshall's discussion by equating unemployment with redundancy (p. 237), but that apart, his own summary of these studies does not support this conclusion; neither do the studies themselves support such a conclusion. Marshall's equation of unemployment and redundancy mean that he is not always comparing like with like, since he draws on studies where unemployment has a broader definition. For example, Daniel (1974) and Daniel and Stilgoe (1977) analyse samples of the unemployed from the register of the unemployed, not all of whom became unemployed involuntarily.
20. Cragg and Dawson (1984, p. 19) also quote a woman who exhibits feelings of guilt and shame similar to those described for men, although they point out that such a response was not typical: 'Being unemployed is boring, miserable, depressing. Very, very, boring: Actually I feel bad about it when they mention something about unemployment. I feel guilty . . . There's a stigma attached to it.'
21. *See* Roberts (1981) or Dex (1978).
22. For example, Amranand (1979). A more extensive analysis which circumvents the problem of unregistered women is contained in Joshi (1982).
23. *See* Field (1977a) for the details of these arguments.
24. *See* Phillipson (1982) for a description of the way retirement policies seek to redefine unemployment and economic inactivity and how these have fluctuated over time in a way that approximates to the reserve army of labour notion.

25. Had women's work been the subject matter under investigation when neoclassical theories were being developed, it is difficult to imagine that 'leisure' would have been the label attached to the non-market household chores which take up so much of women's time.
26. Economists have an elaborate set of concepts to describe these predictions and relationships; for example, replacement ratios, non-linear budget constraints and marginal tax rates etc.
27. New developments have taken place in simultaneous equation models as a result.
28. For example, Joshi and Owen (1982), Elias and Main (1982).
29. Some commentators make a point of stressing the differences in results but given the range of variables, techniques etc. there is a large measure of consensus in the direction of the effects.
30. Most of these results are summarised in Greenhalgh and Mayhew (1981), Heckman *et al.* (1981) and Joshi (1984).
31. Elias and Main (1982).
32. There are even calculations of the effects of marriage on women. The results are undoubtedly reflecting, almost wholly, the effects of childbirth.
33. Wachter (1972) found that higher unemployment increases women's participation, Blau (1978) that it decreases participation, Shaw (1983) that it has no effect and Dex (1984) that it delays re-entry after childbirth.
34. *See* Brown (1983, Ch. 8).

4 Which Occupations?

In the chapters that follow, the sociology of work will be treated primarily as the study of those social roles which arise from the classification of men by the work they do.

(Caplow, 1954, p. 4)

That men work and the sociology of work will need, therefore, to focus on men's work is a view that has influenced and dominated the discipline until recently. It goes unstated that women do not work and therefore are not the focus of studies of work or occupations. Whilst Caplow (1954) made such a clear statement of women's hidden position, he was not the worst offender of those who neglected women and their work, since he in fact incorporated a chapter in his text on women's occupations. Nevertheless, the dominance of these definitions of work and occupations has been all pervasive; work is what men get paid to do, and occupations and careers are ways of conceptualising men's paid employment over time. If women were recognised as entering the realm of paid work at all, they were viewed as facing a very biassed choice between a career or motherhood, with most choosing motherhood. Their period of working before childbirth has been viewed as a time of waiting to get married.

Marxist analysis has not treated women any better, in that domestic work was for a long time viewed as unproductive labour, which meant that it was not a part of the surplus-value calculation, not a part of the class struggle and therefore not terribly important to understanding the dynamics of socio-economic or historical change.

The effects of this foundation on the sociology of work and occupations has meant that women have been neglected from the analyses which came under this heading. They were ignored in studies of the mechanisms of occupational choice, the reasons for downward occupational mobility, the process of recruitment to undesirable occupations, career contingiencies, occupational attainment and the actual experiences of working in different occupations. Economists, in their discussions of occupational choice and occupational attainment have similarly neglected women, and their initial attempts to incorporate women into traditional neoclassical analysis have been fraught with problems and inconsistencies which reflect a lack of empirical understanding of women's choices and constraints; the lack of understanding has thus been common to both disciplines.

The extent of the recent changes has been great. Some major reconceptualisations have occurred in the sociology of work and occupations which have gone hand in hand with new empirical examinations of women's work, all of which have shown the poverty of earlier non-empirically based conceptualisations. Women's paid employment has been examined empirically, and their occupational mobility, their occupational attainment and their experiences of employment are all beginning to be documented. New concepts and measures have been formulated to describe women's occupational position more accurately; for example, the concept of occupational segregation. This work has also given a new spur to the collection of work-history data required for such investigations, and consequently the value of collecting men's work-history data is now being seen. On the theoretical level there has been a questioning of the occupational classification's relevance to women's employment; an argument has been made for including in the list of recognised occupations housework, motherhood and other work done by women. There has also been a challenge to the conventional division between paid and unpaid work which equates work with pay and thereby devalues women's domestic work. Likewise, the concept of skill has been analysed instead of taken for granted. Marxist feminists have argued a case for a more central recognition of the role of domestic labour in Marxist theory. These conceptual changes have generated a further set of empirical studies— for example, of the experience of housework, childbirth and motherhood—and have provided a foundation upon which empirically based notions of women's careers can properly build. Some of the developments are in their infancy. All this suggests that the future will offer more exciting developments. Some of the details of these changes are charted below.

CAREERS

A girl may see it as more important that she be acceptable to the kinds of people who matter to her, so that the kind of man she wants to marry will be likely to propose to her than that she find just the occupation that best fits her talents and aptitudes.

(L.E. Tyler, quoted by Slocum, 1966, p. 214)

The concept of 'career' has been central to the study of occupational sociology, although its meaning has undergone modifications and refinements over time. A 'career' seems to suggest some progress through a series of occupations or maybe staying in one occupation over time. At this level the notion is equivalent to a work history and, as such, it would be a descriptive concept. 'Career' has not always been used in this way, however, and the dominant meaning attached to the concept has been prescriptive. Following Hughes (1937), Becker (1970, p. 165) defined a career as 'the patterned series of adjustments made by an individual to the network of institutions, formal organizations and informal relationships in which the work of the occupation is performed'.

Miller and Form (1949) did one of the early studies which tried to conceptualise men's succession of occupations as a whole by charting empirically their occupational movements. Wilensky (1961) wanted to restrict the notion of 'career' to professional occupations only. Slocum's (1966, p. 5) definition is typical of the prescriptive and hierarchical overtones which later became attached to the concept: 'An *occupational career* may be defined for this discussion as an ordered sequence of development extending over a period of years and involving progressively more responsible roles within an occupation.' Slocum's concept is a more abstract and non-empirical concept than earlier notions, as he himself recognised. Empirical work when it took place consisted of case studies of single occupations or investigations of particular aspects of an individual's behaviour or work history, and as such the longitudinal or developmental nature of a career got lost, as did the potential patterns or shared experiences of individuals. In the light of more recent developments, some of the earliest formulations of 'careers' and 'career patterns' now turn out to have been conceptually more sophisticated than their immediate successors.

A multitude of case studies of one or a very few occupations, firms or industries emerged in the 1950s and 1960s all focusing on men at work; for example, Walker and Guest (1952), Glaser (1964), Fichter (1961). Taking the lead from Becker (1960), other studies focused on crucial points in a career or the performance of some critical tasks which were peculiar to certain occupations; for example, policemen mediating squabbles, poolroom hustling or taxi drivers sizing up customers. Becker introduced the notion of 'career contingiency'. There is a wealth of detail about men's occupations contained in these studies, which are often fascinating to read. They reveal the variety of mechanisms which have been devised to accomplish the same essential task of socialisation of a new entrant to a job or occupation or, indeed, socialising men out of work as they approach retirement.

Alongside the large number of case studies, a theoretical development took place which began to construct typologies of the mass of individual case studies. The typologies set out to reduce the large number of ethnographic accounts to a smaller number of categories which usually had at their basis a division according to how the study resolved a key issue in the organisation of work or careers. For example, Caplow (1954) constructed a typology around the themes of the manner of recruitment, returns to seniority, evaluation of merit and control over occupational behaviour, amongst other issues raised in his investigations. Caplow thus arrived at four categories of occupations: independent fee-taking professionals, building craftsmen, semi-skilled machine-tending factory workers and small retail merchants. Slocum (1966) also suggested a set of categories which focused on the different institutional environments (e.g. the bureaucratic career), and many others exist, some only being modest variants °of the US Census Bureau's major occupational groupings.

Hearn (1977) provided another career typology but as a criticism of earlier forms. Hearn was critical not only of the assumption of any necessary hierarchy in the concept of 'career' but also of whether an ordered sequence was necessarily involved and the conscious, rational pursuit of goals which an ordered sequence implies. Hearn suggested that a typology of careers could be constructed along the two main dimensions of whether jobs are intrinsically meaningful or not and whether work has meaning or no meaning in the wider context. A set of four career types are then possible; the pure career is the career definition of Caplow, where there is a structuring of time in the past and in the future. Hearn's other career types recognise the decline of work as a 'central life interest' and they include 'the careerless' who accept the rules of the game but who do not seriously compete; the 'uncareer', where *both* work and career are neither coherent nor meaningful as seen in the individuals' wider environment; and the 'non-career', where work and a career are no longer meaningful in either an immediate or in wider terms. At least one of Hearn's career types appeared earlier in a study of the transition from school to work by Ashton (1975). Ashton's use of the term 'career' is restricted to the first few years of working life and does not parallel, therefore, other life-cycle uses of the term; the term 'career' has thus been applied in a wide range of contexts.

A later article by Hearn (1981) further extended the range of types to include the 'guerrilla career' and the 'cop-out career', although these are not set within the same dimensions as the first four types. Hearn successfully extended the notion of a career, removing at the same time a necessary link with upward hierarchical progressions, but he also took a further step away from empirically based typologies. Whereas Caplow and Slocum were constructing typologies to make sense of empirical studies, Hearn, as is the danger with all typologising, is offering typologies of the logical possibilities, although he does try and offer examples to fit each. There are, however, grave dangers in such an approach if it locks our thinking into grooves which have little relation to experiences.

Spilerman (1977) reviews many of these developments in an unfavourable light for a number of reasons. He is critical of the trend away from empirically based career descriptions, and he suggests that where empirical work has taken place, through the ethnographic accounts, there is a bias in the types of career discussed. Most of the accounts are concerned with careers within institutional structures, and few if any consider career lines which transverse institutional boundaries or change maybe in mid-life.[1] As such, the careers described are little help to understanding the determinants of industry structures and labour-market distributions of workers. Spilerman (1977) thinks as does Grandjean (1981) that the very notion of career is and should be about an individual's relationship to the structure of employment; Spilerman (p. 553) sees 'the career notion', therefore, 'as a strategic link between structural features of the labour market and the socio-economic attainments of individuals'. Few of the previous studies are useful in uncovering labour-market structures, although there are some exceptions which are mainly studies of actual job changing or labour-mobility behaviour; for example, Lipset and Bendix (1952a and b), Palmer (1954), Parnes and Nestel (1974).

A recent study of male white-collar employees by Stewart, Prandy and Blackburn (1980) has contributed to the concept of 'career' whilst being primarily about the place of men's clerical work in the class structure. They pointed out how uneven the occupational classification is, particularly as a basis for measuring a man's class affiliation since some occupational categories encapsulate careers over a man's life time; they use the analogy of the railway lines here. Other occupations are merely stops along the way; using the same analogy, these are stations. Stewart *et al.* are critical of Slocum's definition of an occupation because he incorporates the notion of a (railway) line into it and thereby confuses lines and stations. It has not been clear whether it was necessary to make this point about women's occupations, since there were no data on women's occupational mobility over their lifetime with which to examine the issue. Stewart, Prandy and Blackburn (1980) were firmly in the mainstream discussions of occupations and class analysis in paying attention solely to men's employment and only lip-service to the importance of women's work.

Women's Careers

Women were neglected by this line of development within the sociology of work. The earlier views of 'career' as a descriptive concept could have incorporated women, and indeed, Hughes (1937, p. 411) pointed out that 'A woman may have a career in holding together a family or in raising it to a new position'. Whilst this view is one which sees women playing only a limited role, it has the virtue of at least putting women's domestic work on a par with men's paid occupations. However, the empirical work of this Chicago tradition did not build upon this foundation. Their commitment to a sociological analysis which recognised the links between jobs, even though some would not be thought of as bona fide occupations or professions by the general public (e.g. call girls), was a foundation upon which a consideration of housework could have built. Unfortunately, their work extended to women only insofar as they were prostitutes, who were not exactly a representative sample of all women.

With the move away from using 'career' in a descriptive sense, even these minority women's groups were no longer represented in sociological studies of work. It is not too difficult to see why women were neglected by this line of development within the sociology of work, especially if the discipline initially intended to investigate men's work. If women were more likely to be in the cross-institutional career trajectories or make less obvious progressions up an occupational hierarchy, they would also be more likely to be excluded. As the move away from empirical descriptions of career paths progressed, it would have cemented further the tendency to ignore women, since if women were assumed not to work or have careers, little other than empirical examination would be likely to challenge such a view. Some of Hearn's (1981) types of career are meant to apply to women, but since they are not derived from empirical work, we can only speculate on their validity.

Spilerman's (1977) reconceptualisation of the notion of 'career' is one which is more open to considering women, but it has come late in the story, when alternative lines of development have now been plotted by feminists and others. It is interesting to note that Spilerman's review of the use of the term 'career' in sociology does not mention the problem of its exclusion of women, and neither does his offered solution specifically include them. There is a sense, therefore, in which part of the tradition of career analysis is still male-centred, but alongside this are a growing number of empirical studies of women.

Rosenfeld (1979, 1980) offers empirically based conceptualisations of women's careers. Dex (1984, 1984a) shows how women's work histories can be analysed within a similar framework to that advocated by Spilerman, although she substitutes the term 'profile' to avoid the male-centred connotations which attach to 'career'.

More fundamental criticisms have been levelled at this neglect of women by the sociologists of work. There has been a concern to tackle the assumptions which lock the discipline into perpetuating a neglect of women, as well as filling in many gaps about women's place in, and experience of, occupations. There are studies now of women in factory work in a variety of industries (Pollert, 1981; Cavendish, 1982; Purcell, 1979; Wajcman, 1983; Coyle, 1982), of women in the professions (Theodore, 1971), in banking (Llewelyn, 1981), in journalism (Smith, 1976) and of women in clerical and secretarial work (Silverstone, 1974, 1975; McNally, 1979). Studies of women in service occupations and part-time work are currently sparse, although Beechey and Perkin's (1983) unpublished work on part-time work in Coventry will help to fill this gap, and Terkel (1974) includes ethnographic descriptions of hairdressers, waitresses and some other service occupations. An overview of women's occupational histories from a national sample of women between the ages of sixteen and fifty-nine can be found in Dex (1984) and Martin and Roberts (1984).

It is clear from many of these studies that a great number of the earlier assumptions and stereotypes about women's experiences of work and about their commitment to working were erroneous. Purcell (1979) suggested that women's militancy and acquiescence both at work and in the home was a function of their experiences as workers rather than as women. The assumption that women are content and even prefer doing boring repetitive tasks has been found to be false when examined empirically. Silverstone (1976, p. 101) reported that the Post Office management held these stereotypes; Charles (1983, p. 5) quotes an example from a TGWU male shop-steward. But in studies by Charles (1983) and Cavendish (1982), women clearly do not all prefer such work, nor are they content with it, although their protest can sometimes be silent, enacted by leaving their emloyer rather than speaking out. The idea that women have no long-term occupational commitment as suggested by Slocum (1966) is shown to be erroneous in the occupational profiles described in Dex (1984a). There are many more examples of demythologising women's work through undertaking empirical studies to replace the previous speculations.

Oakley (1974) has made a fundamental criticism of sociologist's notion of an occupation because it excludes women's work in the form of housework or motherhood, childrearing etc. She argues for adding housework to the list of occupations on a par with others and has contributed much to the sociology of these women's occupations. Oakley has written about the experience of housework (1974), motherhood and childbearing (1979) in a way that shows that these activities are work in the same sense as any paid occupations are and that many of the experiences of working are common across all types of work. Oakley's (1974) discussion of housework contains chapters on 'work conditions' and 'standards and routines'. Under the heading of 'work conditions' she considers the topics of monotony, fragmentation and excessive pace, social interaction or isolation at work, working hours and the technical environment. One of Oakley's (p. 51) respondents even likened housework to factory work:

Cleaning a house is just like working in a factory—you dust the same thing every day and it's never appreciated. I mean I could get this whole place so tidy and the kids come home from school and it's like a bomb's exploded, and nothing's appreciated about it . . . as far as actual housework goes, I don't see how anyone can like it. It's boring, just like a robot.

Oakley has demonstrated empirically what other feminist writers like Barker and Allen (1976) have argued more theoretically, that there are more things in common across the wage–unwaged work divide than there are differences. Focusing on whether the work is paid or not merely obscures these commonalities and, moreover, serves to relegate women's unwaged work to obscurity. The results of the 1980 Women and Employment Survey suggest that many women have a view of domestic work which corresponds with Oakley's claim. The survey asked women who were not working whether they saw themselves as unemployed, and if not why not. The vast majority of women did not see themselves as unemployed; approximately two-thirds said that their reason was that they worked at home and were employed as a wife and mother. Empirical studies like those of Oakley, Gavron (1968) and Hobson (1978) highlight, in contrast, the great importance of women's domestic work in the socialisation of men and women and for understanding men's work. These studies of domestic work have stimulated the interest in informal economies and their links with the formal paid-work sector, and an interest in time-budget studies has also emerged in Gershuny (1983). One could not hope to find interrelationships between the formal and informal sector more vividly displayed than they are in the family.

The reconceptualisation which has taken place is about both women's and men's work since it seeks to pull down an earlier divide which was assumed to lie between them. Whether a job is paid or not has serious implications and is of interest to sociologists, but an obsessive focus on this topic led to a restrictive view of both financial and other relationships. The reconceptualisation of work and occupations as activities, not necessarily paid, has been a liberating influence in the sociology of work, and a serious interest in women's work has been largely responsible for these changes.

OCCUPATIONAL CHOICE

occupational choice can be understood in terms of two theoretical limits. At one extreme, the occupation of the father determines that of the son, and no problems of individual choice are allowed to arise. At the other, occupational functions are rigorously allocated according to individual characteristics, as determined by testing and observation.

(Caplow, 1954, p. 214)

This quotation from Caplow indicates that the development of the study of occupational choice parallels the story told about the concept of 'career' as far as women are concerned. Investigations were made in the 1950s and 1960s of the choice of an initial occupation, usually on leaving school, but later also on graduating from college at the beginning of an individual's labour-market experience. This subject has been studied by sociologists, psychologists and economists to an extent that only a small proportion of issues and studies can be mentioned here. Amongst others, topics which are usually considered under this heading include occupational aspirations, educational aspirations, intergenerational occupational mobility and the transition from school to work. Much of the interest has focused on providing better vocational and careers guidance to school-leavers. The early studies of occupational choice employed the same assumptions as the study of careers; namely, that an occupation is what one is paid for, and that young women are not that interested in their jobs since they are just filling in time before getting married. The studies of occupational choice reviewed by Caplow (1954) and Slocum (1966) are wholly concerned with young men. A review by Clarke (1980), however, points out that many of the studies of occupational choice from 1968 to 1980 included young women in their samples, but few considered the gender effects on occupational choice; their results were thus presented as having unisex significance. This is a type of sexism we will meet repeatedly in the history of sociological analysis. It has had serious implications, since it means that the results of earlier studies do not help our understanding either of young women or of young men.

The early studies broadly saw occupational choice as an event, but as early as 1951 in the work of Ginzberg (1951) and Super (1953), a move to view occupational choice as a developmental process began. Ginzberg's work outlined three phases in the development of young men's occupational choices: the fantasy phase and the tentative phase, followed by the realistic phase, and these became the framework for much of the work which followed. In the late 1960s and 1970s, developments in the UK and USA began to diverge significantly. The work of Blau and Duncan (1967) in the USA confirmed, if not initiated, a strongly quantitative set of investigations into the factors affecting the first occupations of young workers, usually men, whereas in Britain, studies were less quantitative and theoretical debates took the centre of the stage. When women were eventually recognised as an important group, they were incorporated into the analysis on both sides of the Atlantic in a way that was in keeping with the tradition of analysis already established in each case. We will need to follow the two branches separately to see their different consequences.

US Studies

US studies of occupational choice by Blau and Duncan (1967) and their successors became part of a wider study of occupational attainment and the determinants of occupational status. Blau and Duncan (1967) found that one third of the variation in the socio-economic ranking of the first job of young men aged between twenty-six and thirty-five could be explained by their own educational attainment combined with the education and occupation of their fathers; one-third of the differences in the ranking of their later jobs could be attributed to their first jobs. Later studies sought to refine Blau and Duncan's work by using more sophisticated regression and path analysis techniques, by adding in extra explanatory variables like the quality of education, motivation or information and by more fully considering ethnic differences. The collection of new data sources like the US

National Longitudinal Survey, which led to the Career Thresholds studies, facilitated some of these developments. The number of studies is now immense. The studies concluded that there was some tendency for young men to inherit the occupational levels of their fathers, that young men were found to be strongly influenced by the advice of significant others when they selected jobs and chose occupational aspiration levels, that the general values which young men hold were found to be systematically related to their aspiration levels and to the kind of occupations they chose and that the process differed significantly between racial groups. The quantitative models which were constructed, despite their sophistication, however, could only explain at best one-half of the variation in men's occupational achievement.

When women were recognised as a group worth studying, they were incorporated into the established quantitative model-building framework as an additional variable—sex—often called a 'personal characteristic'. Studies were done to replicate Blau and Duncan's (1967) initial work but on women to see what differences there were in the patterns of intergenerational occupational mobility between the sexes. The first studies by De Jong *et al.* (1971) and Havens and Tully (1972) thought that the replication should examine intergenerational transfers between a father's occupation and the daughter's occupation. The studies argued over which method was appropriate in the light of the fact that sex differences within occupational categories existed, and the ranking of occupational categories which was appropriate for men was not so for women. A further study by Tyree and Treas (1974) suggested that there were differences between the intergenerational mobility between father's occupations and between son's or daughter's occupations but that there were more similarities between the transitions of father's occupations to the husband's of the daughter's and the earlier wholly male patterns of intergenerational mobility. Rosenfeld (1978) has since branched out from this framework, and her empirical work shows that mother's occupations as well as father's are an important influence on daughter's occupations. Other studies of the status attain-

ment of women have found that men's and women's
attainment is influenced by similar factors (see Trieman and
Terrell, 1975, or McClendon, 1976). Some difference in the
extent of the influences has been found, however, by
Featherman and Hauser (1976). US women's achievements
therefore appear to be less related to their family origin,
especially if they are farm origins, than is the case with men.
The net effect of educational attainment on occupational
status appears to be greater for women than for men, and
intertemporal increases in returns to occupational status has
only benefited US men.

The recognition of women's importance in this US line of
development has not involved the same level of reconceptualisation as that seen in other fields. Treating women more
seriously within the US framework of quantitative sociological study, however, has contributed to the development
and sophistication of some of the techniques employed, and
certainly new things have been learnt about the process of
women's occupational choice. Some of the more pathbreaking developments like that of investigating the
mother's influence are only just beginning and the full extent
of a mother's influence on a son's achievement can now be
examined. The results of these analyses have been slowly
moving towards a conclusion reached in other fields; that
both the mother's and the father's status are important
elements in understanding both a daughter's or a son's
development. Whilst this might seem a rather obvious
conclusion, it has taken the women's studies movement to
establish a place for mothers and daughters in the tradition.

UK Studies

The UK studies of occupational choice are reviewed in
Clarke (1980, 1980a). Where they are empirical in nature,
they use less sophisticated statistical techniques than the US
studies, although they reach most of the same conclusions—
that home background, ethnic origin and education have
strong influences on the level of occupational choices and
aspirations of young men, and weaker influences are found
from certain family factors and from the geographical
environment. Personal characteristics like intelligence or

ability, personality, interests, values, occupational knowledge and, in the few cases where it was included, sex, were
all found to be important variables.

A theoretical debate took the centre stage of UK
sociological interest in occupational choice in the 1970s. A
debate arose about whether this process of occupational
choice actually involved a rational and conscious choice
from a range of known alternatives. Roberts (1968, 1973)
was one of the prime critics of the choice idea, suggesting
instead that the process was one of allocating individuals to
jobs. The idea of an allocation process was meant to suggest
that an individual is almost powerless in the situation and
that factors beyond his control are determining his fate. The
empirical evidence that working-class children get working-
class jobs and middle-class ones get middle-class jobs etc.
was used to support the idea of the allocation process.
About the same time a similar set of points began to be
made in the USA by the radical economists Bowles and
Gintis (1976) about US education, but their attack was
directed largely towards orthodox economic analysis and
formed a part of the segmented labour-market literature, so
it had less impact on US sociological interest in occupational
choice.

The debate in Britain was not fully resolved, although it
did die out and things moved on. A study of working-class
boys by Willis (1977) illustrated that the so-called allocation
process was complex and that it included active resistance to
school culture on the part of working-class boys. Paradox-
ically, this resistance permitted the boys to adjust easily into
the work culture of mundane and low-skilled working-class
jobs. Little discussion can be found in this debate about girls
or young women's occupational choices; they are either
ignored, or workers and young people are treated as unisex,
as we saw previously.

Some empirical studies of young women were taking place
in the 1970s, and these are gradually starting to fill in the
gaps about how British young women choose occupations
and make the transition to work (e.g. McRobbie, 1978;
McRobbie and Garber, 1975; Sherratt, 1983).[2] Oakley's
(1974, 1979) work is also beginning to uncover the sense and

ways in which young women choose motherhood or house-work as an occupation. This latter development has taken place since the waged versus unwaged divide has been broken down and women's occupations have been added to the list of occupations. Empirical studies are beginning to give us an understanding of women's occupational choice, and as with other fields, the picture turns out to be far from the stereotyped assumptions about young women which dominated and precluded serious study for so long. Sherratt (1983) found from a small sample of young women taking up FE that there was little evidence of any kind that they had domestic orientation, but instead an orientation in which getting a paid job was central. Their concept of 'glamour' goes a long way towards explaining their occupational choices, and even through their failure to achieve their aspirations they remain orientated to working and end up in so-called women's jobs with low pay etc. Two of the young women interviewed by Coyle (1984, pp. 102–3) illustrate this process:

They kept asking you what you'd like to do and they kept saying wouldn't you like to work in a factory, and I ended up in a factory.

I thought of being a model. I was a beauty queen you see, but my mum wouldn't let me. I'll stay in tailoring now, the money's good and me and my boyfriend are almost engaged. You can always get work in tailoring.

A feminist interest in women's occupational choice has also injected something into the debate on allocation versus choice. It is that both of these aspects of occupations must be considered and are important particularly for women. This view suggests that it is erroneous to see any process wholly deterministically since it is important to allow the actors to play an active rather than a passive role—in this case young women are the actors. A development along these lines has been occurring in many fields of sociological interest, and whilst a study of women is not wholly responsible, women have certainly given a considerable impetus to this reconceptualisation.

The changes which have been occurring in the British sociological discussions of occupational choice linked to taking women's occupational choice as a serious subject for study, constitute a thorough-going set of reconceptualisations, the extent of which is not yet complete. Economists have also begun to examine occupational choice using human capital theory. This discussion is reserved for the next chapter, where human capital theory is described more fully. We will see there that the discussion of occupational choice serves to highlight weaknesses in the neoclassical tradition of economic analysis.

OCCUPATIONAL SEGREGATION

The concept of occupational segregation is one which owes its origin wholly to the growing interest in women's employment and, in particular, to the way women are distributed through occupational categories in comparison with men. We discussed earlier in this chapter the way labour markets are divided by sex and the way workers' choices of occupation can contribute to the division. Measures of occupational segregation have been devised to specifically register the extent of this division and whether it has changed in size over time. It has become a central concept in the debates occurring in the USA over whether equal opportunities and civil rights legislation in the 1960s and 1970s have had any effects on women's occupational distributions.

In Britain and the USA, women have been concentrated in certain occupations. This is sometimes called 'crowding' by economists. Joseph (1983, p. 140–44) sets out the figures for women in Britain from the 1971 census and points out that 70 per cent of the women's workforce was concentrated predominantly in service and clerical work and 40 per cent of the total women's workforce were in occupations in which 75 per cent or more were women workers. This picture is little changed in 1983.[3] The list of occupations where women constitute 75 per cent or more of the workforce included typists, secretaries, maids, nurses, canteen workers, charwomen, office cleaners, sewing machinists, hairdressers, laundry workers, waitresses and kitchen hands. In 1981 women constituted 70 per cent of the labour force in clerical work and these other occupations. The occupational distributions of women over time show some important variations. Over this century the category of domestic servants has declined almost to extinction and employment in clothing and textiles for women have also declined. Clerical and retail work have grown in importance as occupations for women over the same period.

These broad changes in occupations do not permit us to see the extent of changes in women's occupational distributions, however; for that, a more precise measure is required. While researchers into occupational segregation generally agree that the majority of jobs can be categorised as stereotypically female or stereotypically male, there are large numbers of operational definitions of how to measure the amount of segregation. Jusenius (1976) in the USA and Hakim (1979) in Britain reviewed the alternatives which have or could be used. They include definitions of occupational segregation which count the following:

1. The proportion of occupations in which no woman (or man) is employed, as Hakim (1979) suggested.
2. The proportion of occupations in which women form a higher proportion of the workforce than they do in the population. It is possible to make a more sophisticated measure using this method if certain prespecified characteristics which are thought to influence the occupational distribution (e.g. education) are added into the calculation of what the expected distribution would look like.
3. An index of segregation based on the index of similarity or dissimilarity used in social mobility tables has been suggested by Joseph (1983) since, unlike some of the other measures, it is not influenced by the relative (or marginal) numbers in each occupational category.
4. The proportion of occupations in which a certain percentage of the incumbents are women. The percentages used in some US studies have included 70 per cent, 32.8 per cent and 45 per cent. They show the arbitrary nature of the criterion used. American studies have more recently been using the concepts of 'typical' and 'atypical' occupations for women provided by Jusenius (1976), where a

'typical' occupation is one which has at least 41.3 per cent of its incumbents as women. An 'atypical' occupation is one which has fewer than 33.1 per cent of its incumbents as women; occupations which fall outside both categories tend to be ignored. The percentages are derived by adding or subtracting 5 per cent to or from the proportion of women in the labour force in 1970.

Hakim (1979) has added to this an important distinction between horizontal and vertical occupational segregation. Horizontal segregation occurs if women and men are working in different types of occupations, whereas vertical segregation exists if men are mostly working in higher grade occupations and women in lower grade ones. Blau (1975) added a further distinction beween interoccupational segregation—that is, between occupational categories—and intraoccupational segregation, within an occupational category.

Hakim's (1979) calculations of occupational segregation measures illustrated that the extent of segregation depends upon the measure used. Nevertheless, the measures provide useful comparisons over time and for this purpose the broad conclusions are not dependent upon which measure is chosen. Hakim (1979) made comparisons between occupational segregation in Britain and the USA over this century and found that similar conclusions applied to both. They are as follows:

1. Britain and the USA are alike insofar as women are concentrated into occupations which are disproportionately 'female'.
2. Over the period 1900–70 a greater amount of change can be seen in the USA than in Britain. US women had higher participation rates than British women by 1970 and the over-representation of women in disproportionately 'female' jobs declined in the USA between 1900 and 1970 to a greater extent than occurred in Britain. The USA started off having more occupational segregation than Britain but overtook Britain by 1961 in progress towards occupational desegregation.
3. Occupational segregation has not changed very much in Britain over this century.

4. The changing pattern of the occupational distribution was similar in Britain and the USA between 1940 and 1970. Women have been increasingly employed in clerical, sales and service-work occupations, and women constitute the whole of the private household workers in both countries.
5. The proportion of women in professional work (lower and higher grades) declined in both countries between 1940 and 1970.
6. The changes in occupational segregation which occurred up to 1970 in Britain and the USA are similar, men having made inroads into women's occupations, but the reverse had not occurred to the same extent.

Hakim (1981) updated the British work on this issue and Beller (1982, 1982a), England (1982) and Shaw (1983a) have updated the US discussion of this issue providing measures of occupational segregation in the 1970s. It is interesting to see that the changes which have occurred in the 1970s are still similar in both countries. The studies all found that occupational segregation had declined in the 1970s, sometimes dating from 1967. The US studies identified the main source of change as being women's increased probability of working in a 'male' occupation, particularly professional and managerial jobs. Recession in both countries was also thought to have caused women's position to deteriorate later in the 1970s decade. All of these writers attribute the improvements to legislation about equal opportunities in both countries, although in the USA this source of improvement is heavily contested by some economists in the neoclassical tradition. The concept of occupational segregation has been drawn into debates about the validity of neoclassical economists' models since no satisfactory neoclassical explanation of occupational segregation, however it is measured, has been offered to date. It will be argued in Chapter 5 that Polachek's (1976) use of human capital theory for this purpose clearly failed. The notion of occupational segregation has also been used in attempts to identify how far women's lower earnings are caused by being in segregated (lower paid) occupations and how far by being paid less than men in the same occupations (e.g. Chiplin and Sloane, 1976).

Despite some improvements, occupational segregation remains widespread. If one adds in intraoccupational segregation from studies like that of Blau (1975), the extent of women's segregation is even greater. A detailed British study of women's work carried out in 1980 confirmed the widespread nature of women's intraoccupational segregation in Britain (Martin and Roberts, 1984). They found that occupational segregation at the workplace is much higher in Britain than is indicated by studies of the national distribution of occupations, and that 63 per cent of women were in jobs done only by women. The equivalent figure for men is as high as 80 per cent. Martin and Roberts also found that higher-level occupations were less likely to find women working only with women and women were much more likely to work only with women if they worked part-time in any occupation.

The introduction of occupational segregation and the analysis using this concept have provided us with a much clearer and accurate description of sexually divided labour markets. We can also see the extent of this division and its relative lack of change over a century of women's employment. The concept itself is not restricted to the sexual division of labour application but can and has been used for other groups (e.g. ethnic divisions) and applied to other fields like housing and crime. It also has wider applications within the area of women's work, as described above. Women's work has undoubtedly given the concept a strong boost, however. The work on the concept and measurement of occupational segregation leaves many unanswered questions about why women's work has developed in this way, some of which are being tackled through particular occupational case studies (e.g. of clerical work).[4] However, the study of occupational segregation has undoubtedly provided a better foundation upon which to tackle these other crucial questions.

SKILL

The concept of 'skill' forms the basis for both occupational classifications and occupational ranking. The research described in this chapter so far has used occupational classifications and rankings as if they were unproblematic, which means that the concept of 'skill' is also being regarded as unproblematic and taken for granted. This concept is also central to the labour-market theories described in the next chapter. Feminist writers have begun to draw attention to the fact that the meaning of 'skill' is not unequivocal. Moreover, in its everyday sense it excludes much of women's work from being counted as skilled. The discussions and empirical work which have focused on its meaning have revealed that the concept is socially constructed, and these discussions are providing a foundation for a reconceptualisation of women's and men's work which make some of the other developments seem insignificant by comparison.

A number of mainly British feminist writers have now started to ask questions about the meaning of 'skill'.[5] In some cases the work has been stimulated by Braverman's (1974) account of a deskilling process, but it stands independently of Braverman's much criticised work. The answers to this question about the nature of skill have illustrated that the notion is far from being clear or unambiguously defined, and more importantly, the meaning of 'skill' is integrally bound up with the sexual division of labour. An understanding of the sexual division of labour requires as a precondition, therefore, a thorough understanding of the meaning and generation of skill distinctions in labour markets.

Some of the empirical work illustrates these issues clearly. A study of the process of producing paper boxes in Britain by Craig *et al.* (1979) found that women who worked on hand-fed machines were considered, classified and paid as unskilled workers. Men who produced cartons on a more automated process which required less individual concentration were classified at a higher level of skill, semi-skilled. Drawing attention to this example, Phillips and Taylor (1980, p. 84) point out that there is a sense in this case study in which the work that women do must, of necessity, be thought of as unskilled, just because it is done by women: 'The women producing paper boxes are simply women producing paper boxes, and however much the work itself might seem to qualify for upgrading, it remains unskilled because it is done by typically unskilled workers—women'.

Studies cited by Phillips and Taylor and a study by Coyle (1982), both of the clothing industry in Britain, reach similar conclusions; that the skill divisions between men and women in that industry have been generated through the struggle of unionised men in often craft-based unions to retain their craft dominance, at the expense of women. Men have retained control and excluded women from working on certain jobs traditionally thought to be more skilled; for example, cutting. Whether they are technically more skilled than women's sewing jobs is highly debatable. The fact that one job has had a lengthy apprenticeship scheme whilst the other has not should not necessarily be the criterion on which a decision is made, especially when the nature of the job has changed. Similarly, it is difficult to accept that machining done by men is so clearly skilled, when machining done by women is labelled as semi-skilled. The doubtful nature of skill divisions in this industry can be seen most vividly through the changes which have occurred through the introduction of new technology. In Birnbaum's study, when men were forced to take on machining work usually done by women and labelled as semi-skilled they fought to redefine the job as skilled. Coyle (1982) demonstrated that men had retained their skilled status as cutters, and the associated pay differential, even after the introduction of new machinery which did all the skilled cutting and which in effect made the men into machine minders. It would seem to be the case within the clothing industry, for a women to become skilled she would have to change her sex.

This process takes on a slightly different form outside the manufacturing industry, where craft-based unions are not present. On the whole, the non-manufacturing sector has been the one which has grown and offered the growing women's workforce new jobs. The idea that women's work is unskilled or semi-skilled can be built in from the start, and this tertiary sector has created, therefore, a whole set of low-skilled women's jobs, often white-collar semi-skilled and certainly low-paid jobs. The outcome is the same; that the work is categorised as less skilled because women are doing these jobs. The cost advantages to employers are obvious. Crompton, Jones and Reid (1982) and Davies (1975) have started to document these distinctions in clerical occupations. At a more general level, part-time jobs are often regarded as lower in status than full-time jobs when it is the same job, and since a large proportion of women work part-time, women suffer status degradation here also. Women part-timers can often be working harder than full-timers, sometimes doing the same amount of work in their restricted hours as full-timers do in a day. The caring occupations, like child-care, nursery nurses and the whole array of social service jobs done by women (e.g. home-helps) are also thought to be generally fairly unskilled. What this means is that the skills involved are not recognised as skills by either the employers or society—and certainly the remuneration would tend to identify such jobs as low skilled. Of course, the ultimate area of women's low-skilled work is in the home in unwaged child-rearing and domestic responsibilities.

It is worth considering how the different sexual valuations of work have arisen and why they persist. It is perhaps surprising when one recognises Novarro's (1980) point that women historically and contemporarily are doing the work which is vital to human survival; childbirth, childrearing, food provision, clothing provision and caring are all jobs in both the waged and unwaged sector which are done by women. Men, as Novarro notes, have traditionally contributed to the production of the unnecessary luxury items of life. We have accepted that these unnecessary although enjoyable aspects of men's production have a higher value and involve more skill. It is not the case that women are unable either physically or otherwise to do what have become classed as men's jobs. Women's experiences in the two world wars and in countries like Sweden, China or the Soviet Union clearly demonstrate that women are able to do a wide range of jobs, although the evidence suggests that women's work is segmented in these countries also.[6]

Part of the reason for the skill division men's and women's work is undoubtedly related to the fact that men's work is paid and that women have often gone unpaid for their contribution. Since our economic system measures its wealth and value by adding up the paid work done, it is not surprising that being paid takes on a particular value of its own. Obviously there are skills to be learnt in order to find paid employment and fulfil one's work effectively, and insofar as these skills are scarce or difficult to learn we might expect some differentiation between the payment and value attached to jobs. Richards (1980) is partly right in recognising the fact that virtually anyone can do housework will mean that it is not highly valued; however, her point is not a sufficient explanation of skill divisions within paid work. The scarcity value of so-called men's skills would not be an acceptable basis for women's continuing exploitation to most feminists. Neither is it clear that child-rearing is unskilled or something which anyone (of either sex) can do efficiently.

The empirical work on skill divisions, some of which has already been described, points to the importance of male-dominated craft trade-unions as a source of perpetuating skill divisions between the sexes. Trade unions have and are contributing, therefore, to sexually divided labour markets (examined in more detail in the next chapter). Armstrong (1982, p. 32) noted that in manufacturing, these skill divisions overlap with the degree of capital intensity of the production: 'Men tend to monopolise both craft work *and* capital-intensive processes, whatever the level of skill involved in the latter. Correspondingly, women's work tends to be unrecognised as skilled (whatever the actual levels of skill) *and* of a labour intensive kind'.

That women and men have accepted these status distinctions has been documented in a number of studies. In his study of electrical fitting Armstrong (1982) added a further dimension to the characteristics of women's work. Women were regarded by the men as being disposable in a time of recession and as such faced greater insecurity in manufacturing industries; Armstrong (1982, p. 27) quotes a fitter: 'Oh well, if it's only women it doesn't matter so much'. Thus, women's work was devalued because women are dispensable. A large-scale British national survey of women carried

out by the Department of Employment and Office of
Population Censuses and Surveys in 1980 (Martin and
Roberts, 1984) asked women about the nature of their work
and whether they saw it as 'women's work' or not. They
found that women who worked only with women or who
worked part-time were more likely to think of their work as
'women's work'. Women working in high-level occupations
were least likely to think of their work in this way. Whether
a woman worked with men or not influenced her view of
whether a man could or would want to do her job, but
women realised that men were not doing 'women's jobs'
because they were not prepared to do women's work with
the low pay it entailed. Husbands, on the other hand, who in
fact were more sex-segregated at work than the women,
were more likely to think that women could not do their
work rather than that they would not be prepared to do it. It
is not surprising that men have these attitudes about women
if they hardly ever come into contact with women workers
who might dispel their false stereotyped perceptions.

There are a series of factors which maintain the sexual
division of skill. These include, amongst others, the societal
valuation of paid work, union-negotiated labels of skill for
certain men's jobs and the attitudes and acceptance by
women and men of the sexual division of labour. We are
only beginning to formulate the parameters of the social
construction of skill divisions and we have yet to incorporate
such insights into labour-market analysis more generally.
There is much scope for further research into the effects of
gender-role ideology and how that ideology is modified
and/or reinforced in practice.

THE DOMESTIC LABOUR DEBATE

The role played by women's unwaged domestic labour has
been the subject of debate within a Marxist framework of
sociological analysis. Recent feminist analysis has been
critical of the generations of Marxist analysis which used
Marx's and Engel's analysis of the family under capitalism as
its theory about women's roles. They have thus engaged in a

thorough critique of this Marx-Engels view of the family in order to reorientate the tradition to a more central and appropriate consideration of women, both in their domestic and waged-labour roles—a Marxist-feminist analysis. Only the role of domestic labour is considered here. Unlike the other traditions of sociological analysis considered in this chapter, traditional Marxist analysis did recognise that women's domestic labour existed and needed to be part of an overall analysis. Marxist-feminists have argued that women's domestic labour should be considered of central importance in capitalist relations of production. This involves questioning some of the traditional analysis which gives a central place to 'productive' labour and thereby marginalised 'unproductive' domestic labour.

Beechey (1977) and Humphries (1977) both summarise the Marx-Engels traditional view of the family. We can only note a few of the relevant points in this review. Marx and Engels suggest that the family grew out of property relations and is itself a property relation. The family therefore had a somewhat ambivalent role in Marx's analysis, since by definition the proletariat were propertyless, so it would seem that only the bourgeoisie could have families. There was no material reason for the existence of the working-class family. Humphries (1977, p. 142) calls this the 'invisibility of the proletarian family', and she goes on to show how Marx's analysis of the reproduction of labour power was like a black box in consequence, whose inner workings, like neoclassical economists' models, are unknown. Humphries (p. 142) quotes from Marx to illustrate this point: 'The maintenance and reproduction of the working-class is, and must ever be, a necessary condition to the reproduction of capital. But the capitalist may safely leave its fulfillment to the labourer's instinct of self-preservation and of propagation.'

Engels gave a more detailed analysis of the process by which women are drawn into the wage-labour force or social production, which he saw as a precondition for the emancipation of women. He suggested that male domination would disappear in the epoch of modern industry, partly through women becoming independent because of their wage labour and through the absence of private property.

He was suggesting that women's position was determined by their position in the production process and by the family in an early mode of production but failed to recognise, like Marx, the persistence of the working-class family and the role of women's domestic labour in reproducing labour within the family in the era of modern industry. Humphries (1977, p. 143) neatly summarised the way in which this neglect of women's domestic labour arose:

Marx abstracts from the problem of domestic labour by dealing with a situation in which all workers are engaged in capitalist production and perform no domestic labour whatsoever. No use-values are produced within the household and the capitalist sector provides everything required to replace the labour-power used up in production. This gives the reproduction cycle of labour-power a distinctive feature in that value is neither created nor destroyed but merely recycled. Wages are used to purchase a subsistence bundle of commodities whose 'consumption' mysteriously leads to the replacement of used-up labour-power. This new labour-power is then exchanged for a new bundle of commodities which is in turn consumed, and so the process continues indefinitely, with labour power being used up in capitalist production and replaced through the act of consumption.

Both Beechey and Humphries conclude that an analysis of domestic labour is vital to explaining the continued existence of the working-class family and for understanding women's oppression under capitalism. Humphries makes some further observations of how Marx's neglect of domestic labour seriously weakens his theory in other areas. A reconceptualisation of women's domestic labour within the Marxist tradition is thus seen as vital to the credibility of the tradition.

Attempts to incorporate women's domestic labour into the Marxist framework preceded Beechey's and Humphries' analyses, and a debate was already under way when they wrote considering the best way to proceed. The domestic labour debate, as it has been called, is a difficult one to review since it is not simply one debate but several and participants have not necessarily been aligned in their positions on all issues; they have found themselves both allied and opposed to the same writer, depending upon the issue considered. Articles which have reviewed the debate cite the earliest discussions as being in 1966, 1969 and 1972, but the main debate did not really commence until the publication of Seccombe (1973) in *New Left Review* and Harrison (1973), followed by Gardiner (1975), Coulson *et al.* (1975), Adamson *et al.* (1976), Smith (1977) and Humphries (1977). Only the broadest outline of the issues at stake can be sketched in this chapter.

One central issue has been concerned with whether domestic labour is value producing or not; that is, whether it is productive labour. Marx's definitions of the value of labour power are thought to be inconsistent, which means that both views could claim Marx's support. Seccombe (1973) argued that domestic labour produces value but is unproductive labour. (An earlier view was that domestic labour was both value producing and productive.) Gardiner (1975), Coulson *et al.* (1975) and Adamson *et al.* (1976) argued against Seccombe. Smith (1977, p. 200) called this the 'orthodox' Marxist response, but the authors in question see the issue as one of developing a Marxist-feminist response to Seccombe. The basis of Seccombe's position is that domestic labour has a definite product, labour power, which it is engaged in producing (or reproducing) as a commodity for capitalist production. Thus, the family takes part in social production, the product of the labourer being sold in the future is capital (e.g. in Coulson *et al.*, 1975). The counter argument suggests that domestic labour is a set of services partly consumed and partly use-values (e.g. cooked meals) for consumption and not for exchange.

Smith (1977) reviews this argument, pointing out that both sides are not wholly satisfactory. He suggests Seccombe's argument is confused in places and that the other side do not always argue their case against him but merely assert it. Smith points out, for example, that whilst Seccombe thinks he is applying Marx's theory of value in subscribing to the view of social production, with the labourer being the exchanged (future) product, in fact Seccombe is proposing a serious challenge to Marx's theory of value.' This is because his view suggests that one commodity, labour power, will always be sold below its value. The wage paid to the labourer to maintain subsistence will not include the domestic labour previously put into making the labourer.

Smith goes on to argue the case for the so-called orthodox position by showing the Seccombe's view about the value of domestic labour cannot be the case. What is needed, he thinks, is to show that a particular concrete and private individual labourer (i.e. domestic labour) cannot also be its opposite of abstract, social and socially necessary labour, so it must in the end be concrete labour producing use-values for immediate consumption. His argument then rests on a number of points from agreed Marxist analysis which establish that domestic labour does not achieve qualitative equivalence with other forms of labour, and that it cannot attain quantitative equivalence as socially necessary labour in the magnitude of its value. Smith (1978, p. 211) ends by concluding that 'Domestic labour is, then, not problematic for Marx's theory of value because it is not part of its object, the production and exchange of commodities'. He suggests (p. 215) that 'It is not Marx's theory of value which marginalizes domestic labour but the capitalist mode of production'.

Some of the earlier writers in this debate (e.g. Gardiner, 1975; Coulson *et al.*, 1975) raised some other points as part of their criticism of Seccombe which are not incorporated into Smith's analysis, and these suggest they would not be entirely content with his satisfaction with the orthodox position. Gardiner (p. 52), for example, challenges Seccombe to have a more radical reappraisal of Marx's theory rather than merely attempting to integrate an additional component, domestic labour. Gardiner's outline of such a theory involves the recognition of sexism in relations between working-class men and women and women's economic dependence. It would also focus on a historical perspective of the family and women's domestic labour under capitalism and ask questions about why domestic labour has been maintained. Coulson *et al.* (1975) add to this the need to recognise the contradictory nature of women's labour under capitalism, which arises from the fact that they are *both* domestic and wage labourers.

The domestic labour debate as such ended in the 1970s.

By 1979, reviewers were considering why it had reached an impasse or cul-de-sac.[7] The main issues were largely unresolved, however. A satisfactory integration of domestic production into a Marxist analysis of production had not been offered, nor had an answer been found to the question of why women are the ones to perform domestic production. Mackintosh (1979) suggested that some progress could be made by distinguishing between work done in the home and the type of tasks being considered, rather than considering both things together under the heading of domestic production. Mackintosh also suggested that a resolution to the issues needed to be sought through comparative and historical analyses of these two aspects of domestic production. Few authors took up this particular challenge. However, some authors have worked at an integration.

Humphries (1977) satisfied some of the requirements of a Marxist-feminist analysis through taking a historical perspective. In seeking to address the issue of why the working-class family has persisted, she focused on the sensitivity of the value of labour power to the employment structure which Marx's analysis abstracted from. Humphries thus focused attention away from the domestic labour debate but complemented existing literature by 'beginning from the capitalist mode of production, but nevertheless looking at the proletarian family from its own perspective' (p. 146). She argues then that what is important is that the working-class has successfully resisted alternatives to the family because they would have weakened its participation in the class struggle and lowered its standard of living. Hunt's (1980) study of class consciousness in a community has also provided the sought-after integration of domestic and industrial production. She points out that households must be seen as units of production when one notes that most consumption goods going into a household have to be changed through work before they can be consumed. It is interesting that new developments in neoclassical economic analysis have begun to regard the household as productive. Studies like those of Humphries and Hunt are thus providing a major reconceptualisation within Marxist analysis and are serving to confirm the strength of the Marxist-feminist position over and above the orthodox position.

Another development in this debate has been that the issues have shifted their location in two ways. They have re-emerged as part of a consideration of sexual politics and as more central concerns of the debate about gender in class analysis. The consideration of sexual politics has been building on the notions of public and private spheres of life, and women are thought to be predominantly in the private sphere.[8] Domestic work is obviously a private sphere activity. Studies have been examining the relationships and interdependence of these two spheres, illustrating in particular that public male-sphere production relies on private sphere servicing. Wives act as unacknowledged personnel officers, secretaries, researchers and, of course, cooks, housekeepers and laundresses. There is a sense in which a wife gets vicarious achievement from her husband's career and the husband's employer appropriates the wife's domestic contribution.[9] Two-person careers are established in this way. Whilst the model is most clearly illustrated in the middle-class, Finch (1983) argues that it has wider relevance.

A discussion of domestic labour has emerged in the debate over women's role in class analysis. This debate is described more fully in Chapter 6. The European tradition of class analysis has argued for a continuation of wives' class positions to be subsumed under their husbands' positions.[10] but this is not thought to be satisfactory, especially to feminist authors. A variety of alternatives have been suggested to replace or improve the tradition, but the most recent have the most relevance to the issues raised in the domestic labour debate. Walby (1984) has suggested that housewives and husbands (but not women and men) be regarded as classes who are antagonistic in the traditional sense. As Walby (p. 18) points out: 'The housewife is then engaged in a patriarchal mode of production in which she is a member of the direct producer class and her husband is a non-producer and member of the exploiting class'. Housewives are dependent wage labourers since they work in the house for income from their husband and they have little direct control over the amount that they are paid. Negotiation is presumably possible, however. Other writers have also argued that the family should be the starting point for class analysis because of the hierarchial relationships within it.[11] This is a far-reaching reconceptualisation of class analysis which has a better chance of integrating women's paid and unpaid work and has obvious overlaps with the developments described in Chapters 2 and 5 of conceptualising labour markets and the origin of orientations to work.

NOTES

1. Spilerman (1977, p. 555), in reviewing this development, draws attention to the way that the development was anti-empirical He says: 'Such a characterization leaves little room for work histories which do not exhibit an orderly pattern. Moreover, it detracts from the view of career lines as empirical regularities in the labor market, to be determined through the examination of data' Quoting from Ritzer, Spilerman goes on to say: "'the [career definitions] tells us very little about actual career patterns'".
2. There is a related development examining young women's education and its importance for subsequent occupations (e.g. Deem, 1980).
3. *See* Equal Opportunities Commission (1984).
4. *See* Davies (1975).
5. *See* West (1982), Phillips and Taylor (1980), Rubery and Wilkinson (1980), Wilkinson (1980), Cavendish (1982).
6. *See* Adams and Winston (1980).
7. Mackintosh (1979) considers this question. Beechey (1984) suggests that the debate was too abstract and formalistic.
8. For, example, Millett (1977), Siltanen and Stanworth (1984), Finch (1983).
9. For example, Finch (1983), Smith (1983).
10. For example, Goldthorpe (1983).
11. For example, Leonard and Delphy (1984).

5 How Much Pay?

The demand for labour is derived from the product, and there is a downward sloping demand curve for labor at the level of the firm . . . this is the marginal productivity theory . . . The supply of hours offered by the individual is made to depend on the wage adjusted for changes in commodity prices. Movements in the real wages determine the employee's choice between work, effort and leisure . . . Demand and supply are then combined to indicate the equilibrium wage and level of employment, occupation by occupation.

(Addison and Siebert, 1979, p. 2)

Addison and Siebert describe this as the central core of thought in labour economics. We can see, therefore, that the orthodox tradition of economic analysis provides a ready-made tool kit which can be used to determine anyone's and everyone's pay. The conceptual framework is unisex. Even so, the bulk of economists' analyses of labour markets until recently was of men's occupations and the relative wage levels between them. When the framework came to be applied to women's pay and the relative pay of men and women, it was unable to predict the scale of pay differentials found between the sexes in Britain or the USA, nor the persistence of these differentials.

Institutionalist and American radical economists have offered alternative accounts of women's lower wages which link together their wages, occupations and other employment characteristics. These have become known as segmented labour-market theories. Sociologists, coming later to labour-market analysis have taken the links between wages and occupations for granted, and they have taken over institutionalist economists' concerns and interests in labour-market segmentation. In the USA, sociological studies have become increasingly quantitative, and efforts have been directed at incorporating structural elements into models of earnings determination. In Britain, sociologists initially embraced theories of labour-market segmentation, but they are now becoming more critical.

Feminists have welcomed some of these developments insofar as they represent a more serious effort to analyse women's work, but they have also been critical of the lack of innovation, the simplistic applications of sometimes inappropriate theoretical frameworks and the assumptions upon which some of this work has rested. Some of the economists' efforts to incorporate women have done so by including 'sex' as an explanatory variable and as one of a number of personal characteristics.[1] This misses the point rather in that it is the sex differentials which are in need of being explained. Other efforts have floundered on a series of deep-rooted assumptions; for example, about the nature of skill, or the definitions of occupational categories. The level of skill and the nature of women's occupations have been offered as part of the explanation of the sexual division of labour and of women's lower earnings when they too are part of the subject matter needing to be explained. The reconceptualisation which has been occurring, therefore, involves a suggestion that labour-market analysis should have a change of focus and re-examine its component concepts.

These latter developments are still in their infancy. The effects of this reconceptualisation can be seen most clearly in sociological labour-market theories. Changes within economics are less apparent, and central concepts like productivity are still awaiting a thorough re-evaluation. The critical voices in economics are still in a minority and generally outside the mainstream. The nature of the criticisms of orthodox economic analysis are no less far-reaching, however, although they draw upon the 'classical' instead of the neoclassical economics tradition. It is somewhat ironic that the criticisms are built upon the classical view of the economy, so we are now returning to ideas which have been lost as economics has 'progressed'. Critics want to change the focus of economic analysis away from partial analysis of the neoclassical tradition towards a focus on the whole economic system. Labour-market analysis should draw together, it is argued, waged work, unwaged work and public sector involvements and provide a theory of the social reproduction of labour power. Some steps have been made in this direction.

We can examine some of these developments in more detail below.

ORTHODOX LABOUR-MARKET ANALYSIS

The pay of individuals or groups is determined in a labour market according to economic analysis. The forces of supply and demand for labour meet in this conceptual market-place and are equated by allowing the price to vary, which in this case is the wage rate. There will be one wage rate at which the supply and demand for labour will be in equilibrium and at that wage rate the market will be cleared; there will be no involuntary unemployment since everyone who wants to work at the going wage rate will be able to work. There can be excess supply or demand if the wage rate is not at the equilibrium level. Also, restrictions can be imposed on markets to stop them operating effectively; for example, minimum wage laws, trade unions restricting the supply of labour, people not having perfect information about vacancies or wage rates or being unwilling to move to the job vacancies. In the case of market imperfections, the result will be a wage level which is appropriate to the restrictions and frictions which affect its operation.

Given this framework, the questions which economists go on to ask concern the components, the demand and supply of labour. If the components can be specified, then the wage rates will be predictable. In practice, however, it is often a case of working backwards from the wage differentials which we can see exist, to why they are as they are. It is answers to the 'whys' of wage differentials that are provided from the determinants of supply and demand at any one time. Behind economists' supply and demand functions are individual decision-makers, according to the orthodox tradition.

It is worth noting first how inappropriate the central core

of market analysis is for handling women's work. There are of course plenty of theoretical and empirical criticisms of the central core for other reasons.[2] The tradition of labour-market analysis has assumed that the demanders of labour make no distinctions between workers other than on the basis of their marginal productivities. If women have been mentioned at all in the theory of labour markets, therefore, it has been in the discussions of the supply of labour. Women are then assumed to make choices as individuals in a way that is different to men's choices about whether to work or not, and how many hours to work, if they work. The results of empirical work looking at the determinants of women's labour-supply decisions have already been reviewed in Chapter 3.

The core notion that individuals make supply decisions on the basis of their own preferences has been found to be particularly inappropriate for understanding women's decisions, as we saw in Chapter 3, and it is now recognised that men's decisions are unlikely to be as individualistic as previously thought. A brief review of the new home economics which has developed around the household as a decision-making unit is contained in Chapter 3 as part of the consideration of labour supply.

We can see, therefore, that taking women more seriously has promoted a new development within the discipline, especially on the supply side. The implications of this go beyond the original application. The demand for labour on the other hand has remained relatively unchanged. The changes which have been occurring affect the fundamental units of economic analysis and seek to link labour-market wage levels to social relationships within households although they are far from being a comprehensive theory of household relationships. Commentators like Addison and Siebert (1979) have recognised the nature of the changes but do not offer any reason for them. I would argue that it is not coincidental that these changes have occurred as women have become a larger proportion of the labour force, and it is women workers who directly, in some cases, indirectly in others, have promoted the new developments. The changes will leave us within the mainstream tradition, which makes them unsatisfactory to some critics.³ Whether of a fundamental nature or not these are conceptual developments in economists' analyses of labour markets, although we shall review the beginnings of a far more revolutionary change later in this chapter.

In addition to criticism of the fundamental units of the mainstream tradition, labour-market analysis within this tradition has also been criticised and thought inadequate for failing to explain the persistence of large wage differentials between men and women workers. In this traditional view of the labour market, wages have had a central role as the price mechanism which moves up and down to bring supply and demand into equilibrium. Earnings differentials between workers of the same level of productivity would be expected to be eliminated over time through the forces of competition. Employer's preferences for cheaper labour power would bid up wages through their extra demand for these cheaper workers. The fact that employers are assumed to have a unisex outlook would imply that differences between the sexes, when workers are of the same level of productivity, would not therefore last, if they ever existed. When we examine the data, however, we find that average earnings of women are well below those of men in every country for which data are available. In Britain in 1983 the ratio of women's to men's earnings for manual workers was 63 per cent and in the USA in 1976 it was 58 per cent. The rate for non-manual workers in Britain was 60 per cent.⁴ What is more, these differentials prove to have a long history.

Within the orthodox theory, persistent wage differences between groups of workers could be the result of three factors: either workers have differing productivities and are not therefore equivalent, or they may have differing supply preferences and choose lower or higher paid jobs as a preference, or the market may have some imperfections or monopoly elements which prevent the wages being equalised.

Within the orthodox theory, the first source of explanation for persisting wage differentials would have been labour-market imperfections. If monopoly elements prevent women from taking up higher paying jobs, or if they are less mobile as workers or have less information than men about jobs, they would be expected to end up with less pay on the average. The size of the differential was thought to be too great to be explained by market imperfection, however, and other explanations have been investigated. These alternative explanations have developed to the extent that they are now almost sub-branches of the discipline. In this sense, women along with other minority groups with persisting lower-than-average pay have promoted these new developments in labour economics; that is, the consideration of human capital and discrimination in the market-place. Human capital theory has been concerned with how far the differences in wage rates can be explained by productivity differences between men and women and how far men's and women's preferences for different jobs might also explain the differentials. Human capital theory has developed as an elaborate supply-side economic theory. Theories of discrimination focus on the demand side and examine the extent to which employers might have preferences for male workers. Both of these developments are still within the mainstream tradition, which concerns itself with individual preferences and individual rationality. Gary Becker has played a founding role in both of these developments, and American economists have done most of the empirical work on these topics. It is only possible to sketch the broad outlines of the proliferating literature in this field, although some extensive reviews now exist.[5]

HUMAN CAPITAL THEORY

Human capital theories have elaborated the notion of labour productivity in the context of labour-supply decisions in an attempt to provide better explanatory models of earnings. Human capital theory becomes a theory of earnings if one assumes that demand is stable, so differences in worker productivities on the supply side will be the main source of difference in earnings. Chronologically, human capital theory was first described after Becker's founding work on discrimination, so much of the impetus to develop the theories of human capital came from efforts to measure discrimination. In this sense, human capital theories derive at least indirectly, and possibly directly, from the desire to analyse women's and black's relative earnings in the USA. We can examine the notion of human capital below in order to see how and why it makes a difference to wages and then examine the human capital theory of supply choices which women have been argued to be making in order to see how far human capital theory is a sufficient explanation of women's relative pay.

An individual can make an investment in his or herself by devoting time to studying, gaining additional educational qualifications or by acquiring skills and work experience. Such activities do not provide much immediate benefit, it is thought, but they do provide a return in the future and can appropriately be thought of as an investment in one's own human capital. The activities which contribute to human capital are those which the market is willing to reward, of course. The decision about whether to make any particular investment should be made, as with all investment decisions, by comparing the present costs with the future stream of benefits over the rest of one's life. Present costs will most often be measured by the earnings which are foregone in order to gain the capital, and the future stream of benefits will need to be discounted in order to be compared with the present costs.[6]

The predictions of this theory are broadly in agreement with the facts about earnings distributions. One would expect a higher return to be forthcoming from making a larger investment. Jobs requiring considerable educational qualifications or a long training would be expected to pay much more over a lifetime than those which can be done without education or training. This is the case. One would also expect that investments in human capital will be greater in one's youth when there is time to recoup the benefits than they will be in later life. This prediction also accords with the facts about worker's education and training. When one starts to look in more detail, however, at the earnings differentials and education or training differences between individuals or groups, the earnings differences are usually far greater than the theory would lead us to expect, so human capital theories at best explain only part of earnings differentials.

All of the empirical work using the framework of human capital theory follows the same format. Regression analysis is used on individuals' earnings data; either manual earnings, or in some cases income is usually the dependent variable, but in a logarithmic form. The independent explanatory variables are then a measure of education, a measure of labour force experience and a squared term of either experience or schooling. The squared term is put in to reflect the parabolic shape of the age-earnings profiles of individuals over their lifetime, rising initially, reaching a peak and then flattening off and maybe declining with the approach to retirement age. Other personal characteristics are usually added in to these regressions as other independent variables; race, sex and socio-economic status being the most common personal characteristics. After the debates between human capital theory and segmented labour-market theories took place, other studies used the same framework and added in what they regarded to be other structural variables in an attempt to test some of the debated issues. We will return to these modifications to the human capital framework later in this chapter. The results of the simple human capital applications found that the explanatory variables could explain up to two-thirds of the variations in individuals' earnings. The inclusion of women as a dummy variable, sex, was not satisfactory since it only allows men's and women's earnings to vary for one reason when it might be the case that the income–education or income–experience relationships also vary by sex. Later studies ran separate regressions on men and women and found that men and women differed in many respects.

The application of human capital theory to the problem of women's earnings was undertaken first by Mincer and Polachek (1974) and Polachek (1975). The essence of their application was to argue that women have different expectations from men about their lifetime labour-force participation, so women therefore make different investment decisions; in particular, they accumulate less human capital and have lower lifetime earnings as a result. Mincer and Polachek (1974) used data from the US National Longitudinal Survey of men and women aged between thirty and forty-four in 1967. The gross earnings ratio between white married women and married men was 66 per cent, but it could be narrowed to 80 per cent by adjusting for labour force experience and education. Polachek (1975) went further and suggested that additional facts other than work experience could explain more of the earnings gap. A British study by Greenhalgh (1980) using the General Household Survey data found that whilst the actual ratio of average hourly earnings of married men to married women was 1.97, the ratio one could expect (or predict), given their other occupational and educational details, was between 1.27 and 1.91. The expected ratio values are the part of the actual ratio which can thus be explained largely in terms of human capital effects. Main (1984) has recently replicated Mincer and Polachek's work using British data and found that women's wages would be 20 per cent higher were it not for the effects of interruptions over childbirth. However, Main (1984) is critical of the mechanism by which these differences have been said to arise. A gap still remains which is unexplained in all of the studies comparing women's and men's earnings.

Siebert and Sloane (1980) found that simple male and female earnings are fairly similar after controlling for productivity difference, in which case they suggest that the unexplained variation between married men and women cannot all be explained as discrimination. Women's preferences are thought to be part of the difference. Studies at an establishment level reported in Sloane (1980) have found that human capital differences explain between 50 and 90 per cent of the variance in earnings of sex and marital status groups. There is a suspicion that better measures of other variables, like separation rates, might even add to this figure. Human capital theory has thus contributed a lot to our understanding of pay difference between men and women, although it is not the whole story. There are other factors like the level of unionisation and the shift and bonus payments which men receive which would also be expected to contribute to the differentials.

There have been many criticisms of human capital theory. The early work measuring worker's productivity was thought to be extremely crude since education, for example, was measured by years of schooling, which ignores important quality differences. Work experience was calculated by subtracting the years of schooling from an individual's age. This measure of work experience was particularly inappropriate for women if they had spent anytime not working. The desire to improve human capital models for women's earnings has been another stimulus to the collection of longitudinal work-history data. Other problems have arisen in attempting to interpret the results, not least because the size of human capital effects appears to be sensitive to the method used in estimating them; a range of values have been found in the large number of US papers now available. There is also a causality problem about whether women's lower earnings possibilities cause them to make lower investments in human capital or whether their lower earnings are caused by their lower investment levels. Bowles and Gintis (1975) added what they called a fundamental criticism to this list, that human capital theory omits to consider what in their view was a crucial variable, social class. It is not clear that one can condemn a theory on the grounds of omission however.[7]

However, a gap does still remain to be explained, despite the increased sophistication of the measures and with improved data, and women appear to have lower rates of return to education than men. It has been suggested that discrimination against women explains this gap, but this has been debated by some human capital theorists. Even though human capital theories and discrimination theories started off being closely linked in economic theory, they are now posed as competing alternative explanations. A similar debate can also be seen in another application of human capital theory to occupational choice, which is described below.

Economists have applied human capital theory to the process of occupational choice in order to make the suggestion that it is women's preferences for different occupations which in large part explain both their lower earnings and their occupational segregation. Individuals are assumed to choose their occupation with a view to maximising lifetime earnings, given their level of investment in education and training. They might also consider the balance of advantages in any occupation by being prepared to accept lower pay for improved conditions or, conversely, expect higher pay to compensate for dirty or dangerous work. Whilst this framework has been used extensively, it does not fit the facts about earnings differentials between jobs too well. We would expect all earnings differentials between jobs to be explainable in terms of human capital requirements and compensation for disadvantages; but they are not. Since women have joined the paid workforce in greater numbers, economists have turned their attention to applying human capital theory to explaining women's choices, partly as a response to feminist arguments that new concepts are required to handle women's employment. Since women have been posing a challenge to the orthodox neoclassical framework, some response has been thought to be needed.

Polachek (1976, 1979) has offered a neoclassical explanation of why women end up in women's jobs. He suggested that women choose to enter occupations for which earnings losses when one is absent are the smallest. Women are thought to find occupations attractive, therefore, if their skills deteriorate least whilst they are absent from the labour force. Since women are all assumed to plan to be absent from work for childbearing and childrearing, they will be expected to choose these low depreciation occupations disproportionately. Effectively, this means that women will choose to enter women's and not men's occupations. Polachek is implying that occupations differ in the extent to which they penalise labour force absence, and he provided some empirical work which claimed to support his conclusions.

There are some serious problems with Polachek's approach which go beyond the questioning of his assumptions about women's plans. England (1982) has questioned the rationality of Polachek's theory. She points out that nowhere does Polachek explain why women will choose occupations with low rewards for experience, since even if one plans only intermittent employment, the fact is that greater lifetime earnings will accrue in an occupation that rewards what little experience one does accumulate. It is rational, therefore, for women to choose an occupation where the appreciation rate which rewards experience is greater than the depreciation rate which affects time out of work. England concludes that women do not maximise lifetime earnings by working in traditional female occupations. This criticism uses the tools of neoclassical analysis to criticise Polachek's claimed neoclassical theory, and it has thus uncovered the lack of any neoclassical explanation of women's occupational choices or of their segregation into certain occupations. Another paper by Beller (1982) has criticised Polachek's empirical work in which he attempted to estimate the rates of depreciation of women's occupations in order to support his position. Beller points out that Polachek's technique would only provide correct estimates of depreciation if there was no discrimination component in the way women end up in certain occupations or if the discrimination element were the same in all occupations. If discrimination differed systematically by occupation, Polachek would be measuring that and not depreciation. One would need males' earnings data to provide uncontaminated estimates of the depreciation rates for occupations, and Polachek did not use males' earnings. Beller then argues that her empirical work suggests that discrimination did exist, although it is not a direct test.

Nevertheless, England (1982) and Beller (1982) together provide a fairly comprehensive critique of Polachek's theory of women's occupational choice, uncovering at the same time the weakness of the orthodox economics' treatment of women.

It is possible to criticise the notion of 'productivity' embedded in all human capital theory applications. It is essentially a sexist concept since it only counts as productive those skills which the market rewards, and many skills which women have go unrewarded and unrecognised. Even at the level of so-called justifiable market-productivity characteristics, women get penalised if criteria like length of service are used for promotion or recruitment to certain jobs. It is not clear that length of service enhances one's productivity in many jobs, so the human capital assumption that skills depreciate when women are out of work is not clearly true. One might reasonably argue that human capital depreciates whilst workers are at work if they have to do monotonous or stressful jobs. Feminists in particular want to have a thorough discussion, therefore, of the notion of productivity, which is central to human capital theorising, and possibly to discover employers' selection criteria in order to uncover and challenge the depths of sexist assumptions they contain.

The Economics of Discrimination

Economists have suggested that an important factor in understanding the lower pay of women is the discrimination which takes place against them. Discrimination is defined by economists to occur when workers of the same productivity receive different pay (or workers of dissimilar productivity are paid equally). Becker (1957) played a founding role in formulating the neoclassical economic theory of discrimination and saw that one of its applications was to sex discrimination. The tradition which has developed out of Becker's human capital theory now appears to prefer to think that discrimination against women does not occur in the sense described. There appears to be a tendency to think that more sophisticated measures of productivity combined with the occupations women specifically choose will explain almost all of the earnings differences between the sexes, certainly to such an extent that discrimination is then minimal and not worth serious study. This view is certainly unacceptable to the institutionalist and segmented labour-market tradition. Nevertheless, a considerable literature on sex discrimination within the neoclassical tradition exists. We can summarise this area as another contribution which the study of women's work has promoted, and we will return to the debates between economists later in this chapter.

The economics of discrimination was a more direct response to the desire to analyse women and black workers in the USA. Although Edgeworth and Dewey discussed discrimination as early as the 1920s, Becker (1957) produced the first attempt at a systematic theory in the neoclassical tradition. His approach was innovative in that he introduced non-pecuniary motives into economic theory, called by the rather dubious name of a 'taste' for discrimination. A price could be put upon this 'taste' which became equivalent to the wage differentials which could not be found to be explained by productivity differences. The original theory was thought to apply to black–white earnings differentials and male–female ones, although there are some important productivity differences thought to exist between the sexes which do not apply between ethnic groups. There were different theories and predictions according to whether the discriminator was the employer, the employee or the consumer.

Becker's fundamental work received considerable attention and criticism and a number of developments have since taken place. Some writers regarded his main discriminatory concept as unrealistic and they have attempted to modify it in the light of further empirical work.[8] There are others who, on a different level, have challenged the predictions of Becker's theory and have also suggested alternative concepts of discrimination which are meant to constitute more realistic assumptions as well as predictions.[9]

If we summarise these conceptual developments, we can list some of the main features: Alexis (1973) suggested that the motive for discriminating could be argued to be envy or malice, which he calls the economics of racism. Krueger (1963) suggested that discriminators could be argued to benefit from discrimination, rather than lose from it as Becker seemed to imply. It is worth noting that at least some of these elaborations have begun to consider issues of power in economic models, although not in any systematic way. Thurow (1969), Stiglitz (1973) and Madden (1973) have worked on the suggestion that imperfections in labour markets are responsible for wage differentials, so discrimination is then a product of, for example, trade union involvement, minimum wage legislation, monopoly power or imperfect information.[10] The application of monopsony models to sex discrimination has been one of the more innovative developments.

A different treatment of discrimination can be found in Bergmann (1971, 1974). Her contribution is important because it was an attempt, within the orthodox tradition, to link earnings and occupational segregation, or occupational 'crowding' as Bergmann called it. Thinking of discrimination as the exclusion of women from certain jobs, Bergmann estimated the effect on women's earnings of the occupational crowding which resulted. She offered a theoretical argument to explain the lower earnings; women's excess supply in certain industries would end up lowering their marginal productivity/ A paraphrase of her argument would be that women are not paid less than men for a particular job, or less than they should be in women's jobs, they are paid the rate for the job but the rate is low largely because there is an overabundance of women waiting to take up the jobs in question. Nevertheless, the situation was thought to arise because women were excluded from certain occupations, although Bergmann did not elaborate upon the exclusion mechanisms. It would be possible, however, to develop theories of group power alongside this analysis, and one could argue that Bergmann's work is an effective bridge between neoclassical and institutionalist theories of discrimination. Certainly, the decade of empirical work which followed has only served to confirm the insight that earnings inequalities and occupational segregation between the sexes are inextricably linked. The crowding hypothesis of Bergmann and the segmented labour-market theories are not the same thing, however, as Chiplin and Sloane (1982) seem to imply.

Much of the American empirical work on the economics of discrimination has been aimed at quantifying the amount of discrimination in earnings using the residual method. What is unexplained after all the possible productivity differences have been included is attributed to discrimination. There has been a development in statistical techniques through this desire to more accurately quantify the amount of earnings differentials attributable to discrimination. This is another interesting effect of focusing on women workers which, as mentioned in Chapter 3, has parallels in the techniques of analysis of labour supply. Leaving the techniques on one side, we find that studies in the USA have used national samples of the entire labour force as a basis for their estimation (e.g. Sanborn, 1964; Fuchs, 1971; Sawhill, 1973 and many others). Other studies have directed their attention to more restricted groups of workers; for example, academics, professionals or selected age groups. The review of the results of this plethora of studies undertaken by Kohen and Madison (1977) revealed that estimates of the amount of discrimination in the women's to men's earnings ratio varied between 45 and 5 per cent for married groups. The percentage had a higher limit for unmarried workers. This range does not give us a great confidence in the accuracy of the results. Many of the differences are attributed to differences in data sources, in the models or in the methods of analysis.

Kohen and Madison (1977) do suggest that a number of generalisations are warranted. There is a consistent result throughout that sex discrimination in the form of unequal pay for equal work is of little, if any, quantitative significance. The study of sex discrimination within firms is in its infancy, so it is difficult to estimate the extent of discrimination in promotion, which means that women with higher qualifications can be doing the same job at the same pay as their lower-qualified male colleagues. Jusenius (1976) examined women's wages in female-intensive industries and found that after holding productivity factors constant, their average wage was much lower. This confirms that the industries (and occupations) which women hold are important in understanding their low pay. Finally, Kohen and Madison suggest that there is a consensus that differences between men's and women's occupations are an important source of earnings disparity between the sexes. It is not clear, however, to what extent occupational differentials are a result of labour-market discrimination or pre-market discrimination in the home or schools. The conclusions thus illustrate a shift in emphasis away from a sole concern on earnings to one which needs to focus on the position women occupy in the American occupational structure. More recently, the debate has shifted to considering the policy issue of whether anti-discriminatory legislation and affirmative action programmes have had any significant effects on women's earnings.

The British work on sex discrimination is far more restricted. It has largely followed in American footsteps by linking discrimination and human capital theories, adding little to the theoretical issues but rather being concerned to make more accurate empirical estimates of the amount of discrimination. British work on sex discrimination has been hindered by the relative lack of readily available earnings data and the lack of work history data on women from which to calculate their work experience. Both types of data have started to become available more recently. One contribution of the British research has been to clarify and define the possible meanings of discrimination and to codify the variety of settings in which discrimination can take place. A thorough review of the work can be found in Sloane (1985).

The initial estimates of the amount of earnings difference due to sex discrimination in Britain were calculated by Chiplin and Sloane (1974). The gross ratio of women's to men's actual full-time earnings in 1974 was found to be 55 per cent. Redistributing women through the occupational structure in the same proportions as men served to increase the ratio to 83 per cent. Chiplin and Sloane concluded, therefore, that differences in pay between men and women in the same occupation contributed 62 per cent to the differential between their pay, and differences in occupations contributing 38 per cent. This was a fairly crude estimate, however, since the broad nature of the occupational categories means that many productivity differences could have existed between the sexes. A finer occupational classification would also be expected to show a greater proportion of the differential being attributed to the uneven occupational distributions between the sexes. Greenhalgh (1980) suggested that in 1975, sex discrimination of about 10 per cent was operating between single men and women; married men had a 10 per cent differential over single men and married women had twice the labour-market disadvantage of single women relative to single men. Some of these differentials have been called marital status differentials. What is more likely in the case of women is that discrimination varies according to whether or not the woman has children. For the majority of women, having children and being married overlap, but it is not their marital status per se which influences women's employment, so their marital status should not be thought to be the source of the earnings differential. These studies suggest that wage discrimination against women in Britain is fairly high and the occupational structure clearly plays a major part in this. British and US studies have reached similar conclusions in this respect.

Other studies of sex discrimination in Britain have focused on particular occupations,[11] the workplace,[12] the recruitment process[13] or the effects of trade unions on pay differentials.[14] These studies are all summarised in Chiplin and Sloane (1982). On the issue of whether equal opportunities legislation is improving women's pay, the results are divergent. The results of the work on trade unions, limited as it is, form another bridge with institutionalist accounts of discrimination since trade unions have been suggested to play an important role in establishing and maintaining sex differentials in pay, in both traditions.

Before moving on to a consideration of the alternative institutionalist school of labour-market analysis, we can summarise the developments which have occurred within the orthodox tradition. The changes have occurred largely as a result of considering women's work, and in response to the criticism from other approaches that the tradition was unable to analyse women's work adequately.

The inclusion of women's work within the orthodox labour-market analysis has led to a shift from the sole focus on wages. The developments which have been centrally concerned with women's employment are the new home economics, human capital theories and the economics of sex discrimination. The tradition is not without its problems, however, and these new developments serve only to highlight them. Orthodox economic models are at best black boxes of mechanisms and processes which have caused women's employment to grow in the manner it has, and they offer only circular reasoning for explaining changes in some cases. The conceptual developments which have occurred are nevertheless real, however, and should not be dismissed by those who have a preference for radical theories.

It is worth noting that despite any limitations of neoclassical analysis, empirical work carried out from within this tradition has reached some similar conclusions about women's employment to alternative theories. The importance of the occupational distribution is noted by all, as is the influence of trade unions, usually male craft trade-union power. In addition, there is a growing recognition through the new home economics that men's and women's labour-market experiences are interdependent with each other and with their house-based activities. The fact that different traditions are reaching similar conclusions adds considerable weight to those conclusions. There is, however, a long way to go in analysing the whole structure of women's and men's employment before we will have a thorough dynamic understanding of labour markets. It is likely that many more concepts will need to be re-evaluated along the way, and women's part-time work and part-time wage rates have hardly begun to be recognised yet, even though the growth in women's part-time work is probably the single most dramatic employment change of the post-war era.

SEGMENTED LABOUR MARKETS

Theories of segmented labour markets began to appear in the USA in the 1960s, but their roots are often traced back to the 1950s institutionalist economists like Kerr (1954), who suggest the idea of a 'balkanised' labour market. The origins of this idea can also be found, perhaps more significantly, in classical economists like Cairnes and J.S. Mill. Its resurrection is part of a recognition of the value of the classical political economic analysis, which was lost as neoclassical partial economic analysis superceded its classical forebearers. At any rate, segmented labour markets were offered as a distinct alternative to neoclassical labour-market models in 1960s, and they were claimed to be superior in the understanding they offered of persistent wage differentials,

occupational segregation, poverty, and race and sex discrimination. Segmented labour-market theories link together
pay differentials with these other phenomena and offer an
explanation of the whole. Another group of American,
economists began writing around the same time and about
the same issues, calling themselves 'radical economists'.
These writers, Edwards, Reich and Gordon (1975), also
adopted the concept of a segmented labour market as part of
a more radical political economy or class analysis of the US
economy. Whilst there is a need to recognise some distinctions between the institutional and radical schools, it is
convenient to discuss concurrently the value of their shared
notion of a segmented labour market in this section since the
overlaps are greater than the differences. The discussion
is also related to the consideration of class analysis in
Chapter 6.

There are now a wide variety of segmented labour-market
models as Loveridge and Mok's (1979) review illustrates.
They vary mainly in the number of segments they describe
and in the criteria which characterise and identify the
different segments. The initial and most simple dual
labour-market model described two labour markets, but this
was soon replaced by further discussion, although the name
'dual labour market' is often still used of the whole genre of
these models, irrespective of the exact number of segments.
We can examine here the most popularly cited model, the
Piore model, in order to see the essential elements of
segmented labour-market theories.

Piore's (1975) model of a segmented labour market has
two main sectors, but one is subdivided further giving three
segments in all. The first major division between the primary
and secondary sector is described by Piore (1975, p. 126) as
follows:

The basic hypothesis of the dual labour market was that the labour market
is divided into two essentially distinct sectors, termed primary and
secondary sectors. The former offers jobs with relatively high wages, good
working conditions, chances of advancement, equity and due process in
the administration of work rules and above all, employment stability. Jobs
in the secondary sector, by contrast, tend to be low paying, with poor
working conditions, little chance of advancement, a highly personalised

relationship between workers and supervisors which leads to wide latitude for favoritism and is conclusive to hard and capricious work discipline and with considerable instability in jobs and a high turnover among the labour force.

Workers compete within each market for jobs, wages and employment conditions in general. Mobility barriers prohibit the movement of workers from the secondary sector to the primary market. The theory concerns itself, therefore, with the occupational as well as pay divisions in labour markets.

Piore introduced a further division within the primary sector to counter the view that the initial dual formulation of the theory focused too narrowly on the problems of disadvantaged workers at the expense of equally important distinctions between primary jobs. Thus, he suggested an upper or 'primary independent' sector, composed of professional and managerial jobs. These were distinct from the lower tier 'subordinate primary' jobs by their higher pay, higher mobility and turnover patterns which, in some ways, resembled those of the secondary sector. Formal education was a requirement of jobs in the upper primary sector and thus constituted an absolute barrier to entry into these prestigious jobs. The lower primary tier might contain lower-level non-manual jobs or craft-based manual jobs, but they would have much less variety in the context of their work and little opportunity for individual creativity and initiative. The characteristics of the work in the three sectors, Piore thought, were closely related to sociological distinctions between the lower-, working- and middle-class sub-cultures, so one of the essential and interesting elements of this theory is that job characteristics and workers' characteristics match each other—at least they do after workers have started their jobs. The majority of women are part of the secondary sector workforce and this is offered as, in large part, the explanation of their lower pay.

This basic description of labour-market segments is accepted by all writers in the field; writers diverge more in their views about the causes of segmentation in labour markets, although they all see it as part of a historical process. An early work by Doeringer and Piore (1971) described the development of an 'internal labour market', which was suggested to be a feature of the primary market, and its development arose through the negotiation process between labour and management alongside changes in industrial structure and technology. An internal labour market is one where the competition between prospective candidates for a job is restricted to those already employed in the firm. An internal labour market thus charts out a career structure. It has obviously been in the interests of management and unions to promote the construction of internal labour markets; for unions, they provide better conditions of work, promotion prospects and great security of employment; for management, they offer a stable workforce which, if training or recruitment costs are high, minimise these costs and reduce the cost of labour turnover. While the specific reasons for this development are not formalised into a theory by the authors, it has tended to be assumed that internal labour markets and the primary sector of which they are a part have developed alongside oligopolistic markets, unionised and highly capitalised production processes. Secondary jobs, therefore, are thought to be located in unconcentrated industries and competitive firms. The sectoral division is sometimes described as one between the core, large-scale monopolised firms, and the periphery, small-scale competitive marginalised industries.

Radical economists like Edwards, Reich and Gordon (1975) have offered a much more specific theory of the development of segmented markets which shares the description of the segments noted above but clearly locates segmentation in the political and economic forces of US capitalism. They suggest that labour-market segmentation arises in the historical transition from competitive capitalism, with its tensions towards homogeneous labour and that this has lead to tensions and strikes; monopoly capitalism is the outcome. Segmentation, therefore, is seen as part of a conscious effort by employers to overcome labour tensions. Once segmentation is established, it is maintained by the interdependence which grows up between the sectors through large-scale core monopoly firms contracting out their unstable production to peripheral secondary-sector industries. The theorists suggest that segmentation is functional to the perpetuation of capitalist institutions and it prevents workers from uniting to overthrow these institutions.

The segmented labour-market theories were imported into Britain largely through two papers one by Doeringer and Bosanquet (1973) and one by Barron and Norris (1976), the latter looked specifically at the role of women. Barron and Norris adopted the dualistic framework and suggested that the main motivation for primary labour markets to develop was the need for firms to retain their scarce skilled workforce, to reduce turnover and to circumvent disruptive demands for better pay and working conditions. They then suggested that women workers fitted the description of the secondary workforce since they had lower pay, that they were concentrated in unskilled and insecure jobs, that they were more likely to be made redundant than men and less likely to be upwardly mobile. Moreover, women were said to have the necessary attributes which made them a suitable secondary workforce; namely, they are meant to be easily dispensible, they do not value economic rewards highly, they are easily identifiable as a group, they are not very ambitious to acquire training or work experience and they are relatively ununionised and unlikely to develop solidaristic links with their fellow workers. There have been some empirical studies of segmented labour markets in Britain. Blackburn and Mann's (1979) study of Peterborough is probably the most famous, but it largely excludes women and examined segmentation between men's work only.

These studies are unsatisfactory both in the role they give to women as a homogenous mass of workers located in a single segment and because they exclude women and cannot hope, therefore, to gain an accurate picture of the dynamic relationships within labour markets. There are a list of other more general criticisms which have been made of segmented labour-market theories which will not be considered here.[15]

Segmented labour-market theories had obvious appeal to economists who were disillusioned with the seeming unreality of neoclassical models. Instead, they seemed to offer a wide range of variables, an integration of a variety of labour-market phenomena and an inclusion of deprived groups. Segmented labour markets have at their roots, broadly speaking, a very realistic description of the occupational and earnings divisions—and the theory goes beyond this. As such, an impressive reconceptualisation of labour-market analysis has occurred, again in large part through empirical work, which sought to take women (and black Americans) more seriously.

Some neoclassical commentators have tried to minimise the nature of the challenge posed to orthodox theory by segmented labour markets, arguing that segmented labour-market theories have nothing to offer neoclassical theories.[16] Others have suggested that segmented labour-market theories are to all intents and purposes identical with the sort of Bergmann 'crowding hypothesis' described earlier.[17] There are admittedly some problems with the segmented market theories which become visible when one tries to test them empirically,[18] but as Ryan (1981) points out, these problems have sometimes arisen from confusions. Ryan's paper does much to clarify just what is the nature of the identification problem. Ryan has set the empirical work on segmented labour-market theory back on a straight path and has done much to equip it to face any neoclassical backlash.

A series of highly quantitative papers on the subject of earnings determination emerged in the USA in the 1970s, largely in response to the debates between human capital and so-called structural theories of labour markets, the latter being either segmented or radical economists' labour-market theories. Some of these articles set out specifically to test labour-market theories whilst others have been experimenting to see how variables contributed by both neoclassical and institutionalist theories might be combined to increase the variation in individuals' incomes that can be explained in a model. Andresani's test of segmented labour-market theory found some support, whereas a test on British data by Psacharopoulos (1978) found little support for the theory.[19] Bibb and Form (1977) and Wachtel and Betsey (1972) used the basic human capital framework but added in structural variables and regarded the significant results on the structural coefficients as evidence in support of segmented labour-market theories. Beck *et al.* (1978) and other studies taking a different approach also found that structural variables were important. Sorensen (1983) has done a thorough review of the structural effects observed in these and other recent studies only to conclude that they do not have unambiguous interpretations, often because they contain methodological problems associated with inadequate model specifications and the use of inappropriate statistics. We can add to these criticisms the general neglect of women workers. Where they are included, it is usually as a 'personal characteristic' of the labour force; such an approach has been argued previously to be an inadequate treatment of all the potential differences between gendered workers. Some British quantitative studies of segmented labour markets by Brown (1983) and Dale *et al.* (1984) have now started to emerge; these do not make this mistake. On the whole however, the US development of quantitative research on segmented labour markets and earnings determination is a retrograde step as far as the consideration of women is concerned.

Fortunately, this is not the only line of research to emerge from the conceptualisation of segmented labour markets. Whilst other studies in this field have tended to examine the nature of occupational division described by the segmented theory, and not the earnings inequalities per se, they are more promising attempts to provide a basis for a theory of the sexual division of labour markets. This new work builds upon a critique of the original segmented labour-market concept, which it sees as only a first step in considering women workers. Beechey (1978) collected together a series of feminist criticisms.

A Critique

Beechey (1978) suggested that segmented labour-market theories were unsatisfactory because they were not specific enough about women's positions in the industrial and occupational structures; nor do the theories explain the post-war expansion in Britain of large numbers of women's jobs in the state sector, because they concentrate on manufacturing industry. The theories are also criticised because they treat all women as homogenous and they separate a woman's place in the family from her role in the labour market, and in treating the former as an exogenous variable, they do not explain either. Segmented labour-market theories also underemphasise the role of trade unions, since they fail to recognise their ability to constrain capital's capacity to pursue a rational labour-market strategy. Rubery (1978) has expanded this latter point by arguing that too much attention was paid in the initial American version of the theory to the actions and motivations of capitalists; insufficient attention was paid, therefore, to worker's organisation. Beechey summarised her criticism by saying that the dual labour-market theory tends to be static and ahistorical, only explaining very loosely the way labour processes structure the organisation of work in any particular historical circumstance. The theory also ignores an important element—the integral relationship between the sexual division of labour and the role of the family in structuring sexual inequality. It is only right to point out that these criticisms were levelled primarily at Barron and Norris, who failed to offer an empircally grounded account of women's specific position in Britain. Some of the American radical economists' writings are certainly not ahistorical, although they may still lack empirical grounding. In part, therefore, Beechey's criticism is a warning against importing theories as a shortcut to detailed empirical grounding in specific contexts. Some of these problems have received attention in some of the more recent writings of American radical economists.

An important development which is now an integral part of the segmented labour-market framework has come from at least two writers. Both Bonacich (1976) and Edwards (1979) have argued for introducing the negotiation process between labour and capital into accounts of segmentation in order to prevent them being overly deterministic. Bonacich provides some of the historical detail for Edwards's claim that workers and capitalists struggle over issues of control in the workplace and that the struggle in the end determines the outcome. Bonacich suggests that certain outcomes may not be optimum from the capitalist's point of view.

Edwards makes this point as part of a larger theory in which he charts a set of phases through which US capitalism has passed, in the process of which he tends rather to go back to an overly deterministic account. His phases are described in terms of the control which has characterised them; simple control was the first phase and this was superceded by hierarchical or technical control, which was superceded by the last phase bureaucratic control. The phases coincide with the response of industry to the growth in firm size, pressures of competition, increased concentration and increased market power. Whilst these systems of control have appeared chronologically in the order indicated, the earlier forms do not die out necessarily but are kept alongside the new as different sectors of the market. Edwards's theory of the changing control systems is thus a theory of labour-market segmentation.

Women are brought into Edwards' schema during the monopoly-capitalist phase as wage-labour and part of the disadvantaged secondary labour force. Edwards recognised that not all sexual differences are reducible to segment differences and that women workers thus require an analysis which is linked to the history of capitalism but which is not synonymous with it. Edwards hints that patriarchal relations may have a longer and possibly independent history. It may well be an improvement on earlier versions of segmented labour-market theories, but Edwards's theory still has weaknesses as far as its treatment of women is concerned.

Edwards, like others, did not attempt to fully integrate into his account more of the detail about the sexual division of labour, although he, like Rubery, recognised the importance of taking this step but thought it beyond his scope.[20] Whilst we can sympathise that theorists have to draw the line somewhere, the problem is that the line has always been drawn in the same place, between the sexes and to exclude women. The resulting theory is at best a partial analysis on a par with neoclassical partial analysis, and as such its claims of superiority are difficult to substantiate. What is more, Edwards's theory contains serious errors as a result. As Matthaei (1983) points out, Edwards's failure to take women's jobs more seriously means that his choice of labour-market segments are not relevant to women. He ends up placing secretaries, nurses and craftsmen in the same category as managers and doctors! As a consequence of neglecting a thorough analysis of women and perpetuating a tradition of sexism, Edwards makes his theory in large parts irrelevant.

There have been a growing number of smaller-scale empirical analyses of sexual segregation; for example Fuchs (1975), Stevenson (1975), Blau and Jusenius (1976), Coyle (1982), Armstrong (1982), Craig *et al.* (1982) and Rubery and Wilkinson (1980). A more extensive historical analysis has been given to the feminisation of particular occupations, especially clerical work (Davies, 1975).

Women's low level of unionisation and their responsibilities in the home are cited as part of the explanation of sexually segregated labour markets. The accounts are one-sided in this respect since they argue for considering the role of men's trade unions in excluding women in order to strengthen their bargaining power, but women are still seen as playing a passive role. Matthaei (1983) is critical of this treatment and redresses the balance to some extent by documenting the active role of women in breaking into certain professions in the nineteenth century. Women's actions, she argued, thus contributed to a new level of labour-market segmentation in the USA. Studies like those of Lawson (1981) and Freeman (1982) draw attention to the role of paternalism as a system of control for women workers.

These studies all confirm the need to have empirical grounding to replace speculative theorising about women's work if a useful and accurate theory is to emerge. The studies to date lack integration into a framework which explains both women's and men's labour-market changes. There are few studies of part-time pay and its comparison with full-time. One of the initial attractions of the segmented labour-market literature was that it seemed to incorporate women workers in a way that neoclassical analysis did not. Nevertheless, the lack of empirical basis for segmented labour-market theories, especially in Britain, has meant that such theories have been relatively easy targets for critics. However, new empirical studies have been provoked by this conceptualisation of labour markets, and the theory that eventually results will undoubtedly be better as a result.

There are now a growing number of studies of homework, outwork and freelancing.[21] What started out as a study of women's paid work in the home has been extended to include men's outworking. It is difficult to identify the size and extent of such workers, but the Department of Employment has offered some estimates on the basis of a survey, although these are thought to be gross underestimates, maybe only half of the actual number.[22] These workers are in varied occupations and have varied experiences. Whilst Hakim (1984a, p. 149) refers to them as a 'secondary labour force', they would appear to need some other descriptive label since they have, on average, different and lower pay and certainly different conditions of employment than other low paid or casual labour. At the same time, the firms in which they work have been found to be more profitable than those who do not use home or out workers. These firms are also more predominantly service-sector industries. This newly identified sector of the labour market awaits a theoretical integration with the rest.

The changes in labour-market analysis which have been taking place have been documented. There are other developments suggested by feminists which, if incorporated into labour-market analysis, will establish further changes. The re-evaluation of the concept of 'skill' described in Chapter 4 is one of the areas which is problematic for all the schools of labour market-analysis because it is a central concept and yet has been largely taken for granted. In its everyday meaning, skill excludes much of women's work as we have already seen. Armstrong (1982) has gone some way towards recognising the socially constructed nature of skill divisions within a segmented labour-market framework. A thorough analysis of the notion of skill and its social construction points to the neglect in labour-market analysis of women's domestic work and the relationship of informal, unwaged economies to waged work.

Mercato (1980) has advocated a change of focus for labour-market analysis as a way of resolving these issues. In order to allow women's work to have its rightful place, Mercato suggested that the focus of labour-market analysis should be on the process of social reproduction. Women are obviously integrally bound up with social reproduction (as are men), so there is then no problem about adding them in. In the process of social reproduction women's contribution has to be seen as valuable and as equally valuable as men's role, whether as waged or unwaged workers. Mercato's framework holds out considerable promise for the future integration of all of the vitally relevant aspects of economic life, and it has obvious parallels with the developments in class analysis described in Chapter 6.[23] These constitute, therefore, the msot far-reaching reconceptualisation of labour-market analysis to date.

NOTES

1. *See*, for example, Fienberg (1979) and the review of the sociology of labour markets by Sorensen (1983, p. 266).
2. *See*, for example, Addison and Siebert (1979) or MacKay (1971).
3. For example, Bowles and Gintis (1975, 1976).
4. Equal Opportunities Commission (1984).
5. *See* Marshall (1974), Dex (1979), Sloane (1985), Kohen and Madison (1977).
6. For a description of the process of discounting, *see* Dernburg and MacDougall (1980).
7. For a further discussion of the debate between neoclassical and radical economists about human capital theory, *see* Cain (1976) and Dex (1979).
8. *See* Thurow (1969), Alexis (1973).
9. For example, Krueger (1963).
10. The recognition of the importance of information in economics is having wide-ranging consequences on the orthodox tradition. Addison and Siebert (1979) cite this as one of three major conceptual developments. There are grounds for arguing that the study of women's work through the development of theories of the economics of discrimination has played an important role in this conceptual change. Such a link can be seen in the work of Phelps (1972) and Stigler (1961a, 1961b).

11. For example, Chiplin and Sloane (1976).
12. For example, Siebert and Sloane (1981).
13. For example, Chiplin (1981).
14. For example, Nickel (1971).
15. For a list of criticisms of segmented labour markets, *see* Marshall (1974), Wachter (1974), Gordon (1972), Cain (1976).
16. For example, Cain (1976).
17. *See* Chiplin and Sloane (1982).
18. *See* Sorensen (1983), Kalleberg and Sorensen (1979).
19. Psacharopoulos (1978) and Andresani (1973) did not perform comprehensive tests of the dual labour-market theory since they only examine one variable (e.g. income) instead of the cluster of characteristics the theory claims to explain.
20. Of incorporating more of the details of the sexual division of labour, Edwards (1979, p. 195) says, 'such analyses will not be attempted here'. Rubery makes a similar point (1978, p. 258).
21. *See* Hakim (1984, 1984a), Hakim and Field (1984), Cragg and Dawson (1981). Other references to studies of homework are also contained in these references.
22. Hakim (1984) points out that the estimated size of the home workforce varies considerably according according to the definition used; whether the self-employed are included etc., whether only a person's main job is considered and over what time period the count is made. In 1980, 111,000 workers were estimated to be home or out workers within the month of the survey but the figure is 281,000 if the count covers the whole of the previous year. The results of a 1981 survey are considerably higher; 658,250 homeworkers, excluding construction workers, which is approximately 2.8 per cent of the labour force. More generous definitions put the figure higher, up to 7.2 per cent of the workforce. Of these homeworkers, however defined, approximately 55 per cent are men and 45 per cent are women. Hakim (1984a) points out that because these surveys excluded firms with less than 25 workers, they are likely to be under-representing the home workforce, especially of women, by as much as half.
23. For example, Walby (1984), Leonard and Delphy (1984).

6 Which Class?

We simplify by dealing only with men. Married women have the same class positions as their husbands. Unmarried women will here be ignored.

(Kahl, 1953, p. 252)

Ignoring women was a fairly standard sociological technique in the 1950s, and certainly Kahl, in reviewing the US literature on the American class structure, might be justified in neglecting women if only because his sources all did the same thing. In case readers think that this was merely a way of focusing the review, with women being treated separately elsewhere, we must note that the neglect went much further and deeper. Haug's (1973) review of the position of women in American stratification studies, even in 1973, shows how surveys were still ignoring women's positions by failing to collect data about their occupation or their education.

It is perhaps not surprising then to hear feminists and others criticising this tradition, accusing the sociological study of stratification as having a sexist bias and wanting to promote a new approach which integrates women. A mixture of empirical and theoretical criticisms have been made. Criticism of the sexism started in the United States in 1964 with an article by Watson and Barth (1964) and was developed and extended by Acker (1973, 1980) and other US and British writers.[1] Much of the criticism is repetitive. Two criticisms which recur are that sexist assumptions underpin traditional stratification studies, and the empirical accuracy of the traditional studies is also questioned. In particular, critics suggest that the changes which have taken place in women's employment and in household structures make the traditional assumptions appear to be grossly unrealistic. It is the facts of social change, therefore, which are appealed to in arguing a case for changing the theorising and conceptualising of stratification studies. Writers on the British or European tradition of class analysis, which is quite different from US stratification analysis, have also entered the debates, and confusion has arisen from their being at least two types of class analysis. Critics have not always clarified which kind they find unacceptable, or whether it is both.

There is far from being a consensus that a new class analysis in which women play a role is either possible or desirable. Parkin (1971) in his early writing was quite dismissive of the feminist case, and Goldthorpe (1983) has made a more recent defence of the traditional exclusion of women from class analysis. Alongside these replies, many discussions and empirical work on stratification and the class structure have continued in the same traditional vein, as if a case of counter-arguments had never been made. Feminists seem divided even in their evaluations of the stage of development of this field. Acker (1980) and Allen (1982) are agreed that the disadvantaged and subordinate position of women cannot be understood or explained within the confines of the available theories of stratification. Haug's (1973) review of the ways of incorporating women into a single index of social status illustrates that none are satisfactory. On the other hand, Garnsey (1978), Haller (1981) and MacKenzie (1982) are more optimistic that a reconceptualisation is in process.

This whole field is one of amazing complexity. Many commentators start off their work making this point. We will need to tread very carefully through what is a minefield of terminology and tangled argument. British researchers have been quite dismissive of American stratification studies to the extent that 'stratification' has become a word of abuse. The difference between these two traditions of class analysis is sometimes characterised as being an individualistic (US) focus versus a collectivist (European) concern. The US stratification studies are claimed to have their roots in Weber and Durkheim, whereas the European tradition has emerged from Marx's class analysis, although this is an oversimplification. Stratification theories have been interested in explaining the nature of inequality as it has existed since the Second World War, and they have thus had a more static interest than European class theories, which have focused on the causes of social change; the European tradition starts, in particular, with the change from feudalism to capitalism.[2] It therefore overlaps in interest with the theories of social change described in Chapter 7.

Theories about the class structure and stratification in industrial societies have occupied a central place in sociology and its development. Possibly because of this primacy, considerable effort and energy have been put into changing and developing the concepts. Theorists like Giddens (1973) have described the problems of class analysis as a crisis of social theory, where confusion, ambiguity and lack of analytical penetration reign. The role of women in class analysis is integrally bound up with the problems to be resolved in class analysis and therefore with the problems of sociology more generally. It is perhaps ironic that women's work, as a phenomenon of social change, has helped to censure one of the major theoretical considerations of social change in sociology.[3] The sociology of class analysis has not only failed to keep pace with developments in society, but the discipline has even resisted change, as if it would have preferred women to have remained invisible. Needless to say, they have not.

The rest of this chapter will locate the criticisms about the neglect of women with their targets in the different traditions of class and stratification analyses. We will then be able to see where developments are taking place and we can evaluate the extent to which they constitute an advance of this central aspect of sociology.

SOCIAL STRATIFICATION STUDIES

The American analyses of stratification have focused upon describing and explaining inequalities in US society. The tradition is commonly cited as having built upon Weber's criticisms of Marx's class analysis. The work of Talcot Parsons played an important contemporary role. This tradition has described a stratified society as one which is marked by inequalities and differences which are viewed as part of a hierarchical structure. Weber is taken to have indicated that inequalities have many dimensions which, broadly speaking, go under two headings: economic division, for which 'class' was an appropriate label, and prestige or life-style divisions, for which 'status' was a convenient label. The various dimensions of inequality can cut across each other so that a division of the population along occupational lines will not necessarily produce the same groups of people as divisions based on prestige. Nevertheless, American studies have wanted to apply these notions to contemporary industrial societies, despite the fact that Weber introduced them as a way of classifying and describing the transition from pre-capitalist to capitalist societies. Other concepts have been added to the list of dimensions of stratification; for example, personal prestige, possessions (wealth), personal interactions, class consciousness, occupations and value orientations. Kahl's (1953) review of US studies described these six variables as 'dimensions of class' to be used to describe a system of stratification. Using these concepts, research then sought measurable variables which represented these various dimensions. The amount of inequality along each dimension could be calculated by finding the proportion of the population in each group. There were a plethora of small-scale US community studies which conducted such an exercise, starting with Lloyd Warner's study of Yankee City in the 1930s.

Warner and Others

Warner's (1941–59, 1963) study of a New England community provided a set of six hierarchically arranged 'prestige classes'. The sizes of these groups were approximately such that a pyramid structure was found with the highest prestige class being the smallest group (1.4 per cent of the population) and the lowest classes having the largest proportions (25 to 33 per cent). These prestige-class divisions were also found to overlap with a large amount of data on attitudes and behaviour. Warner (1960) later published a manual for describing procedures for measuring social status; in particular, for constructing an index of status characteristics on the basis of which each individual interviewed can be assigned to one of the 'class' categories.

The studies which ensued replicated Warner's technique, applying it to other communities, but they also made use of his classification of prestige classes as an explanatory variable. For example, Hollingshead, who had worked with the Warner team, constructed a set of classes to be used to explain the behaviour of the youth of a Yankee City (although he gave it a new name—Elmtown) in 1941. As research developed along these lines the identification of prestige classes was found to involve problems. People differed too much in their notions of prestige rankings, and since prestige and occupation were highly correlated, occupational classifications and rankings began to replace prestige scales. The use of occupational categories meant that a more uniform scale was available with which to compare communities, and occupations were thought to signify income levels, education and styles of life. The use of an occupational scale thus widened the scope of community-based studies enabling them to classify the whole population; for example, Lynd and Lynd's (1937) follow-up work on 'Middletown'. This interest spread to the census occupational categories and North and Hatt constructed occupational classifications for the National Opinion Research Centre (1947).

In all of these studies the same two aims were held: first, to describe a set of ranked prestige classes based on occupations, and second, to be able to use the scale as an explanatory instrument. Part of the description of each class involved illustrating the correlations between the various class dimensions; that is, between income, wealth, occupations, life-styles etc. The result of these early developments was a whole array of research articles and books which, whilst ostensibly focusing on whole communities, actually described a system of stratification for the men.

The desire to explain individuals' occupational attainments, part of which is considered in Chapter 4, grew out of this tradition. The community focus was gradually dropped to be replaced by large-scale national samples. The question of how individuals are recruited to their class or prestige categories was considered. Research was carried out on the degree of inheritance of class positions, fathers to sons, using occupational scales. The founding studies took place in the 1940s at the National Opinion Research Centre (Lipset and Rogoff, 1954); international comparisons were made by Lipset and Bendix in the early 1950s. The desire to classify American society and compare it with others was growing in popularity, even though the stated aim was to gain insight into the perpetuation or breakdown of inequality and social change. The research in practice remained concerned with static classification rather than with processes of social change. The classification issue was often a question of whether the society was 'open' or 'closed'.

A major landmark in the study of occupations and social mobility in the USA was done by Blau and Duncan (1967). The authors, however, were very reticient about locating their work as a theory of stratification, claiming only that their results would have implications for the theoretical work on stratification. Their caution turns out to be partly based on the idea that international comparative studies of occupations are needed to formulate theories of stratification; but also they saw information about institutions as being necessary to formulating a theory of stratification, information which was absent from their data. Their work has given very solid support to the continuation of interest and analysis in men's occupations, and other researchers in the field are not so punctilious about the relevance of their results for stratification theory. Blau and Duncan's (1967) results were described in Chapter 4.

It is worth mentioning a recent American exponent of stratification studies since he has had considerable influence, if not least in becoming a focus of attack by most European commentators. Lenski wrote on social stratification in 1966, but he was attempting to synthesise two traditions, the dominant structural functional consensus model and the critical conflict models dominant in European writings. His synthesis was captured in two laws of distribution, one expressing a force of consensus and the other a force of conflict, and this process of distribution gave way to a structure of the distributive system in which classes were the structural components. 'Class', Lenski suggested, was too narrowly defined, and so he proceeded to widen it by suggesting that there could be as many class divisions as dimensions of stratification or inequality; hence there could be power classes (the most important), privilege classes, prestige classes and class systems based on property, race, age or sex. He does not elaborate the class system based on sex, but reviewers have taken him to mean that women as a whole form one class and men another.

Lenski's scheme has a number of shortcomings. By widening the definition of the concept of class, he had in effect made it redundant. Lenski could almost just as well have used 'strata' instead of the term 'class' and thereby avoided any confusion. Whilst seeming to give a more central place to sexual inequalities, in fact Lenski ends up leaving such relations undiscussed and opts for regarding, rather than demonstrating, that power classes are the most important. Such an analysis is far from integrating sexual and other inequalities. Lenski's work is not an exception, therefore, to the criticisms levelled against this American tradition of stratification studies. The criticisms are listed below.

Critique

The first critics of sexism in traditional stratification theory, Watson and Barth (1964), drew attention to the two main assumptions in the analysis; first, that the family was the unit of 'equivalent evaluation' in stratification studies, all family members being accorded the same rank, and second, that a person's occupation was the basis of the class identification. Acker's (1973) criticism, building upon this foundation, extended the list of assumptions to six. In addition to the summary points made by Barth and Watson, Acker listed the following assumptions:

1. The family is the appropriate unit of stratification analysis.
2. The social position of the family is given by the status of the head of the household.
3. Women live in families with a male head of household.

4. Women determine their own social status when they are not attached to men.
5. Women are unequal to men in many ways but that this differential is irrelevant to the structure of stratification.

These authors proceed to argue that these assumptions are becoming increasingly unrealistic in the light of the empirical evidence. US statistics show that a large proportion of American households (as much as two-fifths) are in female-headed households and that a sizeable proportion of women in families have occupations with a higher status than that of their husband. Our brief survey of this tradition shows that these assumptions correctly describe most, if not all, of the US stratification studies up to the 1970s. As the opening from Kahl indicated, it is easier to ignore women and examine social mobility from father to son without justifying that selective decision. How are we to evaluate the tradition?

It is important to remember that these criticisms were first levelled at US studies of stratification, so they should be evaluated against that US tradition and not necessarily against British class-analysis. Some confusion has been caused by British sociologists like Parkin (1971) defending the British tradition of class analysis from an attack which was aimed primarily at US stratification studies. Parkin points out at the same time that he was unconcerned with the US stratification studies. These confusions aside, we can ask whether there are any justifications for ignoring women in US stratification studies.

If a single class-indicator per family or household was required to be used in an analysis, or if it did not make any difference to analyses whose occupation was used to classify the household, then the tradition's sexist practice might be justifiable. Haug's (1973) review illustrates that neither of these arguments holds. It makes a large difference whether the man's or women's occupation is used to classify a household and, of course, one has the problem of what one does when the women (or the man) is not employed. It is also becoming clear that a single indicator of the class position of a household leaves much that is unexplained, and by incorporating finer details of men's and women's occupations or incomes and their education, the explanatory power of most models is extended. Such results are particularly apparent in studies of occupational attainment, where a mother's education and status effect the child's attainment, the family's life-style and the family's consumption. It is difficult to think of any topics for study where a single class-indicator would be preferable to a set of variables which described more accurately the position and circumstances of a household and their resources. When the process of occupational recruitment and attainment is considered, it is clear that the tradition also ignored the large gap between the son being born and his first job, a gap in which women have been playing a crucial role. In this context, treating occupational recruitment by comparing the father's transference of occupation to a son is particularly myopic.

Some of the suggested solutions to these issues were that the head of household's status should be used to classify the household, or that the highest occupation of anyone in the household should be used. Multi-dimensional class indices have been constructed in Britain by Osborn and Morris (1979). These suggestions do not go far enough, on the whole, if the ultimate aim is to understand the sexual division of labour in the market-place and its relationship to sexual divisions of labour in the home. Another problem remains: the occupational scales which had their origins in the 1930s community studies in the USA do not reflect the range and nature of women's occupations, and in particular women's occupations in comparison with those of men. Rather than face these problems, there is at least a part of the tradition of stratification studies which are continuing to examine men only, without providing any justification for their selection and without considering the implications for the size of the explained variation in their models.[4]

This review of US stratification studies has shown that the tradition has been built upon sexist assumptions about households and upon an occupational classification which is appropriate for men but not for women. The desire to remove this sexism has led some researchers to examine the implications of these sexist assumptions regarding the amount of explanation offered by models which ignore women, and to begin to try and remove sexism from future studies. The sexist tradition still has adherents, however, who are continuing to take what is the easy route and yet what is also a myopic and limiting option if an understanding of stratification is the ultimate objective. One could argue that stratification studies are an inappropriate framework altogether for asking the central questions about women's employment—which is, why has it changed? This is a question which the European tradition of class anlaysis has been concerned to answer. There are now US writers who fall within this European tradition, as we shall see, because of their desire to dissociate themselves from US static stratification studies.

EUROPEAN CLASS ANALYSIS

The European tradition of class analysis, of which British class analysis is a part, is differentiated from US stratification research but also has a variety of analyses and approaches within itself. The varieties within the European tradition have arisen partly because researchers have set themselves different questions to answer and goals to reach. There has been an interest, originating in Marx, in the causes of social change; there has been a concern by some to modify, even salvage, Marxist analysis in the face of the apparent mismatch between twentieth-century developments and Marx's predictions; others have been concerned to describe and identify the social classes of modern industrial society—what has come to be called 'the boundary problem'. This latter motive has strong similarities with the US stratification studies. Studies of class boundaries seem to stop after a reasonable description of the twentieth-century British class structure has been offered; they are therefore essentially static in nature. Researchers who want to use social class categories to explain other types of behaviour are located outside the realm of pure sociological theory which is reviewed here, and they continue to use but complain about the official statistical social class categories. The official categories appear to have a minimal relationship

with the theoretical debates on class analysis which constitute the mainstream of sociological theory.

In pursuing our task of evaluating feminist criticisms and
the state of class analysis in the European tradition, we will
first go back briefly into the roots of this tradition in order to
see the changing nature of class analysis and, in particular,
to examine the place given to women and sexual inequalities
by some of the more contemporary exponents. Since the
European tradition claims to recognise sexual inequalities,
we will have in mind the question of how far this tradition
has offered either an explanation of sexual inequality or a
framework within which the examination of sexual inequalities can be integrated with the analysis of other inequalities.
The task of reviewing this literature is made more complex
by the variety of analyses which come under this broad
general heading. A brief sketch of some of the major strands
of the European tradition is offered here, and the reader is
left to fill in more of the details from some of the summaries
available.[5] The main strands of analysis to be considered are
displayed in Figure 1. They all have their roots in Marx,
although some have taken Weber's critique of Marx more
seriously and have integrated aspects of it into their class
analysis, but to varying degrees. Parkin, for example, has
identified his class analysis as Weberian, whereas Giddens
prefers to emphasise his links with Marx; Goldthorpe
similarly sees his roots in Marx and shares common elements
with Giddens but has been more concerned than the other
writers with empirical analysis, in particular, of social
mobility. (Goldthorpe's structuralist approach should not

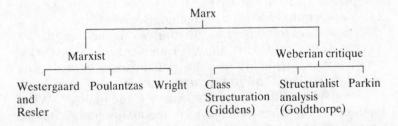

Figure 1. The Generations of European Class Analysis

be equated with the Marxist structuralist tradition from Althusser.)

Marx on Class

As Giddens (1973) aptly illustrates, Marx's concept of class was never specifically articulated. Instead, it is woven through the fabric of his work and must be drawn out by commentators. Giddens portrays Marx's theory of class, in a fairly uncontroversial manner, as having two major components: first, an abstract model of class relations, where classes are defined dichotomously by their relationship to the means of production, and second, specific class analyses are provided by Marx as part of particular historical studies of Western economies. The abstract model provides an axis around which class divisions are orientated: those who own the means of production versus those who do not, the latter being dependent on the sale of their labour power. The specific historical studies introduced more classes in addition to the two which are part of the abstract model. The concept of 'class' in Marx was therefore dynamic, since it was not concerned with static descriptions of particular class characteristics or with demarcating the boundaries of particular classes. Also, class for Marx was an explanatory concept; it explained social change. The dichotomous class division introduced an inherent conflict between the two major classes, and this was meant to promote social change and, in particular, changes in groups' relations to the means of production. Marx's historical analysis of the change from feudal to capitalist society demonstrated the power and relevance of his class analysis. However, many later writers lost Marx's initial focus on explaining social change.

Marx's dichotomous class division is claimed to be an objective division; that is, this division is meant to identify a major line of inequality in industrial societies. Sociologists and Marxists have had to face up to a number of questions. Is class inequality *the* major line of inequality? What significance do other dimensions of inequality have? Should we expect and seek to identify other sub-divisions (social classes) within the dichotomous structure; that is, divisions between wage labourers or capitalists? If we do identify heterogeneities within the two classes, what are their significance for Marx's theory of class and its predictions? Marx, as commentators note, clearly did recognise the existence of other specific class groupings; for example, the petty bourgeoisie. But he did not elaborate the relationship between the abstract dichotomous model and specific historical classes, so we are left unclear as to how to commence answering the above list of questions.

As other commentators have noted (e.g. Garnsey, 1978), Marx did not give any systematic treatment to the position of women's work in class analysis. He did give some discussion to the use of low-paid women's labour power to displace men. Marx did not integrate women's paid employment and their domestic labour into his class theory. Although the nature of women's employment has changed since the nineteenth century, these two aspects of women's work were evident when Marx was writing. Engels did attempt to examine the relationship between the exploitation of women and class exploitation. Engels suggested that the emergence of private property was responsible for sexual domination and that private property overturned the previous matriarchal societies. He saw sexual exploitation as an offshoot of class exploitation and his treatment is far from satisfactory to contemporary critics. Contemporary Marxists have sought to rectify this omission by recognising women's positions and trying to fully grasp their significance.

Marx's class analysis thus left certain questions unanswered, in his treatment both of class identification and the role of women. Weber made a contribution to the first issue which is worth describing next since it has played an influential part in all of the subsequent analyses.

Weber's Critique
Weber is often credited with providing the specific elaboration of a theory of class and social classes which were lacking in Marx, but it was in the context of his criticisms of some of the cruder Marxist analyses of his time. Weber is also partly responsible for the movement away from Marx's interest in explaining social change, towards a more static concern to

describe the major characteristics of different societies at different points in time, although this criticism is more appropriately levelled at Weber's sucessors. Weber sought to describe an identifiable set of social groups called social classes, which he thought were common to industrial societies. They could be described in terms of two dimensions of inequality; economic or class divisions, sometimes described as a group's life chances or market opportunities, and status divisions based on prestige or consumption differences between groups. Both class and status divisions represented a group's differing access to power in the community. It is worth stressing, however, that Weber, like Marx, was motivated by the desire to explain historical social changes, but in addition, he sought to characterise a range of societies in order to arrange them in a typology. Weber's concept of class, like Marx's, was constructed in the process of organising historical data. In Marx, class played the central role in explaining social change, whereas in Weber, the concept of class together with the concept of bureaucracy are both used to characterise modern industrial societies and differentiate modern from pre-industrial societies. Weber, like Marx, did not elaborate the role of women in his class analysis.

The lines of development which succeeded Marx and Weber, to a great extent, revolve around the significance given to Weber's critique. On the whole, Marxists see Weber as a revisionist, although they have taken up more recently some of the same issues Weber was attempting to face—in particular, the location of class boundaries. Giddens (1973) suggested that the US tradition saw Weber's contribution as the beginning of scientific social science, replacing what they saw as the ideological and political propoganda of Marx. In the European tradition there has been a further line of development of those who have valued Weber's contribution. This development builds on Weber's foundation and suggests that the market position of individuals determines their (class) position in the class structure; that is, their access to resources in the distributive process. Lenski (1966) in the USA was in this tradition. In comparison, class in a Marxist framework is essentially determined by the relations of production rather than distribution. Most writers in the Weberian tradition would want to say that both productive and market relationships are important, although their research and analysis tends to concentrate on the latter.

Sexism and the European Tradition

We can now outline the general, largely feminist criticisms made of this tradition; later, we will examine some of the contemporary class analyses in this tradition. European feminist critics repeat their American colleague's criticisms and thus suggest that the assumptions embedded in US stratification studies are also present in European class analyses. Any evaluation of the European tradition therefore needs to consider both sets of criticisms.

Allen (1982) suggests that sexism in class analysis has blinded sociologists from considering important research topics. In spending their time classifying men's occupations into social classes, assuming that the men have dependant wives, sociologists have forgotten to ask questions about household-resource distribution and management and about dependence within marriage. Allen (1982) argues that this has left us ignorant of important processes which maintain capitalist relations.

Delphy (1981) has argued that treating women as dependent wives is effectively giving a greater importance to women's assumed dependence upon their husbands, over and above any attachment they might have to their own occupation. Delphy (p. 127) sees this as a sign that the 'patriarchal class system overrides the industrial one'. Delphy is suggesting, therefore, a major reconceptualisation of sociologists' approach to class analyses in which women are assumed to be dependent. While sociologists have regarded class inequalities under capitalism as fundamental to an understanding of modern industrial society, they have been demonstrating what Delphy regards as something more fundamental, that sexual inequality is primary and more fundamental than class inequalities. Delphy's position is a feminist rather than a Marxist-feminist position.

West (1978) also criticises the Marxist tradition of class

analysis, suggesting that it has either treated women as peripheral to the class structure or that it is there to be used to settle arguments between different camps. The failure to treat women seriously and in an integral way, she claims, has led to inconsistencies in class analyses. All feminist critics have noted that class analyses have not integrated women's dual role as houseworker, or domestic labourer, and paid employee with the rest of the analysis. With these general criticisms in mind we can consider the various strands of class analysis in the European tradition, outlined in Figure 1 (see p. 153), beginning with the Marxists, giving particular attention to their treatment of women.

Marxist Class Analyses

The analysis of Westergaard and Resler (1975) is one of the seminal contemporary analyses of the class structure in Britain. Their work has acted as a foundation for many subsequent Marxist and non-Marxist sociologists. It is essentially an empirical work which claims to show the abiding empirical reality of Marx's dichotomous and objective class division. Westergaard and Resler (p. 18) saw their work as injecting the 'empirical' and 'factual' back into Marxist analysis and, at the same time, acting as a counter to 'an obsession' with re-interpreting Marx's early works.

In gathering together a considerable amount of empirical work, they show that inequalities in British society had not lessened through state involvement since the Second World War and that many inequalities do have a dividing line which coincides with the major class division. One final background point worth mentioning is that they indicated that occupational classifications were insufficient to identify all class divisions. The nature of class inequalities is such that some privilege will be hidden and not a part of the occupational structure they suggested. Thus, one of the major US criticisms of traditional stratification theory, that it relies too much on occupational classifications, does not apply to Westergaard and Resler.

Moreover, Westergaard and Resler pay specific attention to the women's labour-market earnings in their documentation of inequalities, and they specifically wanted to refrain from making false assumptions about women's inequalities. In the conclusion to their examination of the income and occupational scales of women, they say that the class pattern of the inequalities in women's pay complements those in men and even extends them. Women need be given no further special treatment, therefore, since a sex-neutral class analysis will capture all the major inequalities. There are, however, a number of shortcomings in their treatment, some of which are due to the lack of data.

The fact that women's earnings are lower than men's earnings fails to have any significance in their discussion of inequalities. Nor does the fact that women are segregated into certain occupations appear to be important. They suggest, rather than demonstrate, that women's property owning is mediated through men and consequently involves little, if any, economic power. In the light of the recent changes in the age distribution and the fact that women live longer on average than men, there are at least some grounds for being suspicious of this assumption about wealth holding and its influence. An assumption of this sort can often preclude an empirical examination and help to perpetuate a myth.[6] In sum, Westergaard and Resler's claims about the complementary nature of sex inequalities are not demonstrated, since they do not examine men's and women's or husband's and wive's occupations together. The lack of appropriate data for such an examination presumably constrained their analysis. Nevertheless, it would have been judicious to express more caveats about their conclusions. Their approach, as stated, of wanting to focus on empirical inequalities offered the potential for a class analysis which integrated sexual inequalities, but such was not the outcome. What has been most damaging about their work is that subsequent writers cite Westergaard and Resler's conclusions as a justification for now ignoring sexual inequalities, without critically examining whether the documentation for this conclusion is a sufficiently robust base on which to build. Clearly, it is not.

Poulantzas (1973) is another important writer in the Marxist tradition. His notion of class has been elaborated, following on from the work of Althusser as a part of a critique of so-called crude Marxist determinism. Poulantzas is one of a new set of theorists who partly set out to explain why we do not see the wholesale confrontation between the bourgeoisie and proletariat which traditional Marxist theory predicted. Poulantzas is one of the writers who has been attempting to provide a sophisticated theory of social change which relates to twentieth-century developments; in particular, which relates to changes in labour-market relationships. Poulantzas's theory suggests that there are three levels in a class society: economic, political and ideological. While classes are primarily determined in the economic sphere, they contain strong elements of political and ideological elements. In Poulantzas, each class has a 'place' in the structure of relations and a 'position' in a conjuncture; that is, a position in the specific historical situation. The economic basis of classes is defined by their relation to production; in particular, whether a class is engaged in productive or unproductive labour. Poulantzas introduces a further new concept, 'a class fraction'; that is, part of a class which can ally itself with sections of other classes. Poulantzas's conceptual discussion reduces to a description of three social classes in society: the bourgeoisie, the working class and a 'new middle strata' containing the old and new petty bourgeoisie.

As far as women are concerned, Poulantzas recognised that women constitute much of the new white-collar labour which forms part of the new middle strata. This middle-class contains three major fractions: low-level sales and service workers, bureaucratised workers in banking, administration, the civil service and education, and low-level technicians and engineers. Much of the discussion has centred around whether this new class are likely to ally with the proletariat or the bourgeoisie. Women's occupancy of some of these new class positions has been used in arguments both to reject and accept the embourgeoisment (or proletarianisation) theories.

West (1978) provides a good overview of these debates and concludes by pointing out that sexual divisions in the labour market tend to be overlooked in all the discussion. MacKenzie (1982) has made the general criticism that

Poulantzas's analysis is formalistic and mechnanical since it gives no role to actors or their resistance. This general criticism is made more specific by West (1978), who noted that Poulantzas fails to explain why the agents who are filling the class positions and who are becoming increasingly deskilled are mainly women. There are also inconsistencies in Poulantzas's treatment of the sexual division of labour since, at one and the same time, women are regarded as secondary and an important component of the new petty bourgeois class. Women's domestic role is unconsidered by Poulantzas. Poulantzas, whilst considering the contemporary labour-market divisions, therefore fails to consider the question of how sexual divisions affect the class structure. There are several general criticisms of Poulantzas's theory which also cast doubt upon its usefulness.[7]

Wright (1978) is an American who is in the European Marxist tradition of class analysis, since he regards the basis of class as being the individual's relationship to the means of production. Wright criticised Poulantzas but uses his notion of a class fraction. Wright's unique contribution is the suggestion that many positions in the social division of labour will be ambiguous. These ambiguous positions should be recognised as such and given the title of 'objectively contradictory locations within class relations'. Apparently, 50 per cent of the population of advanced capitalist societies appear to be in this contradictory location.

Wright also attempted to overcome Poulantzas's more static analysis by providing a historical analysis of the development of capitalism, explaining why these contradictory locations within the class structure have arisen. Three types of structural changes were identified as contributing to their emergence: the progressive loss of control over the labour process by direct producers, the progressive differentiation of the functions of capital and the development of complex hierarchies of control within business. In the end, however, Wright's approach is static and mechanical, and he has seven categories, replacing the three in Poulantzas, to which individuals are allocated largely according to their occupations. The static nature of Wright's work and some of its limitations appear in the empirical studies which attempt to describe the class structure of the USA.[8]

Wright attempted to incorporate women into his class structure, but women who are not employed at the (cross-section) time he is describing in the US class structure are ignored. Wright argues that these non-employed women have a class position which is mediated through their husbands. Women who are employed are given an individual class position since Wright believes that the individual is the appropriate unit for describing the class structure. He is then able to divide his sample by sex and compare the class distributions of each sex through his seven categories.

Wright has offered a partial solution to the problem of recognising women in the class structure. His solution incorporates women who happen to be employed when he decides to describe the class structure. Since most women are likely to be employed at some time in their lives, Wright's approach does not capture the dynamics of women's employment. Wright's class anlaysis is not one which integrates the sexual division of labour nor women's domestic labour, largely because of its static and boundary-drawing nature. Carchedi (1975, 1977) has attempted to develop Wright's analysis, but he has nothing new to offer as far as women are concerned.[9]

Other American Marxist analyses have been generated through a consideration of labour markets. An outline of some aspects of the work of such writers—Bowles and Gintis (1975, 1976) and Edwards, Reich and Gordon (1975)—is provided in Chapter 5. The attempt to integrate women's labour market roles was argued to be partly responsible for these developments.

In evaluating this line of Marxist class analysis in the light of feminist criticisms, a number of points can be made. The criticisms of American stratification studies concerning the nature of household structures do not clearly apply to Marxist class analyses. Much of the discussion in Marxist analyses is not conducted in terms of single households or at a micro level. Only when theorists begin to document the empirical implications of their analysis do they have to face the issue of what are the appropriate units of analysis. On the whole, contemporary Marxists like Wright have chosen the individual and they thus avoid the earlier criticisms. The other major criticism of US stratification studies, that they depend unduly on occupations as the major class identifier, does not wholly apply to Marxist analyses, since they have often used the distinction of employee versus self-employed and have considered women's occupations as well as those of men. We should beware importing criticisms, therefore, when traditions of analysis vary.

However, some important questions remain unanswered by Marxist analyses. What, in the logic of capitalist development, causes the changes in the sexual division of labour like women's growing monopoly of newer service jobs? What, in this same logic, makes employers stop short of employing more women if they are so much cheaper? The failure to consider these important questions about social change has led critics to suggest that Marxists have lost sight of Marx's method of analysis, which was essentially historical. Insofar as they continue to be seduced into providing static descriptions of class boundaries, they will not be able to offer an integral theory of class analysis and sexual inequalities.[10] Marxist-feminist writers have been attempting to steer the tradition towards such goals.

We can turn now to some of the other major British class-theories in the European tradition and examine the extent to which they have any better analyses of women to offer.

Giddens

Giddens has become a major contributor to the study of class analysis. We cannot do full justice in this short review to the extent and depth of his analysis of other class theorists and of his own treatment of class structuration (1973). Gidden's starting point was a critique of certain developments within Marxist analysis which have, as he sees it, changed the nature of the concept of class from an explanatory term to a descriptive one. He sees his own work, therefore, as a return to the problems in Marx's theory and as a reconceptualisation, but using the same method.

The main problem which Giddens addressed was, how can

one go from a recognition of the diversity of market capacities of individuals to classes as structured forms? It is the problem of relating Marx's abstract model to specific societal analyses but phrased in terms more like a Weberian view of classes. Classes, in Weber, were defined in terms of their market position. Giddens avoids an overly static conception of the class structure by wanting to talk about the degree to which societies have class structuration. By 'class structuration' he means 'the modes in which "economic" relationships become translated into "non-economic" social structures' (1973, p. 105). Nevertheless, he is contributing to the discussion of class boundaries.[11] The structuration of class relationships as a variable depends upon two types of influence: mediate and proximate structuration. Mediate structuration includes factors like the amount of social mobility or the degree of closure of mobility chances, or the ownership of property or qualifications; proximate structuration influences are the localised factors influencing class formation like the division of labour within productive enterprises, authority relations and consumption differences between groups. Giddens shares with Goldthorpe and Parkin the interest in defining class boundaries at least partly in terms of individuals' mobility chances. Although Giddens does not say so, one suspects he means, like Goldthorpe and Parkin, *men's* mobility chances.

Women enter Giddens's analysis in a number of ways. In what has become a well quoted passage, he suggests: 'Given that women still have to await their liberation from the family, it remains the case in the capitalist societies that female workers are largely peripheral to the class system; or expressed differently, women are in a sense the "underclass" of the white-collar sector' (1973, p. 288).

Goldthorpe (1983), in defence of Giddens, has commented on this point, and suggested that Giddens's statement derives directly from a premis which feminists would not wish to deny, even though they end up being critical of Giddens. There may well have been some criticism of Giddens by feminists which was on misplaced grounds, but there is a point which remains undefended in Giddens's writing. It concerns the inconsistency of maintaining, as he does here, that women are peripheral, and suggesting, in other discussions in the same work, that women are part of a central and new concept introduced to help reconceptualise Marxian analysis—the buffer zone between the old bourgeoisie and proletariat classes. Women are brought into Giddens's discussion to argue against the idea that a progressive embourgeoisment of the working class has been taking place, but they are not integrated more positively into the analysis, and inconsistencies about women's positions thus arise.

Giddens's point that women's dependence on men in families makes them peripheral is a direct example of Allen's (1982) criticism that certain assumptions preclude further examination. We do not know the extent to which women are dependent upon their husbands, especially since the majority of women now go out to work and most of them work for 60 per cent or more of their potential working lives.[12] Giddens may be accurately portraying women's employment as often semi-skilled with little training, few prospects, part-time and low-paid. But calling this marginal or secondary work misses the point, as West (1978) notes; irregular labour can be vital rather than marginal to the whole economic system.

Giddens has moved on since his early book on class analysis (1973), although none of his later work has resolved the problems over the analysis of women's roles. In a recent book edited by Giddens and MacKenzie (1982) an article by MacKenzie, already mentioned, looks hopefully to the labour-market analysis of American radical economists for a future integration of a dynamic theory which incorporates human action along with structural analysis and women's roles. As part of his review of the more contemporary treatments of class boundaries MacKenzie (1982, p. 285) says in a footnote: 'A complete theoretical approach to the siting of class boundaries would clearly have to include reference to the media, to the state . . . to patterns of social, ethnic and gender inequality, the structure of the family . . . to name but a few . . . This is a daunting task'. Whilst Giddens does not endorse this view, it is not unreasonable in a jointly edited collection by these two authors to expect a measure of agreement on this issue. If this is the case, Giddens too recognises the lack of development in this field, which presumably will continue until the nettle is grasped.

Goldthorpe and Others

Goldthorpe has contributed to class analysis in Britain through the empirical examination of social mobility. Goldthorpe (1980) traced the largely European tradition of linking class analysis and social mobility. He illustrated that social mobility has been considered as a negative force, precluding the formation of classes and as potentially destabilising and therefore undesirable. Goldthorpe sees social mobility within a conflict model of society as desirable but possibly destabilising. He treats the relationship of social mobility to class formation as an empirical issue. Goldthorpe *et al.* have described the class structure of Britain in the 1970s and 1980s on the basis of detailed empirical analyses of the intergenerational and intragenerational social mobility of British men. They have thus been involved in a description of class boundaries but in the process have modified some of the alternative theoretical concepts.[13]

Goldthorpe's class analysis has been called structuralist in that it has sought to describe a structure of social classes. Whilst this class analysis draws on Marx and Weber, the concept of social classes is defined in terms of market positions and thus derives from Weber. Goldthorpe shares a concept of class with other Weberian writers like Parkin, and they both see the class system as 'a set of institutional arrangements which guarantee a fairly high degree of social continuity in the reward position of family units through generations' (Parkin, 1971, p. 14). Both writers also see the family as the appropriate social unit of the class system, and the occupational system as the backbone of the class structure. Since the family is adopted as the unit of class analysis, women's class position is indicated by their husband's position. The effective exclusion of women from class analysis which this entails has been justified on grounds of expediency,[14] but more recently has been made a virtue by Goldthorpe (1983). Many of the US criticisms of stratification theory thus apply to Goldthorpe and Parkin.

Goldthorpe has more recently engaged in a debate with feminist critics of traditional class analysis, an outline of which will be given below.

There is unfortunately no space to consider the other class analyses; for example, by Parkin (1979) or Stewart, Prandy and Blackburn (1980). These writers advocate different ways of identifying and describing class boundaries, but they are no better at offering an integral treatment of the sexual division of labour, even if they are sympathetic to such an objective.

ASSESSMENT

As described earlier, there have been two sets of criticisms, mainly from feminists, of traditional class analyses: the criticisms of the US stratification studies and the additional set of criticisms from British feminists of the European tradition. Both sets of criticisms have been applied to British class analyses, but as we have seen the stratification criticisms do not clearly apply to the Marxist tradition of class analysis. Whilst most of the contemporary class analysts discussed under the European tradition heading have not offered a satisfactory analysis as far as women's roles are concerned, most of the writers now seem agreed that a better analysis is required; in particular, one which integrates labour-market inequalities and sexual inequalities within marital relationships.

A number of developments have occurred in the light of the criticisms of traditional class analyses. One development has been an adoption of the individual as the class unit, as we saw in Wright's (1982) study. As we saw, women can then be incorporated into class analysis according to their occupation when they are employed, but they are ignored if they are not employed. The use of the individual as a unit of class analysis is at best a partial solution to the objective of integrating sexual inequalities into class analysis. Other studies have tried to repeat empirical studies which have been carried out in the past for men, but using samples of women. Some effort has been expended on providing occupational and class classifications which are more appropriate to women's occupations.[15] These studies do not offer any new concepts of analysis but do offer important empirical results about women's social and occupational mobility.[16]

A development which has involved a greater change in class analysis has come from suggesting that the family be kept as the unit of class analysis but that the categories used to describe the class structure change to incorporate both men's and women's occupations. The list of categories for these analyses allow men and women to be in the same occupational category or to be in different categories, in which case they are called 'cross-class families'. Britten and Heath (1983) have provided the most extensive description of a class structure using both men's and women's occupations and allowing cross-class categories. They allow men and women to be unemployed in their classification. Their empirical analysis also demonstrates that there are correlations between their categories and the voting behaviour of their samples. They suggest that these correlations are evidence that their categories are identifying genuine social groups out of their samples.

Goldthorpe (1983) has presented an empirical analysis to offer a defence of the traditional class analysis. In the light of the feminist criticism, he has made a stronger statement than those contained in his previous writing. He has claimed that the practice of taking the family as a unit of class analysis, using the head of household's (usually male) occupation to indicate the class position and assuming that a wife's class status is the same as that of her husband, best fits the empirical facts of family structure in Britain (or the USA). He draws these conclusions from an analysis of the wives of the men in the Oxford Mobility Study; in particular, he examined the wives' employment histories alongside the social mobility experiences of their husbands. Goldthorpe suspects that he would be prepared to alter his view if the facts were different.[17] Goldthorpe makes clear in his discussions that the debate does not rest upon the issue of whether women are dependent upon men in marriage; on this both sides agree.

On the basis of his empirical work, supplemented by other women's work-history data, he concluded that women's labour-market attachment is still too intermittent to entitle them to a class classification in their own right; women's occupational mobility is such that they cannot be regarded as holding a class position in terms of the continuity required for class formation and classification. Goldthorpe also suggested that when women appear to have higher class classifications than their husbands, in fact it is the fault of the classification system which ranks menial sales work higher than skilled manual work as if sales work is non-manual, when sales work is truly semi-skilled manual work. He suggests that cross-class families are thus rather rare. Insofar as the criticisms of traditional class analysis were made on empirical grounds, Goldthorpe's empirical defence of class analysis is a powerful reply, and he has drawn upon a problem in the usual class classifications which is well recognised. However, the non-empirical criticisms of traditional class analysis remain unanswered.

There have been several replies to Goldthorpe's defence. Stanworth (1984) challenges Goldthorpe's empirical work and the conclusion he draws from it. Stanworth points out that Goldthorpe does not provide any evidence that a wife's employment is conditioned by her husband's employment. She also demonstrates that if one reclassifies all the wives' low-level non-manual occupations as manual and recalculates the husbands' and wives' class comparisons on this basis, then the conclusion is still that a large proportion of cross-class families exist. Britten and Heath (1984) and Goldthorpe (1984) have continued to debate these points and it is clear that they agree on many points. There are still unresolved differences between them which appear to be ones of defining the nature of class analysis. For Goldthorpe class analysis is about identifying stable collectivities which, he suggests, will not necessarily coincide with either socio-cultural differentiation or with socio-political mobilisation and conflict. In this case the dispute must be about the criteria for identifying both a collectivity, and stability. None of the parties consider the parallel problems for men's class identification of men's mass unemployment nowadays.

Walby (1984) has argued that all of these criticisms do not go far enough in their attack on the traditions of class analysis. She argues that it is of limited use attempting to add on women to the central questions of traditional class analysis, which are concerned with why the working-class are not revolutionary, why they do not support the political party claiming to represent them and whether the working-class have experienced embourgeoisment. The central focus of class analysis should be on inequalities between women and men, Walby argues. Leonard and Delphy (1984) would agree, and they criticise the tradition for failing to recognise the hierarchical relations within the family.

Walby argues that the distinctive social relations under which work within the home is performed by women are class relations. Housewives and husbands are classes, therefore, in a patriarchal mode of production, the husband being the exploiter and the wife having no possession of her product. She argues that both full and part-time housewives are a class exploited by their husbands, but it is not all women who are a class, since not all women are housewives. Women and men, in Weberian terminology, are described as status groups. Single women in paid employment should therefore take their class position from their own occupation. Married women have a dual class position; one from their paid work and one as a housewife in relation to their husband. Married men similarly are argued to have a dual class position. Leonard and Delphy (1984) begin to describe the transmission process in class analysis and therefore women's recruitment to their class positions through inheritance and the family structure. Women's position within the family is partly 'created by the differential passing on of family property, which produces a population of successors and non-successors, some of the latter being then transformed into non-holders within each class'.[18]

The issues are far from being resolved to everyone's satisfaction, but a reconceptualisation is definitely underway. Some consensus might begin to emerge if we start to ask, what is the social phenomenon we are seeking to understand? Those who are interested in class boundaries need to ask what it is that such an identification would help us understand. More specifically, what use will a single dimensional class classification have which treats women's class as mediated by their husband? It enables a head-count analysis to be made, but what is left out of the category is as important as what is included, so a single class classification tells us little about social relationships. There appear to be a large set of class-related questions which now necessitate women's earnings and occupations being considered.[19] For example, how far has increased home ownership relied upon women's earnings? To what extent are savings, provision for old age, or children's education dependent upon women's earnings? To what extent is the potential for class action influenced by women's and men's employment histories? How are women as well as men recruited to their class positions in families? These are not the traditional questions about class which have been asked. As feminist critics have pointed out, the traditional class analyses have had the effect of precluding analyses of possibly more important but certainly interesting and relevant questions about class. In particular, intra-family class relations have been ignored. The implication of these theoretical criticisms is that a new focus to class analysis be adopted where these questions can be taken up. Such a focus is more in keeping with the spirit of the concern with social change which the founding fathers of class analysis originally displayed. These questions are a distinct shift away from being concerned with identifying class boundaries. The beginnings of this reconceptualisation are evident and a growing number of empirical studies are appearing which allow for women to take an active role in the process of class formation and allow for both women's influence on men as well as men's influence on women to be recognised.[20]

NOTES

1. For example, Haug (1973) in the USA and Middleton (1974), West (1978), Garnsey (1978), Delphy (1981) and Allen (1982) in Britain.
2. This is not a hard-and-fast division, and some authors fall between the

two types of class analysis. There are also a number of writers who would locate themselves in the European tradition by being interested in the cause of social change, but their work is of a more static nature and is concerned with drawing boundaries around groups in order to identify them as a class because of their position in a structure or hierarchy of inequality; for example, Westergaard and Resler (1982), Wright (1978), Carchedi (1977).

3. There are also other groups which class analysis has failed to incorporate or explain their changing position; for example, ethnic groups, peasants.

4. For example, Kalleberg and Griffin (1980), Baron (1980), Cullen and Novick (1979), McRoberts and Selbee (1981), Hope (1982).

5. For example, Giddens (1973).

6. Studies of wealth inequality and the intergenerational transfer of wealth by economists have all been content to focus upon men or unisex individuals; for example, Harbury and McMahon (1973) and Atkinson (1977).

7. MacKenzie (1982) points out that Poulantzas has strayed away from offering a theory of social change and his analysis ends up being timeless, unchanging and ahistorical. It is not surprising, therefore, that Poulantzas fails to explain changing labour-market division. Finally, as Wright (1982) has pointed out, even even Poulantzas's description of the static class-structure offends common sense by implying that 70 per cent of the US society is in the new petty bourgeoise class and only 20 per cent in the working class.

8. The empirical work is described in Wright (1982). Some of Wright's categories offend at least MacKenzie's (1982) notion of common sense by combining skilled craftsmen and university professors in the same category. Wright's new concept, the 'contradictory class location' is criticised by Holmwood and Stewart (1983) because it fails to explain anything; instead, it shifts the need for an explanation to the new label. Wright also introduced the possibility of double contradictions, which one might expect to cancel each other out.

9. MacKenzie's (1982) assessment of Carchedi is the same as his assessment of Poulantzas and Wright; that they all focus in a static manner on describing class boundaries.

10. Giddens (1973) made the point about the loss of Marx's method by Marxists.

11. The technique of changing a category into a variable in order to avoid overly static analyses was first suggested by Lenski (1966).

12. *See* Martin and Roberts (1984a, p. 202–3).

13. For example, Parkin's (1979) elaboration of the concept of 'social closure' is modified by Goldthorpe *et al.*, as is Giddens's concept of a 'buffer zone'. Goldthorpe's analysis suggests that these concepts did not have a clear empirical base.

14. The Appendix to Goldthorpe (1980) suggests that the women were excluded because resources were unavailable to interview a sizeable sample of both men and women. Parkin's (1971) early work took a

strong position that the majority of women's class positions are given by their husband's occupation rather than their own, and that this procedure was meant to overlap with women's self-perception and identity. Parkin's (1979) later work appears to exhibit a change of mind.

15. *See* Murgatroyd (1982).
16. *See* for example, Rosenfeld (1978) in the USA and Heath (1981, 1981a) and Payne *et al.* (1983) for the study of women's social mobility in Britain.
17. Goldthorpe (1983, p. 470) says he would alter his view if 'the extent and nature of female participation in the labour market is now such that in the more "normal" conjugal family it is increasingly hard to say whether husband or wife could better be regarded as the family "head" or that in many cases there are in effect two "heads" with, quite often, different class positions'.
18. Leonard and Delphy (1984, p. 23).
19. Stanworth (1984) and Walby (1984) make a list of these questions.
20. For example, Hunt (1980), Haller (1981), Pahl (1983), Siltanen and Stanworth (1984) amongst many others.

7 Why the Changes?

That neoclassical forces alone do not determine job design is a view supported by Piore (1968), who found that while the procedures used to select productive techniques within the manufacturing plant were consistent with the assumption of cost minimization, the relative scarcities of different types of labor in the external market did not have much influence on job design. Thus, plants 'mould men to jobs, not jobs to men'.

(Kalleberg and Sorensen, 1979, p. 372)

Much of the discussion of contemporary socio-economic change takes place within a framework which explores and debates the relationship of technology to jobs—men's jobs. The gender of the population which is to fill the jobs has not been thought to be very relevant to a consideration of the motivation for change. Yet one of the major structural changes of industrial economies has been the shift away from manufacturing jobs towards service-sector jobs, and it is women who have filled these positions.

We might expect that theories of socio-economic change would be the strong-point of contemporary social science, but this is not the case. In fact, the situation is quite the reverse and the analysis of social change is a weak link in both sociology and economics. Given that the founding fathers of sociology were almost wholly preoccupied with devising theories of social change which explained the emergence of industrial society, it is perhaps surprising that sociologists do not excel in this area today. It is easier to see why economists are not adept at offering theories of social change when so much of the discipline is concerned with the analysis of comparative static models. It is lamentable, nevertheless.

The magnitude of the changes in women's employment

has been forcing social change back into these two disciplines, and although the analyses which are resulting are far from being comprehensive, there is a promise of better things to come as the tools for the analysis of socio-economic change get sharpened.

There are many dimensions to socio-economic change. The focus here is on labour-market changes and, in particular, change in the industrial and occupational structures and changes in women's participation rates over the cycle of economic activity and as an upward trend since the end of the Second World War. Some theories of social change were implicit in the discussions of earlier chapters; for example, the discussion of class analyses or segmented labour-market theories which are part of a theory which includes technological changes. However, the social change aspects of these theories will not be discussed again in this chapter. Neither will the neoclassical theories of technological change be outlined here, even though the quotation which opens this chapter refers to them. Not only are such theories underdeveloped, but they are highly technical and do not consider their labour-market implications to any great extent. Suffice it to say that the roots of the neoclassical explanations lie in the relative price effects, but to date there have been few efforts to elaborate how such effects might explain women's increased participation. Factors which help to explain the rise in women's labour force participation include their increased potential earnings, partly from having more education, and the slower rate of growth in real earnings of men between the ages of 25 and 35, the ages when wives are increasing their participation. Some work has been done by economists on the demographic causes of women's increased participation by, for example, Joshi and Owen (1981), but relatively little attention has been given to what is, after all, a major change. An American analysis by Shapiro and Shaw (1983) found that this collection of changes explained at best only half the increase in women's participation which occurred in the 1970s.

In the rest of this chapter, the industrial, occupational and participation-rate aspects of labour-market changes are examined separately to see how the theories of each type of change have developed through considering women's employment more fully. What is needed at the end of the day are theories which integrate these various components and offer multidimensional explanations of the gendered labour market changes. Whilst such an objective is far from being achieved, it is significant that women's employment has been the motivation to improve and expand the analysis of socio-economic change. We can look forward to the results.

THE INDUSTRIAL STRUCTURE

The changing industrial structure of Western industrialised economies has been receiving comment from sociologists and economists, and in Britain it is a topic of major concern which is seen as a potential threat to the whole structure of the economy. The phenomenon which receives this treatment is the decline of manufacturing industries and the growth of service industries. American sociologists have discussed this phenomenon under the heading of 'the post-industrial society', and British economists have expressed their concern about this process of 'deindustrialisation' in Britain. Most commentators have noted that the rise in women's labour force participation is in some way linked to these change, but few, if any, have done a thorough analysis of such links. These two aspects of the macro changes will be reviewed below.[1]

The question of what role women's employment is playing in industrial changes is ripe for a thorough analysis, although such a task cannot be undertaken here. In the few cases to date where women are at least given some consideration, in discussions of industrial change, arguments and debates have been clarified and sometimes resolved by the consideration of gender differences in the workforce and the sexual division of labour. A more extended analysis of women's role might provide the elusive breakthrough in the understanding of these issues which has been sought over several decades. Such an analysis would need to consider the vast growth in women's part-time employment, much of which is in the public sector. Given the size and nature of the changes taking place in the sexual division of labour in the industrial structure, it is surprising in some ways that this issue has remained unconsidered. A summary of the developments is provided below before the theories about social change are considered.

The industrial structure of employment has been changing gradually in Britain and the USA for a century or more. If we compare the distribution of jobs by industry over large periods of time, the changes are enormous. Obviously, over shorter time periods the changes appear less noteworthy. The trend is unmistakable over a short period, nevertheless.

Over a twenty-year period, 1940 to 1960, UK manufacturing employment has declined from approximately 39 to 35 per cent and services (including government) increased from approximately 38 to 45 per cent. In the USA over a similar period, manufacturing employment declined from approximately 30 to 25 per cent and services (including government) grew from 41 to 58 per cent. In the 1980s the proportion of employment in services is approaching 70 per cent. It is important to note, however, as Thatcher (1978) points out for the UK, these figures do not necessarily mean that manufacturing employment has declined in absolute terms. In Britain the numbers employed in manufacturing were rising until 1966, since when they have started to fall.

Women's employment has played a large part in these changes. In the USA in 1960, 46 per cent of workers in service industries were women and 73 per cent of all working women worked in services. In Britain between 1841 and 1971 women increased their share of employment in nearly every industry, with the exception of textiles and miscellaneous services. These two cases of decline between 1841 and 1971 result from the decline of the textile industry and the demise of domestic service as an occupation. Since 1961 women's proportion of miscellaneous services' employment has begun to rise again. The growth in women's employment since the Second World War has affected all industries, but services and distribution have seen by far the greatest changes. In Britain over the period from 1966 to 1976 there was a net decline in the employment of manufacturing industries (plus primary industries); of this net decline, 73 per cent were men and 27 per cent were women. Over the same period the net increase in private sector services resulted from a +125 per cent change for women and a −44 per cent change in men's services employment. Of the total growth of the public sector for the same period, three out of every four of the extra jobs went to women.[2]

It is worth noting that in Britain much of the increase in women's services and public sector employment has been in part-time work but this aspect of women's work has been given relatively little recognition in the analyses of socio-economic change. In 1976, 40 per cent of workers in the whole economy were working in part-time jobs; the proportion in the United States was much lower. In Britain between 1971 and 1981 approximately 60 per cent of the employment increases in both miscellaneous services and distribution over the decade were in women's part-time jobs.[3] These figures amount to very large structural changes in the nature of British employment which theoretical analyses of the British economy have yet to face up to. We can go on to examine some of the theoretical work now to see how far it has integrated the changes in employment resulting from women's work into analyses.

Explanations

There are a number of answers to the question of why employment in services has increased. Daniel Bell's (1974) answer is that services increased because as people get richer they come to demand more (personal) services, wanting an improvement in their life-style rather than simply wanting more goods. This explanation for the increase in services was part of a description identifying the characteristics of 'the post-industrial society', a term popularised by Bell. Changes in the industrial structure are one part of a larger set of interrelated socio-economic changes which Bell describes; some of the others being changes in the occupational structure and in the nature of knowledge. Bell was implicitly offering a theory about individuals' consumption preferences to partly explain the changes in the industrial structure, building upon some earlier work by Clark (1940), and he offered some social forecasts on the basis of his identification of the characteristics of social and economic change.

Bell explicitly considers women's roles in these changes, but on one page only of his 489-page book. The extent of his treatment of women is hardly consistent with the importance he appears to attach them in statements like 'the fact is that a service economy is very largely a female-centred economy' (p. 146). Bell's work has a major weakness in this respect and his analysis of socio-economic change suffers as a consequence, although it is not a point which his many critics have chosen to emphasise.[4]

Hirsch (1977) suggested that the expansion of services has reflected new needs. The services are directly associated with the changes in the economic structure which have involved growth, and he generated a set of new concepts to describe the causes of change. Hirsch characterised the industrial growth of the British economy as experiencing an increase in demand for the 'positional goods'—that is, status or prestige. He suggested that since positional goods are finite they are subject to social scarcity; there has to be a distribution of prestige for people to want more of it so that the increase in demand will generate fierce competition to rise or stay at the top. This competition in the positional market increases the relative value of individual's time and effort and makes them demand services to replace their own effort, a change which will push up the price of services and lead to an increasing proportion of family expenditure being spent on them. There is no discussion by Hirsch of women's role in this process.

Baran and Sweezy (1966) and Mandel (1975) are part of what Hirsch calls a 'neo-Marxist' explanation of the increase in services, as they suggest the economy has been expanding in services in order to utilise the economic surplus generated under the phase of monopoly or late capitalism. These writers suggest that the late stages of capitalism are characterised by a rising surplus instead of the older traditional view that a falling rate of profit would result. The surplus is the difference between total social output and the socially necessary costs of producing it. Some way would have to be generated within the system to absorb this additional surplus and Baran and Sweezy identify two absorption areas: first, the 'sales effort'—that is, all the trappings associated with modern consumer society, especially persuasive advertising—and second, the 'civilian government'. Services in this sense are 'unproductive' in this framework and are generated to absorb a surplus. No consideration is given to women's role or employment, even though they are clearly a large part of the overall 'sales effort'.

Galbraith (1973), whilst not working from within a neo-Marxist framework, also sees the increase in services being linked to the large-scale 'planning system' of the new industrial state. The planning system relies on services (advertising and government) and promotes their growth in its search for market stability and dominance. Galbraith recognises changes in household structure from time to time to suit the requirements of the economy. Galbraith also recognises that women are at the forefront of consumption decisions, and as such he goes furthest in this list of writers to incorporate women into his analysis. He stops short, however, as do the other writers, of providing an explanation for the growth in women's employment in the service industries. Rowthorn (1980), in a criticism of Mandel, suggests that the rise in employment in services (in Britain) since the Second World War is because productivity in this sector has grown only very slowly at a time when demand was increasing. There has been what Rowthorn calls a 'technological lag' in services, which has made services more expensive in comparison with industrial products, and this has caused the total expenditure and share of national expenditure going to services to increase. In that service employment can only continue to increase if they start to draw labour away from the industrial sector, they are a potential drain on production and an obstacle to sustained accumulation. Rowthorn's line of analysis is one in which women's employment could be drawn in and integrated into the explanation, but he does not provide such an analysis. As a result of his neglect of women, he suggests that a process of crowding-out is beginning to occur where services are taking away necessary labour from the industrial sector. This conclusion is less appealing when one sees that it is women who work in the service sector, and had he considered the gendered nature of the employed population he might well have offered a different explanation.

British economists have offered a range of explanations for Britain's declining industrial base. Their focus has been on the decline in manufacturing and on the problems this might be creating for the British.[5] There has been some confusion in the debate because some writers have failed to consistently define 'deindustrialisation', which can be either an employment or an output phenomenon. One of the early statements came from Bacon and Eltis (1976) and their argument, in its crude form, suggested that the manufacturing industry in Britain was being forced to contract because resources were being drawn into government spending which was rising at a rapid rate; the argument is one which suggests that crowding-out is the problem. It is difficult to imagine this argument ever being offered if a thorough analysis of the gender-based employment statistics had been thoroughly explored beforehand. Indeed, the main argument offered to counter this view has pointed out that the growth in public sector employment has been largely women's employment and therefore not a drain on private sector men's employment. There is a more sophisticated version of Bacon and Eltis's thesis which is that the crowding-out is a financial effect; this has greater credibility. The crowding-out explanations are not acceptable to the other major explanation of deindustrialisation in Britain, which comes from Cambridge and is often attributed more specifically to Singh (1977).

The Cambridge view rejects the idea that deindustrialisation is a trend in domestic manufacturing (either of employment or output), which is not to dispute that such changes in the industrial structure have been occurring. The problem about Britain's position, according to this view, is that there has been a failure to achieve a sufficient surplus of exports over imports of manufactured goods to prevent the balance of payments from being consistently in deficit. Thus the problem is that the manufacturing sector in Britain is inefficient and uncompetitive in world markets, and British markets have preferred foreign imported goods. A vicious circle of declining market share for British manufacturing can then set in, where profits and investment decline, as does competitive power and employment. This decline, perhaps, would not matter if there was a counter-balancing improvement in other sectors like services, which are saleable abroad, but this has not occurred. North Sea oil, however, has provided a temporary stop-gap for this external balance problem. The question arises, then, of why British manufacturing is inefficient and why services have expanded outside the public sector. Various suggestions have been made to answer the question of British manufacturing's inefficiency, although no consensus exists, and there are arguments from the experience of other countries to discredit any reliance on the explanatory value of most of the options.

In moving away from a focus on employment changes in Britain, the Cambridge school has also moved further away from a consideration of the sexual division of labour and the gender-based employment trends which are integrally bound up with Britain's prospects, and whilst these arguments contain much that is undoubtedly accurate about the British economy, the failure to tackle the women's issues suggests that at best the analysis is partial, and at worst may be a distortion. The debates that still go on amongst British economists about the causes of deindustrialisation cannot be described in more detail here. This review wishes to emphasise the omission of women from all of these accounts. On the basis of past experience, this is a dangerous omission and could mean that many more of the arguments turn out ultimately to have been red herrings.

Finally, Gershuny (1978), partly as a critique of Daniel Bell's thesis, argues that the increase in services has been misunderstood, since many of the so-called services are in fact highly related to production and are not increases in personal services as is often implied. This result was apparent from his disaggregate analysis of the industry by occupation distribution. Gershuny criticised Bell's theory about the change in consumption patterns since Gershuny's analysis suggested that people have been moving away from demanding more personal services and towards a self-service economy based on durable do-it-yourself goods. Gershuny is not entirely accurate in representing Bell's views, although his results certainly point to a picture of micro trends in consumption different from that of Bell.[6] On the basis of a regrouping of the employment figures, by dividing services up into those related to production and traditional (personal) services, Gershuny argues that production-related employment has not fallen significantly, although the organisational structure of employment has certainly changed, with more people becoming self-employed, consultants or technicians for production. Whilst the analysis is of the UK, it is quite likely that the same trend has been occurring in the USA.

To a large extent, Gershuny's innovative analysis has cast the issue of manufacturing decline in a new light. The changes Gershuny has identified are no less important, but they are of a different kind from those discussed and debated by the other authors, and they require different explanations. At the same time, Gershuny's account of industrial change in Britain could quite happily co-exist alongside some of the other analyses we have discussed, like those of Rowthorn or the Cambridge views of deindustrialisation, especially since the problem of Britain's external balance, or imbalance, still remain. It is to be regretted that a thorough analysis of women's employment and consumption roles was not a part of Gershuny's or, indeed, any other analysis.

Assessment

There would appear to be a plethora of explanations of the changes in industrial structure which are visible in the British and US economies, but the position is not quite as chaotic as it might at first appear. Each view has its critics and a comparison between some of these authors can be found in Ellis and Kumar (1983). There is a large measure of uniformity in the trends in industrial structure of all major industrialised countries. Seen in this light, the debate over Britain's deindustrialisation is a mistakenly parochial one, as

Cairncross (1978) in fact implied. Britain may have some unique problems in this context, however; most notably the international balance. Britain is also unique in the Western industrialised world in having such a large growth in women's part-time employment. Such a growth of part-time work is given relatively little, if any, emphasis in the above analyses. It is important to note that the vast increase in part-time work has tended to give an inflated impression of the increase in women's opportunities in Britain because a part-time job is not equivalent to a full-time job. Beechey and Perkin's (1983) analysis of part-time jobs pointed out that over the period 1971 to 1976, counting two part-time jobs as equivalent to one full-time job, the increase in part-time jobs was not significant enough to outweigh the full-time job loss. Whilst more women were working over this period, the working population was not working more. Beechey and Perkins therefore dismiss the idea that part-time work increased because of the shortage of full-time labour.

In seeking a better analysis of industrial change, we can note some of the contributions of the writers reviewed above. Rowthorn pointed out that the productivity of personal services has been low and their relative price has risen. Gershuny's contribution illustrates that people have been substituting goods for services. Galbraith made the point, without developing it to any great extent, that women's role in consumption is important. To these valid points about the industrial structure we need to add a thorough analysis of women's role, in order to understand more precisely the nature of the changes. Several feminist contributions have begun to be offered along these lines, although there is still some way to go in integrating these various contributions.

Women have been drawn into the labour market at the same time that manufacturing production has wanted to sell more domestic durable goods like washing machines. Women's employment provides a rationale for the purchase of such goods and also gives women more control over the household resources with which to purchase these domestic goods. If working women were found to spend their income on such consumer durables, this argument would gain some support. Pahl (1983) has recently opened up the issue of the allocation of money within the household, but the detail of our present knowledge is insufficient to know what women's income is spent on. Beechey (1977) argued that capital could be expected to employ more married women because then the family would be entirely dependent on wages and more dependent, therefore, on capitalistically produced commodities. This would make women preferable to migrant workers, even, because the latter would still have one foot in a subsistence economy when they were working and therefore be less dependent on the employment.

A question which is raised in the process of seeking an explanation of women's increased employment is, why did women not work before? A variety of suggestions have been offered, although as yet there appears to be little consensus. Power (1983) suggests that a mixture of ideological, economic and legislative reasons kept women at home and that the switch from the family's production function to a maintenance function has released women into the labour force. Anthias (1980) disagrees with that analysis on the grounds that the nature of domestic work is such that it is not and never has been clearly work for production. Writers seem agreed, however, that there is a link between the growth of domestic appliances, demographic factors which mean that women have finished childbirth and childrearing earlier, and women's employment outside the home.

When women have been working in manufacturing industries at cheaper wage rates, they have been supporting, in Britain, an ailing manufacturing sector, allowing it to limp along and be slightly more on a par with the cheap labour production of developing countries in textiles and clothing. Given that productivity gains have been restricted in service industries, then women are also the obvious choice of workers to try and keep down costs in these industries. Mallier and Rosser (1980) have suggested that the growth in part-time work is largely a demand-induced phenomenon. There can be a variety of reasons for employer's preferring part-time work, as Rubery and Tarling (1983) note. Where part-time work is part of the structure of the job because of peak periods or anti-social hours, women are the 'ideal' solution since they are pleased to work part-time. Often the part-time hours coincide with children being at school, or husbands being at home to look after children. The growth in part-time jobs in the public sector has strong links with the lack of formal or statutory child-care or its high cost relative to women's wages. Part-time work can also be a way of employer's coping with vulnerability to business-cycle fluctuations and keeping labour costs to a minimum. Beechey and Perkin's (1983) study of part-time work in Coventry suggested that flexibility was the keynote to understanding employers' demands for part-time workers, in manufacturing, services and the public sector. They also found that employers had ways of meeting their requirements which involved gender distinctions. Women's preference for part-time work, given their child-care responsibilities, again make them a highly suitable workforce.

The recent Women and Employment Survey in Britain supported these conclusions by demonstrating that there was a large peak in women's part-time hours at sixteen hours per week, after which employers become liable for more overhead costs associated with women's work. Also, the vast majority of child-care arrangements made by working women involved support from the husband, older children and other relatives. A comparative study of Britain and the USA revealed that the two countries were quite different in this respect; in the USA far more women work full-time and pay for child-care.[7]

Women's preference for part-time work in Britain could easily change in an environment where the child-care facilities were better and more acceptable than in the 1970s. The greater proportion of full-time working women in the USA is partly attributable to differences in child-care, although women's attitudes can also be seen to vary. One of the key points in the women's contribution to the changes in industrial structure is over childbirth. Women in Britain and the USA can be seen to move from full-time manufacturing jobs to part-time services jobs over their first break from work for childbirth. There is a sense, therefore, in which individual women experience deindustrialisation through their participation in childbirth, and the changes in industrial structure are in part relying on women's necessary break from work, however short, which childbirth has involved.[8]

Employers use of the part-time option in Britain might change if women's preferences were for full-time work, but the same advantage of employing women would apply if their labour remained cheaper. One might predict, on these grounds, that as women work more and longer and demand and obtain equal pay, as they are doing, and obtain better child-care, the nature of the industrial distribution of men's and women's work would change alongside these changes. Women have played an active role in bringing about these changes by desiring to purchase new consumer goods, by desiring to have greater control over family resources and their own independent means, by preferring in Britain part-time jobs in order to be able to satisfy their list of desires, described above, alongside shouldering domestic responsibilities. In one sense women have succumbed to the persuasive advertising encouraging them to want new consumer durables, which have become the backbone to modern industrial production. These products are not so obviously labour-saving in a direct way (although it is claimed that they are), but women have nevertheless made significant increases in their standard of living, and they have worked hard, doubly hard, to achieve these increases. It is difficult to assess the size of women's influence on the moves towards a self-service economy, without a thorough examination of this issue, but it is undoubtedly great, and possibly the main impetus moving the economy in this direction. At any rate, women's role in the changing industrial structure cannot be over-emphasised just now, and the analysis which is their due may throw up other reconceptualisations in our understanding of socio-economic changes in industrial societies.

DESKILLING

The *Morning Post* of 30.1.1889 reported that about £10,000 p.a. could be saved in and around Whitehall by the employment of women and typewriters, and in the Civil Service, Probate Office, the work of copying titles which formerly cost £3,000 p.a. by male clerks, could now be done by three women on typewriters at a cost of £300 p.a.

(Silverstone, quoted in Barker and Downing, 1980, p. 70)

We have here a description of some of the elements and some of the ambiguities of the process of deskilling. The notion of deskilling has become part of a neo-Marxist account of socio-economic change, authors claiming that the notion has its origins in Marx's work. There are some undoubted changes, however, in the more recent usage and application of deskilling. Braverman (1974) has become the most famous populariser of this notion. Deskilling involves the idea that jobs have been progressively broken down into simpler and therefore less skilled tasks. Labour is thereby degraded, often as part of the process of technological and organisational change and accompanied by lower relative wages. The ambiguities occur because technological change will mean that new skills are created at the same time that older ones are destroyed. What is missing from the initial quotation is a description of the further breaking down of clerical (or other) skills into simpler components like copy typists, filing, secretarial etc.

Deskilling has been described as occurring throughout industries and underlies the structural occupational changes which have been occurring. Braverman's analysis went as far as drawing the sexual division of labour into this process, and he had specific analyses of women's roles in newer clerical and service occupations; but his analysis has not gone unquestioned. Feminists amongst others have pointed out some of the problems of deskilling if it is offered as an explanation of occupational segregation or of the structural occupational changes which have been occurring in Western industrialised economies. Feminists have called for a more fundamental examination of the notion of 'skill', therefore, and this reconceptualisation is thought to be necessary if we are to understand how some occupations came to be known as women's occupations or work and others as men's occupations.

Marx suggested that modern industry tends 'to equalise and reduce to one and the same level every kind of work that has to be done by the minders of machines'.[9] Nevertheless, this process does not emerge unopposed, and since workers are likely to resist these changes, preferring to hang on to traditional skill definitions, conflict and competition are generated between workers and employers and amongst workers. Marx saw, therefore, that the process of deskilling would be constrained and limited. Marx also documented the way that women and children had been used in order to break down the resistance to deskilling. Beechey (1977) adds the example of the use of women's labour in the First World War to illustrate this point. The introduction of women's labour into the munitions and engineering industries was strongly resisted by the engineers, who reached an agreement with the Government that women should be allowed to enter only unskilled or semi-skilled jobs, except if there was a shortage of men, whereupon they could fill skilled jobs. Part of the agreement was that the women would leave at the end of the war.[10]

Braverman (1974) offered his work as a historical description and analysis of the process of occupational change, mainly in the USA, and to provide an analysis of the labour process to fill a gap left by Marx. The process of the accumulation of capital which is the driving force of change in society effects the working population through two channels: first there is continuous change in the labour processes of each branch of industry—much of which is the degradation or deskilling of jobs. Even the new 'working-class' occupations (e.g. clerical, service and retail occupations) have become standardised, simplified and therefore degraded, according to Braverman. Crompton and Reid (1982) provide empirical evidence of this process occurring in clerical work in Britain. Second, there is the steady redistribution of labour amongst occupations and industries which consists of an overall decline of manual work in the manufacturing industries, a concomitant growth in service occupations and a decrease in the proportion of self-employed (or an increase in the proportion of workers who rely on selling their labour power). Women are part of this process in a way which has been recognised when they became a large proportion of the new service-sector employees. Braverman's account of the changing division of labour and deskilling is integrated with his analysis, in the same volume, of the growth of a universal market as capital takes over areas of consumption previously located within the family. There is also a parallel analysis of the class structure, which we have already mentioned in Chapter 6. The wide-ranging nature of Braverman's work has earned him considerable acclaim,[11] and at the same time, perhaps for the same reason, he has drawn considerable fire. We will also consider the criticisms of the notion of 'deskilling' here,[12] recognising that there is clear empirical support for the descriptive elements of deskilling to which Braverman draws attention.[13]

One criticism of Braverman which has been made by a number of commentators is that he has tended to portray the capitalist class as omniscient and the workers as malleable.[14] Critics have argued that he offers an overly deterministic account of the process of occupational change which tends to ignore organised resistance by workers. Other writers want to recognise that the interests of capital and therefore deskilling can be limited by trade union and other forms of shop floor organisation. In addition, organised labour can fail to represent the interests of sectors of its membership. This last general point has particular significance for women, who historically have often been unrepresented by male (craft-based) unions. Women can then be used as pawns in a struggle of male trade unions against employers such that women's deskilling can be the compromise reached with men keeping something of their former skilled status, at least in name.

Several case studies have illustrated this process more recently. Coyle's (1982) account of technological change in the clothing industry shows the way that organised male cutters managed to retain a label of skilled workers, along with the higher remuneration for skilled work, even though the skilled aspects of their jobs had been taken over by computerised cutting machines. Coyle's (1984) later work suggests this may not be the end of the story and men too may ultimately lose their status. In the same context, women sewers were probably doing far more skilled work, defined in a technical sense, and yet were classed as semi-skilled if not unskilled workers. Cavendish's (1982) account of women's work in a car components factory has made similar points about the labelling of jobs done by women. The jobs Cavendish did herself, and which she describes in her biographical account, involved considerable skill to achieve, certainly a great amount of manual dexterity, and yet they were labelled 'unskilled' or 'semi-skilled' jobs and given relatively low pay.

As feminist writers have begun to examine the notion of 'deskilling' they have found it to rely heavily on a particular notion of the nature of a 'skill' which almost by definition excludes women from being skilled workers, as outlined in Chapter 4. Beechey (1982) pointed out that the notion of 'skill' embodied in Braverman's analysis is that derived from a male artisan. As well as being centred on particular male skills, and excluding women, this is nowadays a somewhat idealised and romanticised notion about the nature of men's skilled work. Case studies like that of Coyle (1982) described above and Armstrong (1982) highlight the fluid nature of the definition of 'skill' and the way that it can be a socially constructed outcome of organised male trade unions' struggles with capital; calling a job 'skilled' may then bear little relationship to any technical aspects of the job in question. As outlined in Chapter 4, feminist writers, amongst others, have thus wanted to suggest that the notion of 'skill' is problematic. It cannot be assumed to have a clear-cut meaning.

Beechey (1982) has offered some further points of clarification about the use of the term skill. She points out that skill is used in Braverman, and others, in at least three ways: in a technical sense to refer to the conception and execution of a task, in reference to the control over the labour process, as in Coyle's (1982) example of cutters, or as applied to the conventional definitions of occupational status. We might add to this list that labour shortages of particular kinds have contributed to labelling a job as 'skilled'. The failure to clarify which of these aspects of skill is being referred to has meant that the notion of 'deskilling' is very ambiguous. It is crucial to make these distinctions if one is seeking to analyse women's work and understand its nature and generation. Cooking, for example, is not generally defined as 'skilled' when done by women in the home, whereas if done by a chef in a restaurant it will warrant the term 'skilled', even in cases where there are no differences in the nature of the technical competence, of the food produced or the scale of the cooking. The difference in this example is in the control over the process. The chef has argued for the title of skilled worker within a system of relationships within capitalist commodity production. It is also important to clarify what is meant by skill when one is seeking answers to questions about why particular groups have been included or excluded from occupations traditionally labelled as 'skilled'.

At the same time, it would be naïve to think that the usage of 'skill' never represents any genuine technical competence where men are concerned. Clearly this is not the case. It must be remembered that women have not pursued education, training and apprenticeships to the same extent as men, just as they have not successfully used the collective bargaining strategy to acquire 'skilled' labels. Neither have they been in a position to enforce a restricted supply of labour and gain the title of 'skill shortage' as a result. There is a tendency, however, to fail to recognise certain activities as skilled; for example, caring for people, childrearing, providing comfort and warmth, all of which are traditionally done by women (Finch and Groves, 1983). More often nowadays, women are paid to do these jobs, yet the skills do not gain recognition and they are mostly very poorly paid. When women take up the new skills which have resulted from technological change, as with the case of typewriters in the initial quotation (and word-processing today), there is a tendency for the jobs to be thought of as less skilled than the earlier form of technology if women fill the jobs. In the case of typewriter operators, one could argue a case that using a typewriter involves greater skill than that involved in the hand copying of the superseded male clerks. Without a clear conception of the possible meanings of skills and without clearly defined objective criteria for describing the technical competence involved, we will not be able to understand or even describe the process of occupational change which has been occurring. Nor will we be able to understand how occupational segregation and the definition of women's and men's work have come into being and are maintained or changed.

Uses of the term 'deskilling' by theorists of social change have only served to highlight the inadequacies of our understanding of occupational change and its relationship to the sexual division of labour. Previous conceptions of the term 'skill' and its assumed unproblematic nature have served to obscure our analysis of these processes. The term 'skill' is a highly complex concept and the construction of gender-based occupational labels is also complex and has varied origins. The recent questioning of the meaning of 'skill' and the new case studies of women's work which have illustrated its varied meanings, are part of a reconceptualisation of skill which is having wide-ranging implications. We may some-time in the future return to formulate a meaningful concept of 'deskilling', or maybe several aspects of the notion of 'deskilling', and use this work as part of a theory based upon crucial and relevant gender distinctions.

THE RESERVE ARMY OF LABOUR

The 'reserve army of labour' is a concept from Marxist theory which has been brought into analyses of socioeconomic change and the role of women in two ways; both were explicit in Marx's analysis. The 'reserve army' is used first to explain why married women have been increasingly drawn into the wage-labour force; there are those who argue that it is a helpful concept (e.g. Power, 1983; Beechey, 1978), and those who argue that it is not (e.g. Anthias, 1980). The second area in which the concept is used is in discussions of what happens to women's employment relative to other groups over the cycle of fluctuations we have come to expect in industrial economies. It is relevant, therefore, to include a discussion of the concept here, and we can see how traditional Marxist concepts have been receiving criticism and modification in the light of women's employment changes. Before going on to examine the two areas of application of a 'reserve army', a summary of Marx's description and use of the concept will be offered.

Commentators have noted that Marx did not define the concept of an 'industrial reserve army' very precisely, and this has allowed a number of interpretations to coexist. There is no doubt that Marx saw the reserve army as a product of the process of capital accumulation and that once formed, it was useful to that process. At a basic level, the reserve army constitutes 'every labourer . . . when he is only partially employed or wholly unemployed' (Marx, quoted in Anthias, 1980, p. 51). It is, therefore, a relative surplus working population.

When total capital is increasing, the demand for labour is expected to fall. Some workers will become redundant in the industry of their current employment, and workers will also be engaged at lower rates than previously. This 'freed' population is then available to be absorbed into new industries. There is also a cyclical function for the reserve since the alternate periods of high production and stagnation both effect and rely upon the reserve's formation.[15]

While Marx's discussion was mainly conducted at an abstract level, he offered some concrete categories of this reserve, although without saying which types of workers might fall into each category. The industrial reserve could take one of three forms:

1. The floating category, 'whereby labourers are sometimes repelled and sometimes attracted into the centres of modern industry. This is linked to the argument that the demand for labour in the centres of modern industry tends to substitute unskilled for skilled labour' (Beechey, 1978, p. 188).
2. The stagnant category, 'comprising labourers who are irregularly employed, whose members are recruited from the supernumary forces of modern industry and agriculture' (Beechey, 1978, p. 189).
3. The latent category, 'which exists among the agricultural population, which is displaced by the capitalist penetration of agriculture' (Beechey, 1978, p. 189).

These types of reserve indicate some of the functions of a

reserve. In addition, the degree of intensity of competition between workers for jobs is affected by the size of the reserve such that a reserve army can depress wages, it is suggested, and force workers to submit to higher rates of exploitation through the fear of unemployment. The existence of a reserve is also thought to counteract the tendency of the rate of profit to fall.

In assessing whether women constitute part of the reserve army, we should note that Marx directed attention away from thinking of the reserve as a separate, discrete group: 'the relative surplus population exists in "every possible form", and every labourer is part of it whenever she or he is unemployed or only partially employed' (Marx, quoted in Power, 1983, p. 74). Authors who have argued that women are part of the industrial reserve have done so on the grounds that they have examined empirically women's experience in their concrete social formation in order to reach this conclusion; in particular, since the end of the Second World War, women have constituted part of this reserve. At least two arguments have been offered; one is that women's experiences have made them part of Marx's latent reserve category over this period.[16] An earlier argument by Beechey (1977) was that women became part of the reserve army but in a different form than those described by Marx. Beechey was therefore arguing a case for changing the concept of a 'reserve army' in order to make women one of its components, whereas Power has argued that women fit into one of Marx's existing categories. Both writers are arguing from within a Marxist-feminist framework, and the fact that Power is concerned with US women and Beechey with the UK is not a sufficient explanation of their differences. The phenomenon of married women being drawn into the paid workforce is the same in both countries.

Power's (1983) argument that women over the twentieth century fit Marx's category of a latent reserve rests on her analysis of the changes in the content of housework over this period. She charts a change from the situation where housework was concerned with 'production' to one where it is concerned with 'maintenance' or domestic reproduction tasks. This process has occurred, she argues, as the home-based production activities have been taken over by capitalist manufacturing organisations in factories, the process being complete in the USA by approximately 1920. The effect of this change was to tie the family more closely to capitalist production, and in some cases reduce family income, removing any last vestiges of women's independence. As the process has continued, the family has become even more dependent on capitalist production for its maintenance tasks, in the form of cleaning materials and household consumer durables. Power sketches this development, but Gershuny describes it in more detail, although in another context.

Power argues that there is a parallel with Marx's concept of a latent reserve in the description of these changes, since capitalist production has taken over a pre-capitalist home-based area of production, releasing women to join the latent reserve army. She also suggests that the demand for labour over the twentieth century was the main force drawing women into paid employment. This demand had a number of components: a growth in occupations already defined as 'female', a creation of new female occupations and the redefinition of some male occupations as female. Power's reasoning about why women did not enter the paid labour force before has already been summarised earlier in this chapter. Power was constructing, therefore, an account of an actual social formation, rather than proposing an abstract general theory within the Marxist framework. One of the implications Power wished to emphasise was that women are no longer a marginal or temporary workforce. The nature of the changes in the content of housework mean, she argued, that there is little for women to do in the home now and so women are likely to remain part of the paid workforce from hereon.

Beechey (1977, 1978) suggests in two articles that women, like men, can occupy any of Marx's categories of reserve army, but that they also constitute a group outside of Marx's categories because of the special advantages married women have regarding capitalist production. Married women, Beechey argues, are uniquely flexible and disposable workers because their domestic role is seen as their primary role in the family. Women are thus distinct form other semi-proletarianised workers. Beechey adds a list of further institutional reasons why British women are particularly disposable as workers; they are less strongly unionised, less likely to qualify for redundancy pay and less eligible for state unemployment benefits. In her first article (1977), Beechey argued that women's dependent status made them an attractive low-paid workforce available for being drawn into the labour market. Beechey does not give a name to her description of women's unique or specific position in the reserve army, but she would see such a position as necessary to any conceptualisation of women's work. She argues that unless women are given this specific consideration one cannot begin to answer the question of why the demand for labour which drew women into the twentieth-century workforce was a demand for women's labour.

Anthias (1980) proposed a different argument. Her contribution is offered partly as a criticism of Beechey's (1977) first article on this topic and partly because other writers since Beechey had begun to adopt, almost unquestioningly, the notion that women were a reserve army.[17] Anthias (p. 50–1) argues that the concept of the reserve army of labour 'can only refer to a determinate active labour force that is made unemployed and *then* used as a "reserve", and that the concept cannot refer to 'racial or sexual groups, but rather to categories of labour that become unemployed these of course may be filled primarily by race or sex groups but the concept cannot explain "why" these groups fill those particular categories'. Anthias further recognises that Marx's category of a latent reserve is the one which could most closely fit women's position, but she argues against its use for women; first, she suggests there is a sense in which women have always been a latent reserve, as are children, so the term loses any explanatory value; second, Anthias thinks that women have not become relatively underemployed in a domestic labour mode, in the same sense that agricultural workers become underemployed, largely because domestic labour cannot be treated as a mode of production in the same sense.[18]

Anthias concludes that Marx's concept of a 'reserve army of labour' has little explanatory power in relation to women's employment. She thinks that Beechey's efforts to rescue the concept were unsuccessful and even confusing. Anthias's criticism is in two parts: she argues that Beechey ends up with a functionalist ideological argument which treats the economic dependence of women in the family as given and unproblematic, and she suggests that Beechey is inconsistent in conceptualising women as both a cheap labour force and a reserve army since women cannot in practice be both a cheap and a disposable labour force. Anthias ends by making a case for a new framework for analysing women's employment which incorporates political, economic and ideological conditions rather than focusing on narrow 'technicist analysis of the mode of production' (p. 61). She also wants to move away from the marginalisation of women's employment which was implicit in the concept of a 'reserve army of labour'. Anthias is reasserting the desire of other Marxist-feminist writers to reconceptualise the Marxist framework in order to integrate women and take their position seriously.

The discussions about whether women are a reserve army form an interesting case study in the development of Marxist-feminist arguments. They illustrate the struggles women are having in breaking new ground in their theorising about women's employment in a way that is appropriate to their subject matter. There is a desire to avoid the theoretical domination of and subordination to earlier male or abstractly constructed theories, without automatically dismissing all previous efforts. The application of these earlier concepts to women's work, whether that be Marxist or other concepts, leaves obvious cracks in the analysis. Most writers are agreed that economistic or functionalist-Marxist theory is not a solution and that women's work is not merely of marginal importance. Yet a framework which links women's position in the home and their position in the labour force to men's positions in both of these spheres and which explains the changes which have been occurring, is far from being fully outlined.

WOMEN THROUGH THE CYCLE

The fact that the study did not distinguish between responses by sex and marital status, as well as the comparative mildness and brevity of recessions during the short sample period under study, should not detract from the value of this early attempt to test the cyclical sensitivity of labour supply.

(Joseph, 1983, p. 42)

The failure to recognise the importance and distinctions between the sexes was common in early attempts by economists to examine the labour-supply implications of cyclical fluctuation in economic activity. Few commentators today would be as generous as Joseph in regarding these early studies, dating back into the 1940s, as having value. The issue of cyclical fluctuation in women's labour-force participation is also part of the Marxist 'reserve army' notion, and there women are thought to be worth singling out as distinct. This notion might lead us to expect that women's participation would be more sensitive than men's to fluctuations.

A consideration of these issues raises two related questions: are women drawn into the labour market during periods of tight demand and are they more disposable workers than men during the recession? The questions are, in effect, asking whether women are a marginal workforce. Beechey (1978) was suggesting that answers to these questions were in the affirmative but without providing empirical evidence. The evidence which exists on these questions has come mainly from economists, although not necessarily Marxist economists. We should beware thinking that any fluctuation in women's employment is evidence that they are a marginal workforce. Unless they are very unusual, there is almost bound to be some fluctuation in women's employment if the aggregate employment figures of which they are a part fluctuate. We are interested, therefore, in how women's employment fluctuates over the cycle in comparison with other groups' employment; notably men's employment.

Measuring women's fluctuating employment in theory could be done in one of two ways: their employment or their unemployment rates could be examined over the cycle. We might expect these two cyclical indicators to mirror each other's movements but in an opposite direction. This is certainly not the case in Britain, however. We have already noted that the published statistics on women's unemployment in Britain are notoriously inaccurate because they rely on women registering as unemployed, and clearly women who are looking for jobs do not all register as unemployed.[19] In pursuing the issue of women's employment fluctuations in Britain one has to either use the employment figures, which are not collected very regularly, or find some way of adjusting the unemployment figures.[20] Information on women's employment and unemployment is far more detailed and systematic in the USA because American unemployment statistics are constructed from a regular survey of households. Insofar as American women say that they are not seeking work when interviewed, however, they will be excluded from the unemployment count.

Orthodox economic theory has considered women's employment fluctuations initially by attempting to test out two hypotheses: the discouraged worker hypothesis and the additional worker hypothesis. The discouraged worker is one who in times of recession, after finding it difficult to obtain a job, will stop looking and withdraw from the active labour force. The additional worker makes a more concerted effort to find a job during the recession in order to maintain family income over a period when the husband may be unemployed. Both theories seem to refer to married women. Some evidence exists for both of these effects, although the general view has been that the net result is a discouraged worker effect.

Brown and Finegan's (1969) review of US studies and their own work concluded that women's employment was more sensitive than men's to aggregate unemployment fluctuations. They also suggested that the responsiveness to demand or economic climate conditions was greatest in population groups whose 'normal' participation rates were low. The estimates of the effects varied, however, depending upon the period chosen for the analysis and according to whether time-series or cross-sectional data were used.

Ferber and Lowry (1976) note that the aggregate US unemployment figures suggest that women have faired relatively better than men during periods of high unemployment and worse in period of low unemployment. The gap between men's and women's unemployment, women in the USA having the higher rate, has decreased as unemployment has increased. Their analysis suggests that the phenomenon, in part at least, is a product of women being more often discouraged workers, so that during times of high unemployment they drop-out and are not recorded as unemployed to the same extent as men.

In conclusion, Bowen and Finegan offer the suggestion that maybe some women behave like discouraged workers whilst others behave like additional workers. This final point, that women may be heterogeneous, is an important one, although the studies Brown and Finegan reviewed did not pursue this issue. In fact, the idea that all women constitute one homogeneous mass as far as their employment behaviour is concerned is stretching credibility somewhat, although perhaps not to some economists.

A study by Joshi (1982) managed to overcome the British data problems by using a special British data source, the national insurance scheme records which used to attach a stamp to a card for each week a person worked. Married women were not obliged to pay for the stamp and could thus opt-out of the scheme. The cards were collected quarterly at Newcastle until 1974, when the scheme was stopped. Joshi examined a 0.5 per cent sample of these quarterly national-insurance-card exchanges for a number of different groups of women, many of whom would be 'missing' from the unemployment register.[21] By comparing the fluctuations in the activity of these women with that of the population as a whole it was possible to estimate the size of those missing from the register and see more accurately how women's unemployment fluctuated over the business cycle. Joshi's results fround that for every 100 increase in the unemployment register, an *extra* 114 people became 'unemployed'; women constituted approximately 76 and men 35 of this total of missing workers. Whilst there was a greater tendency for women to drop out of the labour force, the cyclical elasticities of men and women, which are estimates of the sensitivity to fluctuations, were not significantly different between the sexes, and older married women were found to be a particularly stable workforce.

Joshi's results stress the importance of recognising that women are not a homogeneous workforce, and she suggested that a different hypothesis was needed about cyclically induced movements in the women's labour force which distinguished between age groups. Women should be seen as permanently attached to the labour force she argued. In the case of younger women with children, there is a once-and-for-all flow of women leaving and joining the register over childbirth. The adjustments to women's participation rates come from a speeding-up or slowing-down of the flows into and out of women's permanent membership, rather than drawing on a pool of reserves which have an enduring state of loose attachment. Joshi's findings act as a critique of the tendency of labour economics text-books to lump all women together, or even all married women, and consider them under a subheading of 'marginal' or 'secondary' workers.[22] They also support the conclusion, which is general in both Britain and the USA, that cyclical sensitivity declines as more comprehensive measures of labour supply are used.

A study by Bruegel (1979) used the yearly British employment changes from 1950 to 1978 to examine the issue of whether women are a more disposable workforce than men. This study is interesting in that it distinguished between manufacturing and service industries and between part-time and full-time work. Bruegel concluded that where men and women both work in manufacturing industry, women seemed more susceptible than men to unemployment; but in the service sector, where women predominate, women were shielded from the impact of recession because of the growth in this sector. These results were also found by Rosenfeld (1979) in the USA and in other OECD countries. An analysis by Rubery and Tarling (1983) confirmed that women have amplified cyclical fluctuations in manufacturing, but not in all sectors, nor in all countries. Dex and Perry (1984) used the same data source as Bruegel to examine the same issues, but in a more disaggregate form and up to 1981.

They found that women did not unequivocally suffer in recessions more than men even in manufacturing industries. The conclusions were found to vary according to which manufacturing industry was examined, and according to whether absolute or percentage, or part-time or full-time changes were compared by sex. Part-time jobs underwent greater proportionate fluctuations than full-time in manufacturing, but the result was the same for both men and women. The group which suffered most varied in different year-to-year changes. As the recession deepened over 1978 to 1981 they found that the conclusion did not vary, as Rubery and Tarling (1983) had suggested it might, and women's service-sector employment still remained relatively bouyant over the period. A measure of substitution of part-time for full-time work in manufacturing could be seen in the upswings.

These results confirm Joshi's claim that women are not a marginal workforce and should be viewed as permanently attached to the labour force. The sectoral distribution of women between occupations has been found to be an important factor in how they are affected by fluctuations in the business cycle. In services, women's employment has been found to be relatively unaffected in recent times by economic fluctuations. There is no evidence suggesting that British women are a more disposable workforce than men. In fact, the results suggest that 'disposability' is not a characteristic which applies to population groups as such: it may be better to discuss the vulnerability of certain industries. As to the future, several studies have suggested that things will get worse for women with the introduction of new microtechnology[23] or as services decline[24]. These predictions lack a clear understanding of why women's employment has changed in the way it has. Until that is obtained, predictions about the future are mere speculation.

The issues of whether women are a reserve army of labour or a disposable workforce buffeted by economic fluctuations have both been found to be asking the wrong questions about women's employment. The questions have been informed too much by existing male-centred theorising. More specific gender-related questions need to be formulated about women's and men's work as a further step to an adequate reconceptualisation of the socio-economic changes which are occurring.

NOTES

1. There is a discussion of the microeconomic implications of changes in the industrial structure which focuses on individual's response to relative industrial wage changes. The concern of this literature is largely to test the functioning of labour-market clearing mechanisms, and it will not be considered in this discussion of the industrial structure.
2. These trends are documented in detail in Joseph (1983) and Thatcher (1978).
3. *See* Dex and Perry (1984).
4. An issue of the journal *Survey* (1971, Winter) was devoted to critically evaluating Bell's work. It includes papers by an international collection of academics; for example, Floud, Bourricaud, Sartori, Wiles and others. The papers are a collection from a 1970 conference held to consider Bell's ideas, largely before they were published in 1974.
5. It should be remembered, as noted earlier, that the absolute numbers of employees in British manufacturing only began to decline since 1966. The decline in the share of total employment in manufacturing has a much longer history.
6. Gershuny accuses Bell of not understanding that personal services have in fact declined over time rather than increased, and that modern services are integrally linked with manufacturing and production rather than being services in the traditional sense of the word. Whilst Bell (1974) does not have a well-articulated view of the nature of the change in services, he does recognise these points. Bell makes the distinction between modern-day services and personal services, pointing out also that services in industrial society increase because of the 'need for auxiliary help for production' (p. 15).
7. *See* Dex and Shaw (1984).
8. *See* Dex and Shaw (1984).
9. Marx's *Capital*, Vol. 1, quoted in Beechey (1977, p. 54).
10. This argument is elaborated in Beechey (1977).
11. *See* Wood's introduction to Wood, ed. (1982).
12. For a list of critics, *see* Wood (1982a).
13. For example, Crompton and Reid (1982).
14. *See* Beechey (1978) and Wood (1982a).
15. *See* Power (1983) and Beechey (1978) for the relevant quotations from Marx to substantiate these points.
16. *See* Power (1983).

17. Anthias (1980, p. 50) cites the following authors in support of this claim: Bland *et al.*, Ferber and Lowry, and Mackintosh.
18. Anthias (1980) suggests that domestic labour is not task-specific and does not have clear limits. The categories of underemployment and unemployment cannot be applied to it because there is no contract of work. Although Anthias's paper precedes an article by Power (1983), Anthias would be opposed to the stand taken by Power on production.
19. The problems are reviewed in Dex (1978).
20. There have been a number of studies in Britain attempting to model hidden unemployment as it has become known. These are reviewed in Joseph (1983).
21. Joshi's (1982) four groups were women aged under thirty-five, wives aged between thirty-five and forty-four, wives aged between forty-five and fifty-nine and widows aged between thirty-five and thirty-nine. All groups were opted out.
22. Sapsford (1981) is a recent example of such an approach. After describing married women as secondary workers, he says: 'This classification of workers as primary or secondary corresponds to a partition of the total labour force into its permanent and transitory components' (p. 21).
23. For example, Arnold *et al.* (1982).
24. For example, Rowthorn (1980).

Bibliography

Acker, J. 'Women and social stratification: A case of intellectual sexism' in *American Journal of Sociology* LXXVIII (1973) 4, pp. 936–45

——'Women and stratification: A review of recent literature' in *Contemporary Sociology*, Vol. 9 (1980)

Adams, C.T. and K.T. Winston, *Mothers at Work: Public Policies in the United States, Sweden and China* (Longman: New York and London, 1980)

Adamson, O., C. Brown, J. Harrison and J. Price, 'Women's oppression under capitalism' in *Revoluntionary Communist* 5 (1976), pp. 2–48

Addison, J.T. and W.S. Siebert, *The Market for Labor: An Analytical Treatment* (Goodyear Publishing Co.: Santa Monica, 1979)

Agassi, J.B. *Women on the Job: The Attitudes of Women to Their Work* (D.C. Heath and Co.: Lexington, Mass., 1979)

Alexis, M. 'A theory of labor market discrimination with independent utilities' in *American Economic Review* (May, 1973)

Allen, S. 'Gender, inequality and class formation' in A. Giddens and G. MacKenzie eds. *Social Class and the Division of Labour* (Cambridge University Press, 1982)

Amranand, P. 'Female unemployment in Britain' (Centre for Labour Economics, London School of Economics, Discussion Paper No. 64, 1979)

Andresani, P. 'An empirical analysis of the dual labor market theory' (Ph.D. dissertation, unpublished, Ohio State University, 1973)

Anthias, F. 'Women and reserve army of labour: A critique of Veronica Beechey' in *Capital and Class* 10 (1980)

Anthony, P.D. *The Ideology of Work* (Tavistock: London, 1977)

Armstrong, P. 'If it's only women it doesn't matter so much' in J. West ed. (1982)

Arnold, E., C. Huggett, P. Senker, P. Swords, N. Isherwood and C.Z. Shannon, 'Microelectronics and women's employment' in *Employment Gazette*, (Sept. 1982)

Arnot, M. 'Male hegemony, social class and women's education' in *Journal of Education* 164 (1982), 1, pp. 64–89

Ashton, D.N. 'Careers and commitment: The movement from school to work' in D. Field ed. *Social Psychology for Sociologists* (Nelson: Walton-on-Thames, 1975)

——and D. Field, *Young Workers* (Hutchinson: London, 1976)

Atkinson, A.B. *The Economics of Inequality* (Clarendon Press: Oxford, 1977)

Bacon, R. and W.A. Eltis, *Britain's Economic Problem: Too Few Producers* (MacMillan: London, 1976)

Baran, P.A. and P.M. Sweezy, *Monopoly Capital* (Pelican: London, 1966)

Barker, J. and H. Downing, 'Word processing and the transformation of the patriarchal relations of control in the office' in *Capital and Class* 10 (1980), pp. 64–99

Baron, J.N. 'Indianapolis and beyond: A structural model of occupational mobility across generations' in *American Journal of Sociology* 85 (1980), 4, pp. 815–39

——and W.T. Bielby, 'Bringing the firms back in: Stratification, segmentation, and the organization of work' in *American Sociological Review* 45 (1980) pp. 737–65

Barrett, M. and M. McIntosh, '"The family wage": Some problems for socialists and feminists' in *Capital and Class* 11 (Summer, 1980)

Barron, R.D. and G.M. Norris, 'Sexual divisions and the dual labour market' in D.L. Barker and S. Allen eds. *Dependence and Exploitation in Work and Marriage* (Longman: London, 1976)

Beales, H.L. and R.S. Lambert eds. *Memoirs of the Unemployed*, (Victor Gollancz: London, 1934)

Beck, E.M. P.M. Horan and C.M. Tolbert, 'Stratification in a dual economy: A sectoral model of earnings determination' in *American Sociological Review* 43 (1978), pp. 704–20

Becker, G.S. *The Economics of Discrimination* (The University of Chicago Press: London and Chicago, 1957)

——'A theory of the allocation of time' in *Economic Journal* 75, (1965)

——*Human Capital*, 2nd ed (National Bureau of Economic Research, 1975)

Becker, H.S. 'Notes on the concept of commitment' in *American Journal of Sociology* 66 (1960), 1

——*Sociological Work: Method and substance* (Allen Lane: Chicago, 1970)

Beechey, V. 'Some notes on female wage labour in capitalist production' in *Capital and Class* 3 (1977), pp. 45–66

——'Women and production: A critical analysis of some sociological theories of women's work' in A. Kuhn and A.M. Wolpe eds. (1978)

——'On patriarchy' in *Feminist Review* 3 (1979), pp. 66–82

——'Women's employment in contemporary Britain' (Paper given to BSA Conference, Bradford, mimeo, 1984)

——and T. Perkins, 'Women's part-time employment in Coventry: A study in the sexual division of labour' (Report submitted to the Joint EOC/SSRC Panel, 1982)

Bell, C. and H. Roberts eds., *Social Researching: Politics, Problems, Practice* (Routledge and Kegan Paul: London, Boston, 1984)

Bell, D. *The Coming of Post-Industrial Society: A Venture in Social Forecasting* (Heinemann: London, 1974)

Beller, A. 'Occupational segregation by sex: determinants and changes' in *Journal of Human Resources*, Vol. XVII (1982), No. 3, pp. 371–92

——'Trends in occupational segregation by sex' (Working Papers in Population Studies No PS 8203, School of Social Sciences, University of Illinois at Urbana-Champaign, 1982(a)

Bennett, R. 'Orientation to work and organization analysis: A conceptual analysis, integration and suggested application' in *Journal of Management Studies* 15 (1974), pp. 187–210

Berger, P. and H. Kellner, *Sociology Reinterpreted* (Penguin: Harmondsworth, 1981)

Bergmann, B.R. 'The effect on white incomes of discrimination in employment' in *Journal of Political Economy* 79 (1971), pp. 294–313

——'Occupational segregation, wages and profits when employers discriminate by race or sex' in *Eastern Economic Journal*, Vol. 1 (1974), Nos. 2–3

Beynon, H. and R.M. Blackburn, *Perceptions of Work: Variations Within a Factory* (Cambridge University Press, 1972)

Blackaby, F. ed., *Deindustrialisation* (Heinemann/National Institute of Economic and Social Research: London, 1978)

Bhrolchain, M. 'Birth spacing and women's work: Some British evidence', (Centre for Population Studies CPS Research Paper 83–3, London School of Hygiene and Tropical Medicine, 1983)

Bibb, R. and W.H. Form, 'The effects of industrial occupational and sex stratification on wages in blue-collar markets' in *Social*

Forces 55 (1977), pp. 974–96

Blackburn, R.M. and M. Mann, *The Working Class in the Labour Market* (MacMillan: London, 1979)

Bland, L., C. Brunsdon, D. Hobson and J. Winship, 'Women "inside and outside" the relations of production' in Women's Studies Group *Women Take Issue* (Centre for Contemporary Cultural Studies, University of Birmingham, 1978)

Blau, F. 'Sex segregation of workers by enterprise in clerical occupations' in Edwards, Reich and Gordon eds. (1975)

———and C.L. Jusenius, 'Economists' approaches to sex segregation in the labor market' in M. Blaxall and B. Reagan eds. (1976)

Blau, F.D. 'The impact of the unemployment rate on labor force entries and exits' in *Women's Changing Roles at Home and on the Job* (National Commission for Manpower Policy, Special Report No 26, 1978)

Blau, P.M. and O.D. Duncan, *The American Occupational Structure* (Wiley: New York, 1967)

Blauner, R. 'Work satisfaction and industrial trends in modern society' in W. Galenson and S.M. Lipset eds. *Labour and Trade Unionism'* (Wiley: New York, 1960)

———*Alienation and Freedom: The Factory Worker and His Industry* (The University of Chicago Press, 1964)

Blaxall, M. and B. Reagan, *Women and the Workplace: The implications of Occupational Segregation* (The University of Chicago Press, Chicago and London, 1976)

Blundell, R. 'Modelling family labour supply with micro data' (unpublished, mimeo, Dept. of Econometrics, University of Manchester, 1983)

Blundell, R.W. and I. Walker, 'Modelling the joint determination of household labour supplies and commodity demands' in *Economic Journal* 92 (1982), pp. 351–64

Bonacich, E. 'Advanced capitalism and black/white race relations in the United States: A split labor market interpretation' in *American Sociological Review* Vol. 41 (1976), pp. 34–51

Boulet, J. and A. Bell, *Unemployment and inflation* (Economic Research Council: London, 1973)

Bowen, W.G. and T.A. Finegan, *The Economics of Labor Force Participation* (Princeton University Press, 1969)

Bowles, S. and H. Gintis, 'The problem with human capital theory—A Marxian critique' in *American Economic Review* (Papers and Proceedings, May, 1975)

———, ———*Schooling in Capitalist America*, (Routledge and Kegan Paul: London, 1976)

Brannen, P. ed., *Entering the World of Work: Some Sociological Perspectives* (Department of Employment, HMSO, London, 1975)

Braverman, H. *Labor and Monopoly Capital* (Monthly Review Press, 1974)

Britten, N. and A. Heath, 'Women, men and social class' in E. Gamarnikow *et al.*, *Gender, Class and Work* (Heinemann: London, 1983)

Brown, C.V. *Taxation and the Incentive to Work*, 2nd ed (Oxford University Press, 1982)

Brown, J.A.C. *The Social Psychology of Industry*, (Penguin: London, 1954)

Brown, R. 'Women as employees: Some comments on research in industrial sociology' in D.L. Barker and S. Allen eds. *Dependence and Exploitation in Work and Marriage* (Longman: London, 1976)

——'Work histories and labour market segmentation' (paper given at SSRC Symposium on Work History Analysis, September, 1983)

Brown, R.K., M.M. Curran and J.M. Cousins, *Changing Attitudes to Work* (Department of Employment, Research Paper No. 40, 1983)

Bruegel, I. 'Women as a reserve army: A note on recent British experience' in *Feminist Review* 3 (1979)

Cain, G.C. 'The challenges of segmented labor market theories to orthodox theory: A survey' in *Journal of Economic Literature* Vol. XIV, No. 4 (December, 1976)

Cairncross, A. 'What is de-industrialisation?' in F. Blackaby ed., (1978)

Campbell, B. *Wigan Pier Revisited: Poverty and Politics in the 80s* (Virago: London, 1984)

Caplow, T. *The Sociology of Work* (McGraw-Hill: New York, 1954)

Carchedi, G. 'On the economic identification of the New Middle Class' in *Economy and Society* 4 (1975), 1

——*On the Economic Identification of Social Classes* (Routledge and Kegan Paul: London, 1977)

Cavendish, R. *Women on the Line* (Routledge and Kegan Paul: London, 1982)

Charles, N. 'Women and trade unions in the workplace' in *Feminist Review* 15 (1983), pp. 3–22

Chiplin, B. 'An alternative approach to the measurement of sex discrimination: An illustration from university entrance' in *Economic Journal* (Dec. 1981)

——and P.J. Sloane, 'Sexual discrimination in the labour market' in *British Journal of Industrial Relations* (Nov. 1974)

——, —— 'Personal characteristics and sex differentials in professional employment' in *Economic Journal* (Dec., 1976)

——, ——*Tackling Discrimination at the Workplace: An Analysis of Sex Discrimination in Britain* (Cambridge University Press, 1982)

Clarke, C. *The Conditions of Economic Progress* (MacMillan: London, 1940)

Clark, G. *Working Patterns: Part-time Work, Job Sharing and Self-Employment* (Manpower Intelligence and Planning, Manpower Services Commission, 1982)

Clarke, L. *Occupational Choice: A Critical Review of Research in the United Kingdom* (Department of Employment, Careers Service Branch, HMSO, London, 1980)

——*The transition from School to Work: A Critical Review of Research in the United Kingdom* (Department of Employment, Careers Service Branch, HMSO, London, 1980a)

Coch, L. and J.P. French, 'Overcoming resistance to change' in *Human Relations* 1 (1948), pp. 512–32

Cotgrove, S. and S. Box, 'Scientific identity, occupational selection and role strain' in *British Journal of Sociology* 17 (1966), No. 1, pp. 20–28

Coulson, M., B. Magas and H. Wainwright, '"The housewife and her labour under Capitalism"—A critique' in *New Left Review* 89 (1975) pp. 59–71

Cousins, J.M., M.M. Curran and R.K. Brown, *Working in the Inner City: A Case Study* (Department of the Environment, Inner City Research Programme, 1982)

Coyle, A. 'Sex and skill in the organisation of the clothing industry' in J. West ed., pp. 10–26 (1982)

——*Redundant Women* (The Women's Press: London, 1984)

Cragg, A. and T. Dawson, *Qualitative Research among Homeworkers* (Department of Employment Research Paper No. 21, London, 1981)

——, ——*Unemployed Women: A Study of Attitudes and Experiences* (Department of Employment, Research Paper No. 47, 1984)

Craig, C., J. Rubery, R. Tarling and F. Wilkinson, *Labour Market Structure, Industrial Organisation and Low pay* (Cambridge University Press, 1982)

Crewley, J.F., T.E. Levitin and R.P. Quinn, 'Facts and fiction about the American working women' (Survey Research Centre, University of Michigan: Ann Arbor, 1973)

Crompton, R., G. Jones and S. Reid, 'Contemporary clerical work: A case study of local government' in J. West ed. (1982)

Cullen, J.B. and S.M. Novick, 'The Davis-Moore theory of stratification: A further examination and extension' in *American Journal of Sociology* 84 (1979), 6, pp. 1425–37

Cunnison, S. *Wages and Work Allocation* (Tavistock: London, 1966)

Curran, J. and J. Stanworth, 'Job choice and the manual worker—Where the theories break down' in *Personnel Management* (1978)

Dale, A. and N. Gilbert, 'Labour market structure in the UK: A consideration of some theories of segmentation' (unpublished paper, mimeo, 1984)

Daniel, W.W. 'Industrial behaviour and orientation to work—a critique' in *Journal of Management Studies* 6 (1969), No. 3, pp. 366–75

——*A National Survey of the Unemployed*, (Political and Economic Planning, Vol. XL, Broadsheet 546, London, 1974)

——'Employers' experiences of maternity rights legislation' in *Employment Gazette* (July, 1981), pp. 296–301

——and E. Stilgoe, *Where Are They Now? A Follow-up Study of the Unemployed* (Political and Economic Planning, Vol. XLIII (1977), No. 572, London

Davies, M. 'Women's place is at the typewriter: The feminization of the clerical labor force' in Edwards, Reich and Gordon eds. (1975)

Davies, R., L. Hamill, S. Moylan and C.H. Smee, 'Incomes in and out of work' in *Employment Gazette*, Vol. 90 (1982), pp. 237–43

Deem, R. ed., *Schooling For Women's Work* (Routledge and Kegan Paul: London 1980)

De Joug, P.Y., M.J. Brawer and S.S. Robin, 'Patterns of female intergenerational mobility: A comparison with male patterns of intergenerational mobility' in *American Sociological Review* Vol. 36 (1971), pp. 1033–42

Delphy, C. 'Women in stratification studies' in H. Roberts ed. *Doing Feminist Research* (Routledge and Kegan Paul: London 1981)

Dennehy, C. and J. Sullivan, 'Poverty and unemployment in Liverpool' in F. Field ed., (1977)

Dernburg, T.F. and D.M. McDougall, *Macroeconomics*, 6th ed. (McGraw-Hill: Kogakusha, 1980)

Dex, S. 'Measuring women's unemployment' in *Social and Economic Administration* Vol. 12 (1978), No. 2, pp. 136–41

—— 'Economists' theories of the economics of discrimination' in

Ethnic and Racial Studies vol. 2 (1979), No. 1, pp. 90–108

——*Women's Work Histories: An Analysis of the Women and Employment Survey* (Department of Employment, Research Paper No. 46, 1984)

——'Women's occupational profiles' in *Employment Gazette*, Vol. 92 (1984a)

——and S.M. Perry, 'Women's employment changes in the 1970s' in *Employment Gazette* Vol. 92 (1984), No. 4, pp. 151–64

——and L. Shaw, *A Comparison of British and US Women's Work Histories* (Report submitted to the Equal Opportunities Commission, unpublished 1984)

Doeringer, P.B. and M.J. Piore, *Internal Labor Markets and Manpower analysis* (D.C. Heath and Co.: Lexington, Mass., 1971)

——and N. Bosanquet, 'Is there a dual labour market in Great Britain? in *Economic Journal* (June, 1973)

Dubin, R. 'Industrial workers' worlds: A study of the "central life interests" of industrial workers' in *Social Problems* Vol. 3 (Jan., 1956)

——A. Hedley and C. Taveggia, 'Attachment to work' in R. Dubin ed. *Handbook of Work, Organisation and Society* (Rand McNally: Chicago, 1976)

Edwards, R.C. *Contested Terrain* (Basic Books: New York, 1980)

——M. Reich, and D.M. Gordon eds., *Labour Market Segmentation* (D.C. Heath and Co.: Lexington, Mass., 1975)

Eisenberg, P. and P.F. Lazarsfeld, 'The psychological effects of unemployment' in *Psychological Bulletin* (1938), pp. 358–90

Elias, P. and B. Main, *Women's Working Lives: Evidence from the National Training Survey* (Institute for Employment Research, University of Warwick, 1982)

Ellis, A. and K. Kumar eds., *Dilemmas of Liberal Democracies: Studies in Fred Hirsch's Social Limits to Growth* (Tavistock: London, 1983)

England, P. 'The failure of human capital theory to explain occupational sex segregation' in *Journal of Human Resources* Vol. XVII (1982), No. 3, pp. 358–70

Equal Opportunities Commission, *Eighth Annual Report 1983* (Equal Opportunities Commission, HMSO, Manchester, 1984)

Erhlich, C. *The Conditions of Feminist Research* (Reseach Group One, Report No. 21, Baltimore, 1976)

Esland, G. and G. Salaman eds., *The Politics of Work and Occupations* (Open University Press: Milton Keynes, 1980)

Featherman, D.L., and R.M. Hauser, 'Sexual inequalities and socio-economic achievement in the US 1962–1973' in *American*

Sociological Review 41 (1976) pp. 462–83

Feinberg, R.M. 'Market structure and employment instability' in *Review of Economics and Statistics* Vol. 61 (1979), pp. 497–505

Feldberg, R.L. and E.N. Glenn, 'Male and female: Job versus gender models in the sociology of work' in *Social Problems* Vol. 26 (1979), No. 5, pp. 524–38

Ferber, M.A. and H.M. Lowry, 'Women: The new reserve army of the unemployed' in M. Blaxall and B. Reagan eds. (1976)

Fichter, J. *Religion as an Occupation* (University of Notre Dame Press, 1961)

Field, F. 'Making sense of the unemployment figures' in F. Field ed. (1977a)

——ed., *The Conscript Army: A Study of Britain's Unemployed* (Routledge and Kegan Paul: London, 1977)

Finch, J. *Married to the Job: Wives Incorporation in Men's Work* (Allen and Unwin: London, 1983)

——'"It's great to have someone to talk to": the ethics and politics of interviewing women' in Bell and Roberts eds. (1984)

——and D. Groves eds., *A Labour of Love: Women, Work and Caring* (Routledge and Kegan Paul: London, 1983)

Fox, A. *A Sociology of Work in Industry* (Collier-MacMillan: London, 1971)

——'The meaning of work' in Esland and Salaman (1980)

Freeman, C. 'The "understanding" employer' in J. West ed. (1982)

Fuchs, V.R. 'Differences in hourly earnings between men and women' in *Monthly Labor Review* 94 (1971), 5, pp. 9–15

——'A note on sex segregation in professional occupations' in *Explorations in Economic Research* 2 (1975), pp. 105–11

Gagliani, G. 'How many working classes?' in *American Journal of Sociology* 87 (1981), 2, pp. 259–85

Garmarnikow, E. *et al.*, *Gender, Class and Work* (Heinemann: London, 1983)

Gardiner, J. 'Women's domestic labour' in *New Left Review* 89 (1975), pp. 47–58

Garnsey, E. 'Women's work and a theory of class stratification' in *Sociology* 12 (1978), 2, pp. 223–43

Garside, W.R. *The Measurement of Unemployment: Methods and Sources in Great Britain 1950–1979* (Basil Blackwell: Oxford, 1980)

Gavron, H. *The Captive Wife* (Pelican: Harmondsworth, 1968)

Gershuny, J. *After Industrial Society? The emerging Self-Service Economy* (MacMillan: London, 1978)

——*Social Innovation and the Division of Labour* (Oxford

University Press, 1983)

Giddens, A. *The Class Structure of Advanced Societies* (Hutchinson: London, 1973)

——and G. MacKenzie, *Social Class and the Division of Labour: Essays in Honour of I. Neustadt* (Cambridge University Press, 1982)

Ginzberg, G.E. *et al., Occupational Choice* (Columbia University Press: New York, 1951)

Goldthorpe, J.H. and D. Lockwood, 'Affluence and the British class structure' in *Sociological Review* Vol. 11 (1963), pp. 133–63

——, ——F. Bechhofer and J. Platt, *The Affluent Worker: Industrial Attitudes and Behaviour* (Cambridge University Press, 1968)

——, ——, ——, ——*The Affluent Worker: Political attitudes and behaviour* (Cambridge University Press, 1968)

——C. Llewellyn and C. Payne, *Social Mobility and Class Structure in Modern Britain* (Clarendon Press: Oxford, 1980)

——'Women and class analysis: In defence of the conventional view' in *Sociology* Vol. 17 (1983), pp. 465–88

——'Women and class analysis: A Reply to the replies' in *Sociology* Vol. 18 (1984), pp. 49–99

Gordon, D.M. *Theories of Poverty and Underemployment* (D.C. Heath and Co.: Lexington, Mass., 1972)

——R. Edwards and M. Reich, *Segmented Work, Divided Workers* (Cambridge University Press, 1982)

Glaser, B.G. *Organizational Scientists: Their Professional Careers* (Bobbs-Merrill, 1964)

Grandjean, B.D. 'History and career in a bureaucratic labor market' in *American Journal of Sociology* 86 (1981), No. 5, pp. 1057–92

Greenhalgh, C. 'Male–female wage differentials in Great Britain: Is marriage an equal opportunity?' in *Economic Journal* Vol. 90 (1980), No. 360

——and K. Mayhew, 'Labour supply in Great Britain: Theory and Evidence' in Hornstein *et al.* eds. (1981), pp. 41–46

——and M. Stewart, 'Occupational status and mobility of men and women' (Part 2 of a report submitted to MSC on 'The Effects of Work Experience and Job Training on the Occupations and Earnings of Women 1965–1975', 1981)

Griffiths, M.W. 'Can we still afford occupational segregation? Some remarks' in M. Blaxall and B. Reagan eds. (1976)

Gronau, R. 'The intra-family allocation of time: The value of the housewife's time' in *American Economic Review* 63 (1973)

Hakim, C. *Occupational Segregation* (Department of Employment Research Paper No. 9, 1979)

——'Job segregation: trends in the 1970s in *Employment Gazette* (Dec., 1981), pp. 521–29

——'Homework and outwork: national estimates from two surveys' in *Employment Gazette* Vol. 92 (1984), No. 1, pp. 7–12

——'Employers' use of homework, outwork and freelances' in *Employment Gazette* Vol. 92 (1984a), No. 4, pp. 144–50

——and J. Field, *Employers' Use of Outwork: A Study Based on the 1980 Workplace Industrial Relations Survey* (Department of Employment Research Paper No. 44, London, 1984)

Haller, M. 'Marriage, women, and social stratification: A theoretical critique' in *American Journal of Sociology* 86 (1981), No. 4, pp. 766–95

Hannington, W. *Unemployed Struggles 1919–1936* (Lawrence and Wishart: London, 1977)

Harbury, C.D. and P.C. McMahon, 'Inheritance and the characteristics of top wealth leavers in Britain' in *Economic Journal* Vol. 83 (1973), pp. 810–33

Harrison, J. 'The political economy of housework' in *Bulletin of the Conference of Socialist Economists* Vol. 4, (1973), pp. 35–51

Hartman, H. 'Capitalism, patriarchy, and job segregation by sex' in *Signs* 1 (1976), 3, pp. 137–68

——'The unhappy marriage of Marxism and Feminism: Towards a more progressive union' in *Capital and Class* 8 (1979), pp. 1–33

Haug, M.R. 'Social class measurement and women's occupational roles' in *Social Forces* Vol. 52 (1973), pp. 86–98

Havens, E.M. and J.C. Tully, 'Female intergenerational occupational mobility: Comparisons of patterns' in *American Sociological Review* 37 (1977), pp. 774–77

Hearn, J. 'Towards a concept of non-career' in *Sociological Review* 25 (1977), No. 2, pp. 273–88

——'Crisis, taboos and careers guidance' in *British Journal of Guidance and Counselling* Vol. 9 (1981), No. 1, p. 12–23

Heath, A. *Social Mobility* (Fontana: London, 1981)

——'Women who get on in the world—up to a point' in *New Society*, (12th Feb., 1981), pp. 275–78

Heath, A. and N. Britten 'Women's jobs do make a difference: A reply to Goldthorpe' in *Sociology*, Vol. 18 (1984), pp. 475–90

Heckman, J.J. 'Shadow prices, market wages and labour supply' in *Econometrica* 42 (1974), pp. 679–94

——'Heterogeneity and state dependence in dynamic models of labour supply' (unpublished manuscript, University of Chicago, 1978)

——'New evidence on the dynamics of female labor supply' in Lloyd, Andrews and Gilroy (1979)

——M.R. Killingsworth and T. MaCurdy, 'Empirical evidence on static labour supply models: A survey of recent developments' in Hornstein *et al.*, eds. (1981), pp. 75–122

Herzberg, F., B. Mausner, R.O. Peterson and D.F. Capwell, *Job Attitudes: A Review of Research and Opinion* (Psychological Services of Pittsburgh, 1957)

Hill, M.G., R.M. Harrison, A.V. Sargent and V. Talbot, *Men Out of Work* (Cambridge University Press, 1973)

Hill, S. *Competition and Control at Work* (Heinemann: London, 1981)

Hirszowicz, M. *Industrial Sociology: An introduction* (Martin Robertson: Oxford, 1981)

Hobson, D. 'Housewives: Isolation as oppression' in Women's Studies Group, *Women Take Issue* (Hutchinson: London, 1978)

Holmwood, J.M. and A. Stewart, 'The role of contradictions in modern theories of social stratification' in *Sociology* Vol. 17 (1983), pp. 234–54

Hope, K. 'Vertical and nonvertical class mobility in three countries' in *American Sociological Review* Vol. 47 (1982), pp. 99–113

Hornstein, Z., J. Grice and A. Webb eds., *The Economics of the Labour Market* (HMSO: London, 1981)

Hughes, E.C. 'Institutional office and the person' in *American Journal of Sociology* 43 (1937), pp. 404–13

Hughes, J.J. 'How should we measure unemployment' in *British Journal of Industrial Relations* Vol. XIII (1975), No. 3

Humphries, J. 'Class struggle and the persistence of the working-class family' in A.H. Amsden ed. *The Economics of Women and Work* (Penguin: Harmondsworth, 1977), pp. 140–65

Hunt, A. *A Survey of Women's Employment* (Government Social Survey Division, HMSO: London, 1968)

——ed., *Class and Class Structure* (Lawrence and Wishart: London, 1977)

Hunt, P. *Gender and Class Consciousness* (MacMillan: London, 1980)

Hunter, L.C. and D.J. Robertson, *Economics of Wages and Labour* (MacMillan: London, 1978)

Ingham, G.K. *Size of Industrial Organization and Worker Behaviour* (Cambridge University Press, 1970)

Jahoda, M., P.F. Lazarsfeld and H. Zeisel, *Marienthal: The Sociology of an Unemployed Community* (Tavistock: London, 1971)

Joseph, G. *Women at Work: The British Experience* (Philip Allan: Oxford, 1983)

Joshi, H.E. 'Female labour supply in post-war Britain: A cohort approach', Centre for Labour Economics (Jan., 1981)

——*Women's Participation in Paid Work: Further Analysis of the Women and Employment Survey* (Department of Employment, Research Paper No. 45, 1984)

——and S. Owen, 'Demographic predictors of women's work participation in post-war Britain' (Centre for Population Studies, London School of Hygiene and Tropical Medicine, CPS Working Papers Nos. 81–3, 1981

——'Secondary workers in the cycle', in *Economica* 48 (1982), pp. 29–44

Jusenius, C.L. 'The influence of work experience and typicality of occupational segregation on women's earnings' in *Dual Careers* Vol. 4 (US Department of Labor, Employment and Training Administration monograph No. 21, Washington DC, 1976)

Kahl, J.A. *The American Class Structure* (Rinehart and Co.: New York, 1953)

Kahne, H., A.I. Kohen and D.S. Hurley, 'Economic perspectives on the roles of women in the American economy' in *Journal of Economic Literature* Vol. XIII (1975), No. 4, pp. 1249–92

Kalleberg, A.L. and L.J. Griffin, 'Class, occupation and inequality in job rewards' in *American Journal of Sociology* 85 (1980), pp. 731–68

——and A.B. Sorensen, 'The sociology of labor markets' in *Annual Review of Sociology* 5 (1979), pp. 351–79

Kelly, A. 'Feminism and research' in *Women's Studies International Quarterly* 1 (1978), pp. 225–32

Kenrick, J. 'Politics and the construction of women as second-class workers' in F. Wilkinson ed. (1981)

Kerr, C. *Labor Markets and Wage Determination, the Balkanization of Labor Markets, and Other Essays* (California University Press: Berkeley, 1954: reprinted 1977)

Kohen, A.I. and J. Madison *et al. Women and the Economy: A Bibliography and a Review of the Literature of Sex Differentiation in the Labor Market* (Centre for Human Resource Research, Ohio State University, mimeo, 1977)

Kreckel, R. 'Unequal opportunity structured labour market segmentation' in *Sociology* Vol. 14 (1980), No. 4

Krueger, A.O. 'The economics of discrimination' in *Journal of Political Economy* 71 (1963), pp. 481–86

Kuhn, A. and A.M. Wolpe eds., *Feminism and Materialism: Women and Modes of Production* (Routledge and Kegan Paul:

London, 1978)

Kumar, K. 'Unemployment as a problem in the development of industrial societies: the English experience' in *Sociological Review*, Vol. 32 (1984), pp. 185–233

Long Laws, J. 'Work aspiration of women: False leads and new starts' in M. Blaxall and B. Reagan ed. *Women and the Workplace* (University of Chicago Press, 1976)

Lawson, T. 'Paternalism and the labour market segmentation theory' in F. Wilkinson ed. (1981)

Lenski, G.E. *Power and Privilege; A Theory of Social Stratification* (McGraw-Hill: New York, 1966)

Leonard, D. and C. Delphy, 'Class analysis, gender analysis and the family' (Paper presented to ESRC Symposium on Gender and Stratification, University of East Anglia, July, 1984)

Levy-Garboua, L. ed., *Sociological Economics* (Sage Publications: London and Beverly Hills, 1979)

Lipset, S.M. and R. Bendix, 'Social mobility and occupational career patterns. I. Stability of job holding' in *American Journal of Sociology* 57 (1952a), pp. 366–74

——, ——'Social mobility and occupational career patterns. II. Social mobility' in *American Journal of Sociology* 57, pp. 494–504 (1952b)

——, ——*Social Mobility in Industrial Society* (Heinemann: London, 1959)

——and N. Rogoff, 'Class opportunity in Europe and the United States' in *Commentary* (Dec., 1954)

Llewelyn, C. 'Occupational mobility and the use of the comparative method' in H. Roberts ed. *Doing Feminist Research* (Routledge and Kegan Paul: London, 1981)

Lloyd, C.B., E.S. Andrews and C.L. Gilroy eds., *Women in the Labor Market* (Columbia University Press: New York, 1970)

Lockwood, D. *The Black Coated Worker* (Unwin: London, 1958)

Loveridge, R. and A. Mok, *Theories of Labour Market Segmentation* (Martinus Nijhoff: The Hague, 1979)

Lupton, T. *On the Shop Floor* (Pergamon Press: Oxford, 1963)

Lynd, R.S. and H.M. Lynd, *Middletown in Transition* (Harcourt Brace: New York, 1937)

McClendon, M.J. 'The occupational status attainment processes of males and females' in *American Sociological Review* 41 (1976), pp. 52–64

MacKay, D.I., D. Boddy, J. Brack, J.A. Diack, N. Jones, *Labour Markets under Different Employment Conditions* (Allen and Unwin: London, 1971)

McKee, L. and C. Bell, 'Marital and family relations in times of male unemployment' (Paper presented to SSRC Research Workshop on Employment and Unemployment, mimeo, (Nov., 1983)

MacKenzie, G. 'Class boundaries and the labour process' in A. Giddens and G. MacKenzie eds. (1982)

Mackintosh, M. 'Gender and economics: Debates on the sexual division of labour' (Paper given at Sussex Conference on the Subordination of Women in the Development Process, 1978)

——'Domestic labour and the household' in S. Burman ed. *Fit Work for Women* (Croom Helm: London, 1979)

Mackie, L. and P. Pattullo, *Women at Work* (Tavistock: London, 1977)

McNally, F. *Women for Hire* (MacMillan: London, 1979)

McRobbie, A. 'Working class girls and the culture of femininity' in Women's Studies Group ed. *Women Take Issue* (Hutchinson: London, 1978)

——and J. Garber, 'Girls and subcultures' in *Working Papers in Cultural Studies* 7–8 (1975)

McRoberts, H.A. and K. Selbee, 'Trends in occupational mobility in Canada and the United States: A comparison' in *American Sociological Review* 46 (1981), pp. 406–21

Madden, J.F. *The Economics of Sex Discrimination* (Lexington Books: Lexington, Mass., 1973)

Main, B. 'Women's earnings: The influence of work histories on rates of pay' (University of Edinburgh, mimeo, 1984)

Mallier, A. and M. Rosser, 'Part-time workers and the economy' in *International Journal of Manpower* 2 (1980), 3

Mandel, E. *Late Capitalism* (NLB: London, 1975)

Manser, M. and M. Brown, 'Bargaining analyses of household decisions' in Lloyd Andrews and Gilroy (1979)

Marsden, D. *Workless* (Croom Helm: London, 1982)

Marshall, G. 'On the sociology of women's unemployment, its neglect and significance' in *Sociological Review* Vol. 32 (1984), 2, pp. 235–59

Marshall, R. 'The economics of racial discrimination: A survey' in *Journal of Economic Literature* Vol. 12 (1974), No. 3, pp. 849–71

Martin, J. and C. Roberts, *Women and Employment: A Lifetime Perspective* (DE/OPCS, HMSO, London, 1984)

——and C. Roberts, 'Women's employment in the 1980s' in *Employment Gazette* Vol. 92 (May, 1984a), pp. 199–209

Martin, R. and R.H. Fryer, *Redundancy and Paternalist Capitalism* (Allen and Unwin: London, 1972)

——and J.G. Wallace, *Working Women in Recession: Employ-*

ment, Redundancy, and Unemployment, (Oxford University Press, 1985)

Matthaei, J.A. *An Economic History of Women in America: Women's Work, the Sexual Division of Labour, and the Development of Capitalism* (The Harvester Press: Brighton, 1983)

Matthews, S.H. 'Rethinking sociology through a feminist perspective' in *American Sociologist* 17 (1982), 1, pp. 29–35

Mayer, K. and W. Buckley, *Class and Society*, 3rd ed (Random House: New York, 1955: reprint, 1970)

Mercato, A.P.D. 'Social reproduction and the basic structure of labour markets' in F. Wilkinson ed. (1981)

Middleton, C. 'Sexual inequality and stratification theory' in F. Parkin, *The Social Analysis of Class Structure* Tavistock: London, 1974)

——'The sexual division of labour in feudal England' in *New Left Review* Nos. 113–14 (1979), pp. 147–68

Miller, D.C. and W.H. Form, 'Occupational career pattern as a sociological instrument' in *American Journal of Sociology* 54 (1949)

Millett, K. *Sexual Politics* (Virago: London, 1977)

Mincer, J. and S. Polachek, 'Family investment in human capital: Earnings of women' in *Journal of Political Economy* Vol. 82 (1974), No. 2.

Morgan, D. 'Men masculinity and the process of sociological enquiry' in H. Roberts ed. (1981), pp. 83–113

Mott, F.L. ed., *The Employment Revolution* (MIT Press: Cambridge, Mass., 1982)

——A. Statham and N.L. Maxwell, 'From mother to daughter: The transmission of work behaviour patterns across generations' in F.L. Mott ed. (1982)

Murgatroyd, L. 'Gender and occupational stratification' in *Sociological Review* 30 (1982), pp. 574–602

National Opinion Research Center, 'Jobs and occupations: A popular evaluation' in *Opinion News* IX (1947), pp. 3–13

Nichols, T. and H. Beynon, *Living with Capitalism: Class Relations and the Modern Factory* (Routledge and Kegan Paul: London, 1977)

Nickel, S. 'Trade unions and the position of women in the industrial wages structure' in *British Journal of Industrial Relations* Vol. XV (1977), No. 2

Nielson, E.C. and J. Edwards, 'Perceived feminine role orientation and self-concept' in *Human Relations* 35 (1982), 7, pp. 547–58

Norris, G.M. 'Unemployment, subemployment and personal characteristics in *Sociological Review* 26 (1978a), pp. 89–103; (1978b), pp. 327–47

Novarra, V. *Women's Work, Men's Work* (Marion Boyars: London, 1980)

Oakley, A. *The sociology of housework* (Martin Robertson: Oxford, 1974)

——*From Here to Maternity: Becoming a Mother* (Penguin Books: Harmondsworth, 1979)

——*Women Confined: Towards a Sociology of Childbirth* (Martin Robertson: Oxford, 1980)

——'Interviewing women: a contradiction in terms' in H. Roberts ed. (1981)

Ornstein, M.D. *Entry into the American Labor Force* (Academic Press: London, 1976)

Osborn, A.F. and T.C. Morris, 'The rationale for a composite index of social class and its evaluation' in *British Journal of Sociology* Vol. XXX (1979), pp. 39–60

Pahl, J. 'The allocation of money and the structuring of inequality within marriage' in *The Sociological Review* (1983), pp. 237–62

Palmer, G. *Labor Mobility in Six Cities* (SSRC: New York, 1954)

Parkin, F. *Class Inequality and Political Order* (MacGibbon and Kee: London, 1971)

——*Marxism and Class Theory: A Bourgeois Critique* (Tavistock: London, 1979)

Parnes, H.S. and G. Nestel, 'Middle-aged job changers' in H.S. Parnes *et al.* eds. *The Pre-retirement Years* Vol. 4 (Center for Human Resource Research, Ohio State University, 1974)

Payne, G., J. Payne and T. Chapman, 'Trends in female social mobility' in E. Gamarnikow *et al.* eds. *Gender, Class and Work* (Heinemann: London, 1983)

Perkins, T. 'A new form of employment: A case study of women's part-time work in Coventry' in M. Evans and C. Ungerson eds. *Sexual Divisions, Patterns and Processes* (Tavistock: London, 1983)

Phelps, E.S. 'The statistical theory of racism and sexism' in *American Economic Review* Vol. 62 (1972), pp. 659–61

Phillips, A. and B. Taylor, 'Sex and skill: Notes towards a feminist economics' in *Feminist Review* (1980)

Phillipson, C. *Capitalism and the Construction of Old Age* (MacMillan: London, 1982)

Piore, M.J. 'Notes for a theory of labor market stratification' in Edwards, Reich and Gordon eds. (1975)

Piore, M.J. and S. Berger, *Dualism and Discontinuity in Industrial*

Societies (Cambridge University Press, 1980)

Platt, J. 'The *Affluent Worker* revisited', in Bell and Roberts eds. (1984)

Polachek, S. 'Discontinuities in labor force participation and its effects on women's market earnings' in C.B. Lloyd ed. *Sex, Discrimination and the Division of Labor* (Columbia University Press: New York, 1975)

——'Occupational segregation: An alternative hypothesis' in *Journal of Contemporary Business* 5 (1976), pp. 1–12

Pollert, A. *Girls, Wives, Factory Lives* (MacMillan: London, 1981)

Poulantzas, N. 'On social classes' in *New Left Review* 78 (1973), pp. 27–50

Power, M. 'From home production to wage labour: Women as a reserve army of labor' in *Review of Radical Political Economics* Vol. XV (1983), No. 1, pp. 71–91

Psacharopoulos, G. 'Labour market duality and income distribution: The case of the UK' in W. Krelle and A.F. Shorrocks ed. *Personal Income Distribution* (North-Holland, 1978)

Purcell, K. 'Militancy and acquiescence amongst women workers' in S. Burman ed. *Fit Work for Women* (Croom Helm: London, 1979)

Reddaway, W.B. 'Wage flexibility and the distribution of labour' in *Lloyds Bank Review* 54 (1959), pp. 32–48

Reder, M.W. 'The theory of occupational wage differentials' in *American Economic Review* 44 (1955), pp. 833–52

Reid, I. *Social Class Differences in Britain* (Open Books: London, 1977)

Richards, J.R. *The Sceptical Feminist* (Penguin: Harmondsworth, 1980)

Roberts, C. 'Women's unemployment' (paper presented to SSRC workshop on Employment and Unemployment, mimeo, Oct., 1981)

Roberts, H. 'Women and their doctors: A sociological analysis of consulting rates' (SSRC Workshop on Qualitative Methodology, 1978)

——ed., *Doing Feminist Research* (Routledge and Kegan Paul: London, 1981)

Roberts, K. 'The entry into employment: An approach towards a general theory' in *The Sociological Review* 16 (1968), pp. 165–84

——'An alternative theory of occupational choice' in *Education and Training* 15 (1973), pp. 310–11

Robinson, D. ed., *Local Labour Markets and Wage structures*

224   *The Sexual Division of Work*

(Gower Press: London, 1970)

Robinson, O. *Part-time Employment in the European Communities* (Commission of the European Communities, Programme of Research and Actions on the Development of the Labour Market, 1977)

—— 'Part-time employment in the European Community' in *International Labour Review* Vol. 118 (1979), No. 3

Rose, M. *Industrial Behaviour: Theoretical Developments Since Taylor* (Penguin: Harmondsworth, 1975)

Rosenfeld, R.A. 'Women's employment patterns and occupational achievements' in *Social Science Research* 7 (1978), pp. 61–80

—— 'Women's intergenerational mobility?' in *American Sociological Review* 43 (1978), pp.36–46

—— 'Women's occupational careers: Individual and structural explanations' in *Sociology of Work and Occupations* Vol. 6 (1979), No. 3, pp. 283–311

—— 'Race and sex differences in career dynamics' in *American Sociological Review* 45 (1980), 4, pp. 583-609

Roston, M. 'Early neoclassical economics and the economic role of women' (Social Science Working Papers, Open University, 1983)

Rottenberg, S. 'On choice in labor markets' in *Industrial Relations Review* 9 (1956), pp. 183–99

Rowntree, S. and B. Lasker, *Unemployment: A Social Study* (London, 1911)

Rowthorn, B. *Capitalism, Conflict and Inflation* (Lawrence and Wishart: London, 1980)

Rubery, J. 'Structured labour markets, worker organization and low pay' in *Cambridge Journal of Economics* 2 (1978), 1, pp. 17–36

—— and F. Wilkinson, 'Notes on the nature of the labour process in the secondary sector' in *Low Pay and Labour Markets Segmentation* (Conference papers, Cambridge, 1979)

——, ——*Outwork and Segmented Labor Markets* in F. Wilkinson ed. (1981)

—— and R.J. Tarling, 'Women in the recession' (Economic Reprint No. 68, Department of Applied Economics, University of Cambridge, 1983)

Ryan, P. 'Segmentation, duality and the internal labour market' in F. Wilkinson ed. (1981)

Salaman, G. 'The sociology of work: Some theories and issues' in Esland and Salaman (1980)

——*Class and the Corporation* (Fontana: London, 1981)

Sanborn, H. 'Pay differences between men and women' in

Industrial and Labor Relations Review 17 (1964), 4, pp. 534–50
Sapsford, D. *Labour Market Economics* (Allen and Unwin: London, 1981)
Sawhill, I.V. 'The economics of discrimination against women: Some new findings' in *Journal of Human Resources* 8 (1973), pp. 383–96
Scanzoni, J. *Sex Roles, Women's Work and Marital Conflict: A Study of Family Change* (D.C. Heath and Co.: Lexington, Mass., 1978)
Seccombe, W. 'The housewife and her labour under capitalism' in *New Left Review* 83 (1974), pp. 3–24
Shapiro, D., and L.B. Shaw 'Growth in the labor force attachment of Married Women' in *Southern Economic Journal* (1983), pp. 461–73
Shaw, L.B. *Unplanned Careers: The Working Lives of Middle-Aged Women* (D.C. Heath and Co.: Lexington, Mass., 1983)
——'Does working part-time contribute to women's occupational segregation' (Paper presented to annual meeting of the Mid-West Economics Association, St. Louis, Missouri, mimeo, April, 1983.
Sheldrake, P.F. 'Orientations towards work among computer programmers' in *Sociology* 5 (1971), No. 2, pp. 209–24
Sheppard, H.L. and A.H. Belitsky, *The Job Hunt: Job-Seeking Behaviour of Unemployed Workers in a Local Economy* (John Hopkins: Baltimore, 1966)
Sherratt, N. 'Girls, jobs and glamour' in *Feminist Review* 15 (1983), pp. 47–61
Showler, B. and A. Sinfield eds., *The Workless State: Studies in Unemployment* (Martin Robertson: Oxford, 1981)
Siebert, W.S. and P.J. Sloane, 'Shortcomings and problems in analyses of women and low pay' in P. Sloane ed. (1980)
Siebert, W.S. and P.J. Sloane, 'The measurement of sex and marital status discrimination at the workplace' in *Economica* Vol. 48 (1981)
Silverstone, R. 'Just a Sec?' in *Personnel Management* Vol. 7, No. 6 (June, 1975)
——'The office secretary' (unpublished Ph.D thesis, City University, London, 1974)
Siltanen, J. and M. Stanworth, 'The politics of private woman and public man' in *Theory and Society* Vol. 13 (1984), No. 1, pp. 91–118
Sinfield, A. 'Poor and out of work in Shields' in P. Townsend ed. *The Concept of Poverty* (Heinemann: London, 1970)
——*What Unemployment Means* (Martin Robertson: Oxford,

1981)

——'Unemployment in an unequal society' in B. Showler and A. Sinfield eds. (1981)

Singh, A. 'UK industry and the world economy: A case of de-industrialisation' in *Cambridge Journal of Economics* (June, 1977)

Sloane, P.J. ed., *Women and Low Pay* (MacMillan: London, 1980)

——'Discrimination in the labour market: A survey of theory and evidence' in M. Summer *et al*. ed. *Surveys of Economic Theory: Labour Economics* (Longman: London, 1985)

Slocum, W.L. *Occupational Careers: A Sociological Perspective* (Aldine: Chicago, 1966)

Smith, D. 'Women, class and family' in R. Milliband and J. Saville eds. *The Socialist Register* (1983)

Smith, M. and M. Leiper, 'A study of temporarily unemployed girls' in *Occupational Psychology* Vol. XIV (1940), Part 2, pp. 82–93

Smith, P. 'Domestic labour and Marx's theory of value' in A. Kuhn and A. Wolpe ed. *Feminism and Materialism* (Routledge and Kegan Paul: London, 1978), pp. 198–219

Smith, R. 'Sex and occupational role on Fleet Street' in D.L. Barker and S. Allen eds. *Dependence and Exploitation in Work and Marriage* (Longman: New York, 1976)

Sorensen, A.B. 'Sociological research on the labor market' in *Work and Occupations* Vol. 10 (1983) No. 3, pp. 261–87

Speakman, M.A. 'Occupational choice and placement' in Esland and Salaman (1980)

Spender, D. 'Educational research and the feminist perspective' (unpublished paper, British Educational Research Association Conference on 'Women, Education and Research', University of Leicester, 1978)

——*Invisible Women: The Schooling Scandal* (Writers and Readers Publishing Cooperative Society, 1982)

Spilerman, S. 'Careers, labor market structures and socio-economic achievement' in *American Journal of Sociology* 83 (1977), pp. 551–93

Stanley, L. 'Sexual politics in sociology: A content analysis of three sociology journals' (unpublished paper, University of Salford, 1974)

——and S. Wise, *Breaking Out: Feminist Consciousness and Feminist Research* (Routledge and Kegan Paul: London, 1983)

Stanworth, M. 'Women and class analysis: A reply to John Goldthorpe' in *Sociology* Vol. 18 (1984) No. 2, pp. 159–70

Statham, A. and P. Rhoton, 'Attitudes toward women working: Changes over time and implications for the labor-force behaviours of husbands and wives' in L. Shaw ed. (1983)

Stevenson, M.H. 'Relative wages and sex segregation by occupation' in C.B. Lloyd ed. *Sex, Discrimination and the Division of Labor* (Columbia University Press: New York, 1975)

Stewart, A., K. Prandy and R.M. Blackburn, *Social Stratification and Occupations* (MacMillan: London, 1980)

Stigler, G.J. 'The Economics of Information' in *Journal of Political Economy* Vol. LXIX (1961a), No. 3

——'Information in the labor market' in *Journal of Political Economy* Vol. 70 (1961b)

Stiglitz, J.E. 'Approaches to the economics of discrimination' in *American Economic Review* (May, 1973)

Super, D.E. 'A theory of vocational development' in *American Psychologist* 8 (1953), pp. 185–90

Terkel, S. *Working* (Penguin: Harmondsworth, 1975)

Thatcher, A.R. 'Labour supply and employment trends' in F. Blackaby ed. (1978)

Theodore, A. ed., *The Professional Woman* (Schenkman: Cambridge, Mass., 1971)

Thurow, L. *Poverty and Discrimination* (The Brookings Institution: Washington D.C., 1969)

Touraine, A. and O. Ragazzi, *Ouvriers d'origine agricole*, (Editions du Sevil, Paris, 1961)

Townsend, P. *Poverty in the United Kingdom* (Allen Lane: London, 1979)

Trevithick, J.A. *Inflation. A Guide to the Crisis in Economics*, 2 eds (Penguin: Harmondsworth, 1980)

Trieman, D.J. and Kermit Terrell, 'Sex and the process of status attainment: A comparison of working women and men' in *American Sociological Review* 40 (1975), pp. 174–200

Tyree, A. and J. Treas, 'The occupational and marital mobility of women' in *American Sociological Review* Vol. 39 (1974), pp. 293–302

Wachtel, H. and C. Betsey, 'Employment at low wages' in *Review of Economics and Statistics* Vol. LIV (1972), p. 121

Wachter, M.L. 'A labor supply model for secondary workers' in *Review of Economics and Statistics* 54 (1972), pp. 141–51

——'Primary and secondary labor markets: A critique of the dual approach' in *Brookings Papers on Economic Activity* No. 3 (1974), pp. 637–93

Wajcman, J. *Women in Control* (Open University Press: Milton Keynes, 1983)

Walby, S. 'Gender, class and stratification: Towards a new approach', Paper given at ESRC Symposium on Gender and Stratification, University of East Anglia (July, 1984)

Walker, A. 'The economic and social impact of unemployment: A case study of South Yorkshire' in *Political Quarterly* (Jan., 1981)

Walker, C. and R. Guest, *Man on the Assembly Line* (Harvard University Press: Cambridge, Mass., 1952)

Warner, W.L. *Social Class in America: A Manual of Procedure for the Measurement of Social Status* (Harper Torch books: New York, 1960; originally published Chicago 1949)

——et al. *Yankee City* (one volume abridged edition, originals 1941–59, New Haven, 1963)

Watson, J.J. *Sociology, Work and Industry* (Routledge and Kegan Paul: London, 1980)

Watson, W.B. and E.A.T. Barth, 'Questionable assumptions in the theory of social stratification' in *Pacific Sociological Review* Vol. 7 (1964), pp. 10–16

Wedderburn, D. *White Collar Redundancy: A Case Study* (Cambridge University Press, 1964)

Welch, H.J. and C.S. Myers, *Ten Years of Industrial Psychology* (Pitman: London, 1932)

Wertz, D.C. 'Social science attitudes toward women workers, 1870–1970' in *International Journal of Women's Studies* 5 (1982), 2, pp. 161–72

West, J. 'Women, sex, and class' in A. Kuhn and A. Wolpe ed. *Feminism and Materialism* (Routledge and Kegan Paul: London, 1978)

——ed., *Work, Women and the Labour Market* (Routledge and Kegan Paul: London, 1982)

Westergaard, J. and H. Resler, *Class in a Capitalist Society* (Heinemann: London, 1975)

Wight Bakke, E. *Citizens Without Work: A Study of the Effects of Unemployment upon the Workers' Social Relations and Practices* (Archer, Hamden, Connecticut, 1969)

Wilensky, H.L. 'Orderly careers and social participation: The impact of work history on social integration in the middle mass' in *American Sociological Review* 26 (1961), pp. 521–39

Wilkinson, F. ed., *The Dynamics of Labour Market Segmentation* (Academic Press: London, 1981)

Williams, G. *Women and Work* (Nicholson and Watson, 1945)

Willis, P.E. *Learning to Labour: How Working Class Kids Get Working Class Jobs* (Saxon House: Aldershot, 1977)

Wood, D. *The DHSS Cohort Study of Unemployed Men, Working*

Paper No. 1, Men Registering as Unemployed in 1978—a Longitudinal Study DHSS, 1982

Wood, S. 'Redundancy and female employment' in *Sociological Review* Vol. 29 (1981), No. 4, pp. 649–83

——ed., *The Degradation of Work? Skill, Deskilling and the Labour Process* (Hutchinson: London, 1982)

Woodward, J. *Management and Technology*, (HMSO: London, 1958)

——*The Saleswoman: A study of Attitudes and Behaviour in Retail Distribution* (Pitman: London, 1960)

——*Industrial Organization: Theory of Practice*, (Oxford University Press, 1965)

Wright, E.O. *Class, Crisis and the State* (New Left Books: London, 1978)

——C. Costello, D. Hachen, and J. Sprague, 'The American class structure' in *American Sociological Review* Vol. 47 (1982), pp. 709–26

Yanz, L. and D. Smith, 'Women as a reserve army of labour: A critique' in *Review of Radical Political Economics* XV, (1983), No. 1, pp. 92–106

Yohalem, A.B. *Women Returning to Work: Policies and Progress in 5 Countries* (F. Pinter: London, 1980)

Zweig, F. *Women's Life and Labour* (Victor Gollancz: London, 1952)

Index